A Ray of Hope

A Ray of Hope

Helping Dogs with People Problems

Raymond J. McSoley

Clovercroft Publishing

A Ray of Hope: Helping Dogs with People Problems
©2024 Raymond J. McSoley

Published by Clovercroft Publishing, Franklin, Tennessee
ClovercroftPublishingGroup.com

Interior Design and Cover Design by Suzanne Lawing

Printed in the United States of America

ISBN: 978-1-956370-24-9 (print)

Dedication

To Finn
My four-legged friend and true Zen dog,
a companion, a teacher, an associate.
Thank you for sharing your wisdom.

Acknowledgments

A huge thank you to my dear friend, Judy Turmail, who physically took the manuscript off my desk and placed it in my hands, saying, "update this." Special thanks go to Cathy Petz and Richard Muller for putting me in contact with Clovercroft Publishing. Sincere thanks to Clovercroft Publishing, and deepest gratitude to Shane Crabtree and my copy editor, Ann Tatlock. Thanks guys for putting up with me. Thank you, Hillary, for being there when I needed help. Thanks to Col. Robert Peterson, Ret. for planting the seed for a second book. A most sincere thank you to Ray Hunt, who passed over the bar a number of years ago. He was an amazing horseman, and I learned so much about how to handle troubled dogs from Ray. I will always have fond memories from my trips to Best Friends Animal Sanctuary. Thanks. Many thanks to the dozens of Veterinarians and Techs who, through these many years, have graciously referred their clients to me. From deep in my heart, thank you to the thousands of clients I have had the honor of working with. How do I properly thank the dogs, those magnificent animals that opened their hearts to me, and trusted me enough to take me on as their student? Thank you, each and every one of you. This book is for you.

Foreword

It is a rare privilege when one has the opportunity to write true words about the character and life work of someone who has impacted them in such a deep way. Ray McSoley is that person, and I would like to share with you how I have come to know and learn from him.

Our family brought home our beloved dog Duffy from the Animal Rescue League of Boston over 10 years ago. With 4 young children in tow we headed to the South End to meet the new addition to our family. And what a life changing occasion it was. Duffy was an 8-month-old, 90 pound German Shepherd hybrid who presented us with his chew toy through his enclosure the moment we walked in. In an instant we knew that he was to be ours and the wonderful care team at ARL guided our young family through the steps of bringing this beautiful soul home.

Duffy had been relocated from one shelter to another before coming to us and we were committed to making our home and family a steady and stable constant for him. It would not be an easy task, and as I searched for education on training our very spirited Duffy, it became apparent that Ray McSoley was "the holy grail" Dogman. He is highly regarded by many, and I was determined to give Duffy and our family the best guidance available. I listened to my gut, and reached out to Mr. McSoley.

Ray pulled up in his green Jeep and opened the rear hatch. Donned in Wrangler jeans and a cowboy hat, he smiled—kind blue eyes sparkling—and introduced himself. "Hi, I'm Ray." Instantly I felt a sense of calm confidence from him (energy perhaps?), while Duffy jumped, tail wagging, and imposed his now 110 pounds in my small entrance hall. Now the process, what Ray calls 'Stepping onto the Path' would begin.

"One step at a time," Ray said when I, like many dog owners, was so eager to see Duffy grow to his greatest potential, all in a single session. With each practiced step, and with Ray's calm yet firm assistance I found myself feeling more confident. The more confident I felt, the more confidence Duffy seemed to have in his role. Strange. Why did Duffy seem to relax when hearing the word "Heel"? Eventually I knew the answer. He was experiencing my calm energy! He was enjoying the process that Ray calls Quiet Firmness. From that day forward, each new day brought Duffy and I closer to becoming a team, while our weekly sessions with Ray and his yellow Lab Finn (patiently waiting, hatch open) increased the mutual trust and respect between Duffy and myself.

I found *A Ray of Hope* to be just that—Hope. His message throughout these pages is that the dog owner's primary responsibility is to establish a strong leader/ follower relationship. Furthermore, that relationship needs to be achieved without conflict and confrontation. Instead it needs to be achieved through mutual respect, trust and Ray's 'Quiet Firmness.' It worked beautifully with Duffy and my family. It can work with yours as well.

Enjoy and God Bless,
Leslie Dardas Noto

Contents

Introduction

Only after the dog opens your heart can you begin to think as one.
~Ray McSoley, Dogman

Thank you for choosing *A Ray of Hope*. It is a culmination of 50 years of learning and understanding what the dogs have taught me. I feel I have an obligation, a duty, to pass along to you what I have learned from them. They, who have been my tireless, forgiving professors throughout these many years, all 24,000 plus.

During my early years, when my real job was working as a regional vice president for a Fortune 500 truck leasing company, my avocation was training my Labrador retrievers, Jake and Kitt, in retriever field trials. It was difficult and time consuming but I loved it, and so did my dogs. Most Wednesdays and Saturdays you could find us in a field or on a marsh, along with my usual group of retriever friends and their dogs, working hard to compete for that elusive blue ribbon. It was also a chance to get away from my job which was, at times, very stressful. Spending time with my dogs was my fun job. At times, though, I could be a bit rough on them. I learned from a few of the pros back then that you needed to be dominant, alpha, no compromising. That became the foundation for the training I did with my own dogs. I had a wonderful family and my Labs. Life was good.

Suddenly, in early March 1974, a personal tornado hit me. I lost my job; I was fired. The news arrived out of the blue, just a phone call from my boss in Albany, New York. Just like that I was an out-of-work, 34-year-old history major with a wife and three young children—and no job prospects. I was also the sole breadwinner. I recalled some-one once telling me that when one door closes another door opens. I was very frightened and discouraged, and I sure didn't see any doors opening for me anytime soon.

I had been home scarcely two weeks when I took a phone call from Jeanne Tarlow, a good friend and Lab breeder from whom I had pur-chased two wonderful Labs. She called to say that one of her dogs, a 14-month-old yellow male named Simba, was being returned by an older couple named Rutledge because the dog simply was way too much for them to handle. They had had three separate trainers work with Simba but nothing they did solved the problems. Jeanne said Simba would be perfect for me. I mentioned I was recently jobless and it most probably would not be a prudent time for me to arrive home to my wife with a third dog in tow.

Jeanne went on to say that the Rutledges lived just one town over in Dover (Massachusetts) and that I really should drive over just to take a look at the dog. Jeanne made the call and, against my better judgement, I drove over. I arrived a short time later where I ended up spending a couple of hours drinking hot tea with Mrs. Ruth Rutledge, an older, gray-haired, ebullient woman with warm green eyes. I told her I had Labs, did their training myself, and that some Labs can be a bit of a handful. Between tearful sobbing she repeatedly told me how much she loved Simba and mentioned the three prior trainers. Before I knew it, I had offered to work with Simba, asking Ruth, "What do you have to lose?" She threw her arms around me, gave me a hug, and exclaimed, "Oh, thank you, Ray." Fortunately, the biggest problems were Simba's jumping on every human being that entered the house and not coming, the latter being a large issue because, as a result, Simba got next to no exercise.

Fortunately, I was able to resolve both issues, resulting in the Rutledges' keeping their dog. Simba's vet was a young woman named Dr. Susan Steele who happened to be my vet as well. A couple of weeks after the training was finished I received a call from Dr. Steele saying Simba had come to the clinic and the staff remarked about how well the dog's behavior had improved. I asked if she would be kind enough to refer problem dogs to me "until I figure out what I'm gonna do for the rest of my life." She agreed and it wasn't long before I was working with a couple of Dr. Steele's clients' dogs and their issues.

I had some early success and word soon spread. It wasn't that long, however, before I was beginning to get clients with more serious problems, such as aggression toward people and/or other dogs. Since my past training was largely defined by dominating the dog, I knew I could not get really "alpha" with a client's dog because they most probably would not invite me back. I tried working with food; however, even though it would work with simple dog issues, it most certainly did not work with the majority of the problems with which I was now dealing. Indeed, with some dogs I found it to be counterproductive. In my head I knew I was out of my league, taking on those difficult problems.

Still, I was considered to be very successful with the majority of dogs with which I worked. I also had begun receiving a fair amount of publicity, with articles about me in *The Boston Globe* and *Boston Herald* as well as *The New York Times* and even *The Wall Street Journal*. I was receiving referrals from some 30 vet clinics as well. Then, in mid-1984, I was asked to start a behavior department at Boston's famed Angell Memorial Animal Hospital. That was followed in 1988 with my first book, *Dog Tales*. I was now seeing and working with problem dogs at Angell in addition to my regular practice of making house calls, solving problems where the dogs actually lived. The dogs that did not do well with me in my general practice as well as those from Angell continued to confound me. Those dogs simply would not respond well to my dominant approach. Back then I believed it was because those dogs were simply too stubborn or, perhaps, simply not smart enough to understand me. So with those dogs I would get firmer and they would get firmer and with some I would eventually end up in the local emergency room to get put back together.

Angell had an extensive library, open to staff, and I could be found there on days other than Tuesday, reading everything there was on dog behavior. The problem was there was very little, and what little was there was virtually no help. Talking with trainers back then did not help me either. I knew what they knew. By this time I had read close to a dozen books on dog training, but there again, they were training the way I was.

Like a wandering monk I searched everywhere for answers, but found little. Then, one afternoon my daughter Kristen, who was at the time working at Fidelity, called and asked me to dinner. She had picked up a magazine, *Shambhala Sun*, from her boss's desk and said there was an interesting piece I should read. The article she had in mind was about the monks at New Skete Monasteries (known for their excellent dog-training program). Some years before I had spent a day at New Skete, located in Cambridge, New York. Most of that day was spent with Brother Job, a fascinating and dog-wise young monk. We talked dogs and worked with several, but once again, we both trained fundamentally pretty much the same.

I was about to put down Kristen's pilfered magazine when the pages opened to an article titled, "Ray Hunt, the Cowboy Sage." It was about an Idaho cowboy horse trainer who was working with a philosophy of "gentling" unbroken horses. Ray spoke about his mentor, Tom Dorrance, an older, amazing cowboy horseman, a pioneer in using this "gentling" approach. Tom used to say to a student, "First you go with the horse, then the horse goes with you, and then you go together."

A rider myself, those words hit me like a hammer. I quickly realized it needed to be that way with the dogs. But how to get there? Twenty-five years after working successfully with clients' dogs, I discovered I needed to adjust my thinking; I needed to change the prescription in my glasses so I could look differently at the relationship between the dog and me. Maybe, just maybe, with those difficult dogs, perhaps they weren't the real problem. Could it possibly be me?

Desperate, I finally went to the dogs themselves. I became their student and they became my teachers. Eventually, through many years of painful and incredibly difficult work, but with help from the dogs themselves, I began to learn how to get inside the dog's mind and understand what he needed from me. I also began to understand that I needed to listen to the dog, for the dog had much to teach me about what I needed from him. I began calling it Quiet Firmness. It's in this book, and is the foundation for the approach I now use when working with a client and their dog. Throughout these pages I have included anecdotes of clients' dogs with both common and not-so-common problems, and have detailed how I resolved each of them. When I first meet with a client, there are many times I don't know how best to work with their dog, or even with the client. However, after spending time with the dog for a while, I'll know the best way, because that dog will tell me. You see, they're all different and there are no rules that dictate what applies to one dog applies to all. Nor does it come from books. It's really about learning how to communicate respectfully with THAT dog, with my eyes, my body, and my mind.

Thirty-six years after my first book, *Dog Tales*, I've finished *A Ray of Hope*. I know and understand the agony, frustration, and hopelessness many of my clients are experiencing when we first meet. From many I hear, "Ray, you are our last resort." Like the dogs themselves, each client is different, so I need to be both intuitive as well as flexible. I need to be honestly empathetic, at times more with the client than with the dog. Above all I need to be understanding and nonjudgmental.

A troubled dog makes for a troubled dog client, just as a troubled client most often ensures a troubled dog. I have worked with clients whose marriage may well be in crises as a result of the dog's issues; one wants to keep the dog, the partner wants it gone. Vacations are cancelled due to dog issues. Friends no longer visit because the client's dog poses a threat to anyone entering the home. Neighbors, once friendly, now call the police because of a client's constantly barking dog. A single mom is being harassed by the condo association where she lives for the same issue. A board of selectmen (or women) vote to deport a family dog as a result of its behavior. I've pretty much been a witness to it all and have successfully resolved the majority of issues with which I've been asked to help.

I hope this book will awaken in you a desire to become a compassionately firm leader/companion to your dog. May it open you to the awareness that success is not only possible, but achievable, creating the relationship between you and your dog which you've always wanted, yet thought never possible. To get there you will also need to work on yourself. This book is about working with your dog but it is also about you working on you, and that can be the really difficult part. In the end you will understand this book is really about both dog and owner learning from each other.

I'm still at it, still learning. The dogs are my life. It's been a remarkable, 50-year journey, and I'm so grateful to have been blessed with a gift for what I do. To help you, I've put what I've learned into this book. In the chapters that follow you will learn and understand how and why your dog thinks and acts as he does. You will discover how to communicate with him the way he communicates with you. Finally, you will learn what is crucial in establishing a lasting relationship, one based upon mutual trust, respect, love and Quiet Firmness.

Chapter 1

The Nature Of Dog

The first thing you need to know is the last thing you'll learn.
~RAY HUNT, HORSEMAN

*T*he bumper sticker on the Honda parked ahead of me stated, "Dogs Are Little People in Fur Coats." It was an early September evening and I had been invited to speak about dog behavior to members of a well-respected humane society. I climbed the steps to the front door of the public library where I was scheduled to speak, and entered the conference room. There were perhaps 50 attendees, most of them gathered in the rear of the hall where the coffee and pastries were. A few minutes later the chairwoman graciously introduced me as that "well-known and respected dog psychologist." I thanked her and began by telling them I had prepared a talk; however, after seeing that bumper sticker about the little people in fur coats, I told them that was, to me, misguided and how thinking that way can get dog owners off on the wrong foot with their dogs. I said that to hold that concept of dogs as little people is disrespectful to the dog. I said a lot of things that were not in my prepared talk that night. I don't know whether or not I convinced many there that evening, but I do know that, at the very least, I got them talking about it. Several of them told me so.

If the dog were asked whether he would prefer to be treated as a dog or as a person, I believe the dog would answer simply, "Treat me with the respect due me as a dog." I believe that a dog thinks and acts behaviorally, from three areas:

1. Hierarchy, where the dog sees himself in the ascending pack order.

The human understands two types of a relationship. Your wife has tennis friends. You have golfing buddies. These are what I call equal relationships. The relationship is horizontal. The other relationship is vertical. The boss and staff, professor and student. There is no room for an equal relationship in the mind of the dog. God never put that "chip" in the dog's brain. Therefore, the dog sees himself as either leader or follower.

2. The Survival Instinct. Self preservation.

I see this in many of the rescue dogs I work with.

3. Energy, that which in the Far East is called chi.

I speak about this at length in a separate chapter.

So what exactly is the nature of the dog? Somewhere between 30,000 and 50,000 years ago, the wolf became a dog. Over countless centuries, he became increasingly domesticated, with specialized breeds developing over time. Herding, guarding, coursing, and military breeds most probably came first, with vermin hunters, pulling breeds, and retrievers following. For centuries, the dog lived together with man. Most not only lived with us, but worked alongside us. They were with us 24/7. In addition, they knew many, if not all, of the inhabitants of their local village. My, how times have changed.

Dogs are social animals. Their nature is to bond with their human pack. It is to devote their life to members of its pack, and to do so unconditionally. It is also to be either the leader or a follower. There is no middle ground here. In the wild that works perfectly. There is order, which flows from the top down. It is perfection. It is our responsibility, our duty, to emulate that pack mentality, with our dog and our pack. Owners who have true working dogs understand this concept better than the dog owner who has a lap dog. They understand the pack mentality of the dog. Talk with a rancher, for example, about his ranch dog. He will tell you how important it is for the dog to understand clearly where he or she resides in the pack.

After all, when a cowboy's workin' cows, he needs his dog to help keep them in line, not scatter 'em across Idaho. He works with the dog's hierarchy and natural herding instincts. And the dog works happily with him, understanding that the cowboy is the leader.

A few weeks ago, while (lightly) brushing a client's aggressive Miniature Poodle, I was bitten. Not a 911 situation, just a couple of forearm bites. That evening my client was kind enough to text me an apology, telling me that Franco, her dog, was sorry he bit me. Truth is, he's not sorry. If Franco could speak English, he'd give me that great line from the movie *The Godfather*: "It's not personal; it's business." That is the nature of dog.

I've had clients tell me that, "Aztec doesn't think he's a dog; he thinks he's a person" or "Mollie's only nine months old. She's my baby." I hear this and it scares me, because if I'm unable to set them straight on what it is on the other end of the lead, they are heading down a rocky path with that dog. He will, because of what he is, because of his nature, probably become a problem for them.

If I come home after a difficult day, go into the side room, and sit quietly in my chair, Finn, my yellow Lab, will come in and quietly put his big head on my thigh. He's picked up my energy, and he wants to let me know he understands. That is his nature. It's what drives the therapy dog, the dogs for the blind, etc.

This book will, I pray, help you to understand more about your dog's nature, why he does what he does, and how to work WITH him rather than AGAINST him.

Think about the great qualities we humans try to perfect throughout our daily life. I'm speaking about patience, truthfulness, forgiveness, selfless service, compassion, generosity, kindness, loyalty, courage, unconditional love. The dog has already mastered those and more. If we pay attention, who learns from whom? And that is why we love our dogs.

There is a sign over many doors in parts of India, written in Hindi.

Translated it says, "Leave your ego with your shoes." One of the biggest differences between the human and the dog is simply this: the dog has no ego. He lives his entire life without knowing what ego is. Try your best to learn from your egoless dog. That is the true nature of dog.

Let me tell you a quick story. I once was introduced to an individual who worked in a rest home. When he was given the position, part of the contract stated that he would live there with the residents. He was young, and I thought it must be difficult for him to be living with those poor old souls. He didn't seem to mind at all. When I learned what his duties were, his "job description" astounded me. He was in charge of all security and he was also the social and recreation director. In addition, he made the rounds to visit almost every resident daily. He participated in their physical therapy, accompanying them on daily walks; and in fact, he was directly responsible for many of them getting outside and getting some fresh air and exercise. Finally, he filled in, illegally, for the licensed social worker on her days off, listening to their problems with the utmost patience, and always helping them feel better after a session with him. He worked there for 11 years, giving selfless service and never accepting one dime in recompense! He passed away quietly in his sleep three years ago. His name was Barou, and he was a handsome Golden retriever. I had the pleasure and honor of helping him to learn the ropes at St. Patrick's Manor in

Framingham, Massachusetts. All of the great qualities of life of which I spoke of earlier were in this dog. He helped me learn what incredible beings dogs are. You get them to learn SIT, STAY, COME, HEEL, DOWN. They will, if we let them, teach us about the virtues of life. Tell me, who's teaching whom? This is the nature of the dog.

This is why your dog silently says to you, "Have patience with me! I'm trying my best to learn from you." Yet, if you and your dog are not in sync, the dog cannot learn from you, try as he might. There is a responsibility on your part to learn as well as to teach. The Delta Society told us that dogs help us live longer, reduce our stress, help fill that "void" in our hearts. Not always. I deal with clients on a daily basis whose stress is increased because of their dog; their dog is an anchor around their necks. Why? They don't know how to communicate with them; they don't understand their nature.

Have you ever thought what a wonderful gift it is that a dog can, literally, move in and live with humans in their home? We take that for granted, that they somehow, amazingly, adapt to our lifestyle. Thousands of them get through a 10-hour day completely by themselves. I am constantly amazed that they are, somehow, able to adapt as well as they do.

The dog will be comfortable where we tell him to be. If, by our irresponsible actions, we allow him to become the leader, that's where he'll be. If, on the other hand, we accept our responsibility and achieve the leader role, he will naturally be the follower. This is the true nature of dog. Believe me, you are not going to change this nature.

Chapter 2

Mutual Trust And Respect
And Balancing Energy

To gain respect I had to learn to give respect.
~RAY HUNT, HORSEMAN

I grew up in northwest Ohio and, as a seven-year-old, rode the po-
nies at the military boarding school I attended. I never learned how
to ride—I just learned to stay aboard. They were pretty salty, whip-
ping their heads around to nip me, or trying to buck or scrape me off
against a fence post. They were never successful and I learned a bit
from them. They say we learn from our peers. I know this: everything
I know about dogs the dogs have taught me.

It was some 50 plus years ago, and I'd been getting dogs to heel
with what I call the cowboy method—a lot of yanking on the collar
and lead. It isn't that you can't get the job done that way. You can and
I did. But it helps to be strong and it's unpleasant for both dog and
trainer. There can be lots of frustration (low-level anger) as well, and
pretty soon you've got yourself a real battle of wills between you and

your dog. Then you have to get tougher and the process just keeps escalating. Some still believe they need to dominate the dog, to be the alpha figure, the head honcho.

I was tough on my own dogs too, way back, before I learned a better way. I wasn't stupid, just ignorant. I'm not proud of it. I had big, strong, field-bred, hard-running Labradors. Dogs that when you sent them on a retrieve would kick dirt in your face to get there. I was an executive vice president in the transportation field and was pretty much on the go with lots of business pressure. I had little time for my dogs. I had a lot of frustration as well, and took some of that out on them when training—that is, I raised my voice and used a bit of corporal punishment. It worked with all but one of them.

Geordy, was a big, tough Lab weighing north of 90 pounds. I could never get Geordy to heel properly. It was always a battle. He was always out in front a little, with me yanking him back. You see, I didn't know any better. It was always he verses me, conflict and confrontation. I'd get more forceful, and so would he. That was the only way I knew to train—I thought you needed to dominate the animal. It didn't work with Geordy. After a tough, frustrating training session, there were times I really didn't like that dog.

Then, lying in bed one night, staring at the ceiling, I realized something about him. I didn't respect him and I knew he didn't respect me. There was no mutual respect. The following day I tried something totally different with Geordy to help him to heel better. When he began to walk in front of me I let him go and then I changed direction on him. We both did this impromptu, uncoordinated little "dance" for about 15 minutes, and lo and behold, that dog began walking next to me. It worked! The big guy was heeling right next to me, focusing on me, and enjoying himself. We both learned a great deal that day. That was the first time I worked with that big guy using what I call Quiet Firmness.

28

Heeling – Round Penning for Dogs

Horseman Buck Brannaman begins to gain mutual trust and respect from a green (untrained) horse by round penning that animal. Eventually the horse voluntarily begins to follow as Buck turns away from him. The horse follows Buck because he's accepting Buck as his leader. For many years, I have shown my clients the importance of gaining mutual trust and respect from their dogs through my method of teaching dogs to heel. Over four decades, I've been turning away from dogs to get them to turn toward me. With rare exceptions, when I first start working with a client's dog, I begin with helping the dog to learn to heel. Heeling simply means (to the dog) to walk next to your side with zero tension or pressure on the lead (leash), and if you so wish eventually with no lead. (See Chapter 5).

As the dog begins to understand the process, a fascinating fundamental shift begins to take place. First, you will notice that the dog begins turning as you turn, without your needing to help the dog. The dog stops walking out in front of you and CHOOSES to follow you. Second, you will also notice that his primary focus is now on you, and no longer on things going on around him. This "shift" in attitude is a pivotal one, for it shows the beginning of your dog accepting you as the leader. The dog, possibly for the first time in its life, begins to place trust and respect in the human. Watching this happen never fails to stir something in me.

There is no hard force involved, yet neither am I attempting to achieve the desired result through being sentimental. Dogs see through that wishy-washiness for what it is—a lack of discipline and confidence on our part. Neither babying the dog nor physically dominating the dog is the answer. The answer is quiet firmness.

Positive Pressure—Gaining and Giving the Commitment

Your dog is an "into pressure" animal. This means simply that when a dog feels SUSTAINED physical pressure on him one way, he turns into the direction of the pressure rather than backing away from it, and it is precisely why you see so many people walking their dogs down the street with the dog five feet ahead, dragging the owner like he or she was a dogsled in the Iditarod race. Understanding this is critical in helping the dog to learn and helping the dog to begin giving to you.

Try it. Make a fist. Now, face your dog's right shoulder and apply moderate pressure with your fist directly into the shoulder area. Didn't your dog lean into the pressure, rather away from it? I first noticed this years ago. When one of my Labs would come to me for petting if I were squatting, his head would come up against my chest. I would push my chest against his head and he would push back into me. I thought his behavior interesting, and used it over the years with hundreds of dogs.

They all seemed to enjoy it, and they all pushed back, just like the Lab I had long ago. Back then I didn't understand what fundamental dynamic was unfolding right before me. Only years later did I understand it—I was helping to establish trust between the dog and me. When I think back on it, I wonder how I could have been so blind.

I now apply the pressure differently. After heeling the dog for anywhere between five and ten minutes, I will stop, and getting down on one knee will kneel alongside the dog's shoulder—right or left depending on which side I am heeling the animal—and with the back or the side of my fist, will begin applying pressure in a circular motion to the shoulder.

Amazingly, when the correct amount of direct pressure is applied, the dog will move into the pressure, and therefore, toward me. I will continue this pressure up to three or four minutes sometimes. During this time, I may move my face literally inches from the dog's so my nose is partway between his ear and his eye. As I continue to push, I begin speaking in a calm voice, "Am I gonna get a commitment from you today, huh? What do you say? How about that commitment?" I am looking for one commitment—turning and moving toward me.

If I get the commitment, that move toward me—which might seem insignificant to you, but let me assure you it is anything but—that represents a major breakthrough in the relationship! I now have the beginning of his trust and respect—both critical aspects in building a lasting relationship.

Remember, this trust and respect must be mutual. I demonstrate respect to the dog by placing my face close to his (depending upon his temperament and behavior) and by treating him exactly for what he is, a dog. Indeed, the highest form of respect I can grant him is to treat him with dignity and thank him for being the marvelous creature he is.

This doesn't mean I can't lose that respect through anger or stupidity. It's my job to retain that respect and build on it. It's a lifelong commitment to your dog. If you aren't prepared to make that type of commitment, get yourself a cat.

Balancing Energy

Those of you who are or have been students of the martial arts will be familiar with the word chi. For those of you unfamiliar with it, chi is a Chinese word referring to one's inner energy or inner force. This force is very powerful; it is the chi that allows the martial artist to break bricks with the side of his hand. The breaking of bricks is, however, merely a physical outward expression of chi. Chi also refers to the life force within. Eastern mystics believe that when this life force is in harmony, in balance, that balance expresses itself in good health. When the energy is out of balance, poor health is one of the results. The acupuncturist restores good health to the person by balancing the inner energy, by placing the needles in critical pressure points.

Easterners further believe that the entire planetary system (cosmos) is composed of this single energy force, and that this force is the most powerful energy there is. Furthermore, when this energy is in balance, the world is in balance (it would seem that this energy has been out of balance for quite some time).

I strongly believe in this Eastern understanding. We hear people say, "That John McGuire is certainly in tune with his dog." Or we say, "Nancy Saunders is on the same wavelength as her horse." What does that mean? It means that there is balance between the two—the human and the animal. Although the person may not understand the concept of chi, that is what he or she is referring to. The dog, on the other hand, instinctively understands energy. It is what helps him to survive in this world.

I believe that a harmonious relationship between the owner and his dog depends upon their energies being balanced with one another's.

When they are in balance, dog and owner act as one. When they are unbalanced, they are at odds. When we are angry, stressed, frustrated, depressed, irritable, etc., how can our dog remain calm? Our energy affects his energy. Our state affects his state. Allow me to give you an example of how your energy (chi) affects your dog's energy (chi). Let's say your dog is aggressive toward other dogs. The two of you are enjoying a pleasant walk together. Suddenly, up ahead, you see another dog and owner approaching. What is your instant reaction? You tense up. You pull the lead up tight. That's negative energy and, believe me, your dog is aware of your energy shift in a heartbeat. You get tense; your dog instantly tenses up and begins to show aggressive behavior toward that approaching dog.

How do you balance each other's energies? One way is through proper breathing. When I'm stressed my breathing is tight, shallow. When I'm relaxed, so is my breathing, long and deep.

In my opinion, it is precisely the same with the companion dog/ owner relationship. When things between you and your dog get tense, STOP, take in a deep breath, and stabilize your own energy before you take the next step in working with your dog. If you can't manage to do it at that moment, call a 15-minute recess. Never allow your frustration (low level anger) or any emotional pressure to own you. Think about this. If you cannot control your own energy, how can you control your dog's energy?

Chapter 3

Finn's Doghouse Dogmas

Are we smart? Smart enough to wrap an owner 'round our paw.
~Finn, Labrador retriever

*W*hen Finn, my 13-year-old yellow Lab, found out I was writing another book, he wanted to have an active say. I agreed; after all, he accompanies me on my visits with clients, and is an important associate. So when I was ready to do Chapter 3, both he and I got together, and I listened and wrote down what he had to say. Read what follows as if your dog were telling you how best to work with him.

Dogma #1. I need you to learn how to communicate effectively with me.

Dogma #2. I need you to learn how to feel my energy. I already feel yours.

Dogma #3. I need you to learn how to use Ray's Quiet Firmness approach.

Dogma #4. I need you to learn how to lead. I'll be happy to follow. I cannot understand an equal, buddy relationship.

Dogma #5. I will learn either appropriate or inappropriate behavior from you. Please be careful what you are REALLY teaching me.

Dogma #6. Be consistent with me. If at times it's okay to jump on you, don't blame me for jumping on friends.

Dogma #7. Do not expect me to automatically understand what, in your mind, is acceptable vs. unacceptable behavior. I make no ethical or moral judgments.

Dogma #8. I must understand why my behavior is being corrected. Please do not merely assume I know. Be both quietly firm and clear.

Dogma #9. Reward me when I get it right. I like praise—just like you.

Dogma #10. Whatever you give me will come back to you 10x over.

Dogma #11. Treat me as a dog, with the respect I deserve as a dog.

Dogma #12. Please learn from me, for I have much to teach.

The above are just a few important suggestions from me. Ray and I have enjoyed a wonderful relationship these past 13 years. My wish is that both you and your dog(s) enjoy an equally special time together.
—Finn

Finn crossed over the bar on October 4, 2023. He was both my loving companion and my associate. I miss him greatly.

Chapter 4

Tasking: Discovering
A New Path

Humans are the only animals who will follow unstable leaders.
~Cesar Millan

*H*eel, Sit, Stay, Down, Come (Here). What do you call those words? Of course, you call them commands. I was raised with commands at the Catholic military boarding school located in Ohio's northwest corn country on a 600-acre farm. From the time I was seven, in the second grade, until I graduated at the age of 14 in eighth grade, I was both given and giving commands. Later, in the Marine Corps, those commands were reinforced with a seriousness I had never before experienced. Marine drill instructors (DI's) are the very essence of the term alpha dog.

During my early years working with dogs, I was a firm believer in teaching commands, along with a high price to pay for not obeying. Then, in late December 1989, a strange thing happened. I was asked to travel to India to work with a troubled dog living in an ashram. I had been working with both dogs and their owners for over 15 years, and had achieved a high degree of success doing so. I considered myself a highly accomplished dogman, helping dogs with people problems, and my book, *Dog Tales*, further confirmed it. I arrived in what was then Bombay on the 13th of January 1990. I had agreed to spend a month, doing my best to help get the dog patched up and on with life. During my stay, however, I began to experience a subtle yet real shift in my thinking and, as a result, my approach to dealing with this particular dog. I awoke one early morning around 2:00 a.m. thinking about the dog with which I was working. I heard a voice say, "Do you know what bothers you most about Sanchis? It's that he's just like you." It hit me like a mallet. It was right. What I despised most about him was how it was like looking into a mirror. It wasn't so much that I had never before dealt with similar problem behavior, it was more about my reaction when the behavior (aggression in this case) reared up. I began thinking how many dog owners relate to their problematic animals, but in a way I had never thought before. Later, back in the States, I began seeing the dog/owner relationship through a different prism, a different set of glasses. While in India I realized that the word command can easily result in conflict and confrontation between dog and owner, and that results in the relationship becoming increasingly problematic.

Let's use the command, "Sit," as an example. Such a simple command that an eight-week-old puppy learns to sit quickly when reinforced with food. That same dog, however, at five or six months of age, might well begin ignoring commands it once obeyed so well as a pup. Now the owner begins to up the ante, demanding the dog to "Sit." This is typically conveyed by becoming both louder as well as repetitive, "sit, sit, SIT"—commanding the animal to sit.

Totally frustrated, angry, and exhausted, the owner contacts a trainer, who may tell him he's not being firm enough, which might result in one of three possible scenarios. One, the dog resists more or, two, he finally submits to the demands of the "master" through fear and intimidation. Or three, they get rid of the dog. If, on the other hand, they had contacted me, I would have told them what came to me while in India during some of those nights and as a result how I changed my approach working with that dog. I want to share with you the shift I experienced those 34 years ago.

I want you to change your thinking about the word command. I want you to begin to think of those words as tasks. When my daughter Kristen's twins, Evan and Tatum, were between three and four years of age, she would tell them when dinner was over to brush their teeth and to get ready for bed. Did she give them the command, "Evan, Tatum, go brush your teeth"? Of course not. Why? Because it's not a command, but rather a task. When they finished completing the task, they were rewarded, which helped them to succeed, to feel better about themselves, to feel safer and more secure under Kristen and Van's parenting. When you tell your dog, "Sit," that's a task. Not a big task, mind you, but a task nonetheless. When you tell your dog to sit, you're giving him a task. When he sits, he gets rewarded, so he succeeds, feels better about himself, feels safer and more secure under your guidance, coaching, leadership—however you wish to think of yourself. And what if he doesn't sit? Read on, dear reader.

Dogs are social animals. There are four species of canids: wolves, dogs, coyotes, and fox. Three—wolves, dogs, and coyotes—are social (pack) animals. The fox is a solitary (non-pack) animal. The domesticated dog is a highly social animal, naturally gravitating toward the human for companionship. If isolated from good social human contact, the domestic dog becomes a stressed, insecure, defensive shell of what he is capable of becoming. On the other hand, providing that dog with good, positive human contact sets the tone for a contented member of his human family (pack).

So then, what to do when your four-legged family member begins not to sit when told to do so? Simple. Withhold all affection from him until he decides that the smart move is to sit, which is then followed by some affection, but not food (treat). I tell clients, when your dog gets a bit of maturity in him (five to six months), YOU should become the treat. I had a client with a three-year-old English sheepdog that had become aggressive with all family members except the wife. I told them to withhold affection until he decided to sit. It took three days. But down the road? No more aggression toward family members. I'll tell you another story, one that truly amazed me. Lowell is a city northwest of Boston. My clients were both professional people, one of them the president of a large company based in Boston. They had a very large, ancient flock (and shepherd) guarding breed, called a Komondor. When I arrived they began to tell me that Kudzu had, over the past year, become aggressive toward them. He had never bitten them; however, whenever a new large object was brought into the home he would guard it for two or three days. For example, a stainless-steel trash basket in the kitchen could not be used for three days after they brought it home. After the three days they were free to use it as they wished. The same with a new armoire. That bothered them, but the real reason they secured my services was because they had to modify the way they got to their cars in the morning in order to get to work. Originally, they would finish breakfast and coffee, pick up their briefcases, and enter the attached garage through the kitchen. Kudzu had begun guarding the door to the garage. Marie, my client-husband's wife, made it crystal clear to me that she was less then pleased with this arrangement. A major reason they had purchased their new home was because it had access to the garage from inside the house. It was now winter in New England and she was most upset over being forced to leave the house, walk over to the garage, open the garage door from outside to get to the cars. Her husband was none too pleased as well. I inquired about training and they told me they had a trainer helping them when Kudzu was a pup, but that they had not pursued any additional training. The Komondor can be quite willful, with an eye toward being pack leader. I suggested they begin reinforcing his sit before affection. Marie was sitting opposite me, pen and note pad in hand, and immediately wrote, "Sit prior to receiving affection."

"What else?" she queried, eyeing me like a company president addressing an employee way down the chain of command.

"I think that might be enough, for starters," I answered.

"That's ridiculous," she shot back, "he sits very well." Whereupon she called for Kudzu and a minute later the beast appeared in the doorway. She got up, strode over to Kudzu and, in a voice somewhat reminiscent of my company commander when I was still in the Marines, demanded, "Sit, you, sit," whereupon Kudzu turned on his paw and slowly left the room.

"I think working on the sit as I suggested is enough for a start," I repeated, asking them to please keep in touch before our next session. Well, it took three weeks, but then I got a phone call.

"Mr. McSoley, this is Marie ... I'm calling to tell you it took three days before Kudzu responded to my telling him to sit, but since then he has been sitting well for both of us."

"That's great news, Marie. Keep up the good work and let's get together this coming week."

"Next week is fine, Mr. McSoley. Let's set a day and time while we're on the phone, and by the way, there is something else." I knew it, I thought, the other shoe is about to drop. "Three days ago, Leonard got up from the breakfast table, and Kudzu was standing by the garage door as usual, but as Lenard got up, he moved away from the door, and we were both able to go out to the garage without it being a problem. And he has not guarded the door since. We knew you'd like to know and, we are both very grateful to you for your assistance."

Pressure

Whenever you're working on solving an issue with your dog, there is going to be some psychological, emotional pressure, and that pressure can come in one of three ways:

1. all the pressure is on the dog

2. all the pressure is on the owner

3. the pressure is split, some on the dog, some on the owner

Which do you think it should be? Take your time, there's no time limit for your answer. If you're like 90% of dog people, you will pick #2 or #3. What's a synonym for pressure? How about stress. I don't know about you, but when I work with a client's dog, I can't afford to have even a scintilla of pressure on me. Why? you ask. Because I can't do my job. And the dog picks up my stress and interprets it as weak, negative energy (chi). And at that point I cannot be looked upon as leader. So, I put all the pressure on the dog; however, I want to set the dynamic where I provide a way for him to end the pressure. He ends the pressure by simply doing what I ask him to do. No conflict. No confrontation. He succeeds by doing the right thing, with quiet firmness from me. So the correct answer is #1. Put the pressure where it should be—on your dog. And please do not give me that "Ray, is it inhumane" jive. When he learns that doing the correct thing works, he begins to acknowledge you as the CEO, and he accepts his position as executive junior VP. And then life is good.

Chapter 5

Quiet Firmness: Stepping Onto The New Path

By leadership we mean the art of getting someone else to do something that you want done because he wants to do it.
~General (and former President) Dwight D. Eisenhower

$\mathcal{W}$hen my first book, *Dog Tales,* was published in the spring of 1988, my publisher, Warner Books, dispatched me to New York City to be interviewed on *The Good Morning America* TV show. When the producer began to interview me, at one point she said, "I read in your book that you work with aggressive dogs."

"That's true," I answered.

"Well, I can't imagine doing that; you must wear gloves," she continued.

"No," I answered, "I don't wear gloves. Understand, as soon as I put on a glove I'm bitten."

"Explain, please," she asked.

"Well," I said, "putting on the glove sets me up to be bitten, otherwise, there's no reason for me to put on the glove. The mind is a wish-fulfilling tree. What we wish for, we get."

"Oh," she answered, "have you ever been bitten?"

"I have," I answered, as she winced for the audience.

She then queried, "Were any of them bad bites?"

I looked directly at her when I answered. "Hell, lady, none of 'em were good."

It begins with the mind. The mind is everything. It is the computer processor in the human body. The senses are controlled by the mind. Your eyes see an object, but it is your mind that identifies that object, what the object is. "For him who has conquered the mind, the mind is the best of friends; but for one who has failed to do so, his mind will be his greatest enemy"(*Bhagavad Gita*, by Vyasa). Your energy is controlled by your mind. If you do not learn to control your mind, how can you possibly hope to have any control of your dog's mind? When you tell your dog "Sit" and she doesn't, you begin to become frustrated. But what really happens is that you allow your mind to become frustrated because you have no control over it. Now your dog senses your frustration, your negative energy, and so now her behavior becomes worse, and before long, you both are engaged in conflict and confrontation—a battle of wills, people call it. But it is really a battle of your mind and your dog's mind.

So it all begins with you controlling your mind. How can you do that? As I said, if your mind is unsettled, forget the training session with your dog. If you had a rough day, don't train. If your toddler twins got into a five-pound bag of flour while you were downstairs with the laundry, please do not hold a training session later with your dog. When you do, make it easy for your mind. Let's say, later, you're at the stove, reducing your wonderful risotto and your dog is nearby. Simply turn to your dog and, with your mind at ease, ask her to sit. She sits, and you give her some quiet praise. And that is enough. It all begins with your mind. Only when your mind is still can you exercise what I call Quiet Firmness.

To help me still my mind, I meditate. Meditation is a precious gift I received during my stay in India. That gift has assisted me greatly and has resulted in my becoming better at what I do with the dogs. Not long ago someone very special told me, "Your work is not yet finished." Chances are that neither is your work finished. Take time every day to sit quietly and listen. One of the things I heard (while sitting in meditation) at the ashram was, "I have given you the gift of learning to be a simple dogman." Whatever you hear while sitting quietly will help you develop both a quiet mind and Quiet Firmness.

\

Chapter 6

Learning To Learn:
First Steps On The Path

When you get to square ten, all of square one will be in it.
~RAY HUNT, HORSEMAN

*T*his chapter is about helping your dog to learn how to learn. I'll show you how to work with your dog so that he WANTS to comply when you ask him to do something. Remember, we will not be commanding him to do anything, nor will we be begging him to do what we ask and stuffing a treat in his mouth when he does it. As I make clear throughout this chapter, a large part of your responsibility is, by using your mind, to help motivate your dog into completing the desired action. In order for you to be able to control your dog, he first needs to learn five fundamental tasks. Those tasks consist of Sit, Come (or Here), Heel, Down, Stay. That's it. Just those five tasks. Those tasks are the cornerstones to a happy and healthy relationship. Remember, they are tasks rather than commands.

Unfortunately, most dog owners cannot get their dogs to complete those tasks, even though they learned them in "puppy school," or an "obedience" class. Ninety percent of my clients have had their dogs to either one or the other, or both. Their dogs will sit when told to some of the time, and will come some of the time, etc. But, when they REALLY need their dog to respond, nope. Many times, when I tell a client I will help them get their dog to respond 100% of the time, notwithstanding the distraction, he or she tells me it's impossible. Not only is it possible, if you follow carefully what I tell and show you, both you and your dog will achieve greater results than you both ever thought possible!

Throughout all of the following exercises, I want you to think about what you want your dog to learn and how best you can accomplish it. Your dog work should support the concept that you are helping your dog to first learn how to learn. When you begin working with your dog this way, you will also be building mutual trust and respect.

I have broken down the basics tasks into three separate phases (chapters). This chapter is about learning basic structures or tasks. The next two chapters I will be showing you how to use, properly, a Mendota British slip lead (simple reinforcement) and finally, how to properly use the remote collar (e-collar). Your dog does not know automatically how to learn from you. That is what this chapter is about.

I work with dogs six or seven years old who have never learned how to learn. We are never too old to learn. I learn something from every dog with which I have the honor of working.

SIT

Okay, let's get started. A quick but very important point. If your dog is aggressive with you, do NOT use the following method. Okay, I see you've already put Pogo's buckle collar on. Let me check to see if it's snug enough so he can't back out of it, and it can't get caught on an ear. It's good. Now, stand facing Pogo. Bend forward a bit so you can slip the three middle fingers of your left hand (or right, whichever you prefer) around the collar and under his jaw. If you can cradle his jaw with your thumb on one side and little finger on the other side, so much the better. Okay, that's perfect.

Next, place your right hand at your belt buckle, say "Sit" and slowly bring that hand up to your chest, as though you were zipping up your jacket, and at the same time, bringing your left hand (holding his collar) up, which lifts his head up. At this point Pogo is standing with his head tilted up, eyes on you. Perfect! Now hold that position until he sits. It may take a while; after all, he has no idea what it is you want him to do. Holding his head up and a little back is a bit uncomfortable for him, however, and he will eventually move into a sit, at which you instantly release the pressure and give him a "good boy" and a pat or two.

Sometimes it takes a minute or two for the dog to sit, and it also takes a bit of time for the both of you to get in sync with each other. It is, remember, a learning process for you both. Just remember, don't tense up, breathe.

Only give the "Sit" a single time. Do not repeat. If you repeat you let him know you were not serious about "Sit" the first time you said it. Use a firm but normal voice tone. Remember, your dog has hearing far superior to yours. Repeating "Sit" and getting louder is not firmness. It just breaks his ability to concentrate, therefore making it more difficult for him to "Sit." Repeat the procedure five or six times and then stop. Do it twice daily.

Remember, every time he begins to sit, he is the one who relieves the simple neck pressure, not you. Sitting ends pressure. Therefore, the faster Pogo sits, the faster he releases the pressure. Eventually you will say "Sit," raise your hand like zipping your jacket, and Pogo will sit and look at you. He will think to himself, "Hey, what a smart dog I am. I'm so smart I've learned how to beat the system." Why the hand moving up your shirt or jacket? So Pogo learns not only to sit, but to focus on you as well, by following the rising hand with his eyes, so at the end of the sit you have his full attention. Killing two birds with one stone, as they say. At this point you need but say, "Sit," with no hand in the collar, but with the other hand zipping up. Once sitting is consistent, begin having Pogo sit before giving him affection. This way, he learns to request affection rather than demanding it. He no longer demands attention, receiving it for merely breathing in and out. He learns to complete the task first. This builds self-confidence, helps him feel better, safer, and more secure, all under your leadership. Best of all, it really helps the bonding.

STAY

This should be a relatively easy structure for both you and Pogo. All he needs when told "Stay" is to remain motionless. Begin by standing in front of your dog. No, I did not forget to remind you to put your lead on Pogo.

Have him sit. Now, bring both hands up to your shoulders, palms facing Pogo, and tell him "Stay," at the same time moving both hands, palms outward, toward Pogo, and take two steps back. As you step back, keep both palms moving in slow circles. Why? Motion postures tend to hold a dog's focus better than not moving your hands. After two to three seconds, return to the dog's side, standing next to his shoulder. Tell him "Good dog" in a quiet voice. Then back away a couple of feet, tell Pogo "Break" and quietly slap your knees with the palms of your hands. Do not praise him when he releases. Have Pogo repeat the Stay exercise three or four more times, then quit. If Pogo releases before you get back to his shoulder, make certain you do not attempt to correct him, just quietly bring him back and repeat the procedure again. Eventually, he will stay, perhaps out of confusion more than anything else, which is fine because he's still doing it. With both time and repetition, Pogo's confusion will become understanding.

A few points regarding stay. Praise every time you return to him, just make certain you have returned completely prior to giving praise.

If you begin praising him as you return, he may begin to anticipate your return and come halfway to meet you. So, all the way back to his side before the praise. And, most important, don't even think of calling Pogo to you at the end of the stay. Always, always, until we have completely reinforced his stay, make absolutely certain everyone in the family follows that rule! Your dog should be rewarded for staying. Period. Another point. When I work on stay with a client, I work on increasing time, rather than distance. Too many owners can't resist testing their dog's stay too soon, creating greater and greater distance before their dog is solidly secure in the stay. Take my advice. I've been through this, literally, with thousands of clients. Once your dog is steady in the stay for one full minute, only then should you begin adding distance. After you have built up distance straight back, make a change. Now stand at Pogo's side, whichever side is preferable for you, either right or left. Let's say you chose your left side. Now have Pogo sit at your left side, facing forward as you are. Now place your left hand about six inches from his nose, palm facing him. Tell him, "Stay," and move your hand a bit toward his nose, then walk directly away for five to six feet. Do not walk tentatively. Mentally tell yourself that when you turn around, Pogo will be sitting where you told him to stay. If so, wait a bit, then return all the way to where he is, turn so you're facing his way, wait a couple of seconds, then quietly give him praise. Repeat this exercise five or six times, then call it a day. Remember to always end on a high, positive note. If Pogo's not getting this new exercise, then give him one of the originals, facing him and backing away, then returning. He will do that, so praise him and call it a day. When he's getting the new variation, begin walking to the left as well as to the right, but facing him as you do it. You're lined up next to him with him sitting, both facing the same way. Tell him, "Stay," give him the one-hand signal, walk away, then turn, look at him and walk left and right, then return to his side. Eventually, walk around behind him, then return. Keep yourself mentally positive, knowing he is going to do it correctly. Remember, he's reading your energy. Confidence instills confidence. And you want him holding eye contact with you through the exercise. Eye contact maximizes proper focus, and focus is the prerequisite for learning. If I'm at an all boys high school teaching history to 15 boys in the class, and 14 are focused on me but the 15th is looking out the window at a girl walking past, I can teach but #15 cannot learn. Got it? Thought so. Eye contact. Critically important.

HERE

First, allow me to get this off my chest. I do not like the word "Come."

I don't like it one bit. Delmar Smith, one of the finest dogmen ever, said that in his opinion, come is a dead-sounding word. I agree. Back when I was retriever field trialing, none of the field trialers I knew ever used the word come. We all used "Here." Delmar said the word here carried better. Use whichever word you wish; they make Chevies as well as Fords.

Anyway, there's Rocket, the German shorthair over in the next alfalfa field, headed for parts of this hemisphere not yet previously discovered, while Dudley, his normally unflappable owner, is yelling so loud he'd be shattering Waterford crystal within earshot. "Come, Rocket! Rocket, come!! Rocket, get back here, you son of a bitch!!!" And Rocket? Blissfully, he just cleared the second fence in perfect stride and disappeared into the tall stand of Beechnut trees about a quarter mile distant. Many, many years ago that could well have been me, 'cept I had hard-runnin' Labs rather than shorthairs. As the fella said, "Been there, done that." You got a problem like that? I can help. Once again, I've straightened out thousands of dogs whose sole issue was that they did not come when called. I would guess, on a serious note, that the problem results in thousands of dogs being hit and killed by automobiles. The saddest part of all is that it needn't be that way. Most of those dogs would come when called 40%, 50%, or even 90% of the time; however, the one time the owner really needed the dog to come was the one time he didn't. If your dog comes any less than 100% of the time, guess what? He doesn't come when called. Coming when called is a focus drill; if he's not focused on you, he probably won't come. So, like the other tasks, coming when called begins with proper focus.

In the training process, where do things go wrong? Some owners call and call, and when Bullet finally responds, they scream obscenities at him. Now that's smart. Never call your dog and, when he arrives five minutes later, punish him. From the dog's perspective, what have you done? You've taught him not to come when he's called. From his perspective, if he doesn't come, he saves himself a punishment. Others put their dogs out to pee and poop, and then when they return, the owners put the dogs in crates and head off to work. Another thing that goes wrong, I believe, is that owners simply allow way too much time to elapse before they even begin to teach the task. Once I learned the best way, I began teaching my Labs to come when they were 10 weeks old. So begin helping your dog to learn to come when he's young. Coming when called should be the high point of your dog's day rather than the low point.

All my Labs came when called. So can yours.

Here's how to begin. Trip on down to your local sporting goods store or contact an online company like Cabela's (cabelas.com) or Lion Country Supply (lcsupply.com) and purchase a small, black referee's whistle. You can get a metal one, if you wish, but cold metal on the lips around mid-February can be a rather painful experience. I'll stick with plastic. The Acme Thunderer (made in England) has been around since man invented the wheel and is a good one, as is the Roy Gonia Special, my personal choice. I like using a whistle for several reasons. Because of its pitch, it's more exciting than your voice. Plus, your dog hears your voice all the time. Not so with a whistle. A whistle is also consistent. When my kids were young and the dogs might be in the back yard, if one of them called the dogs, they may or may not come; however, if they trilled the whistle, those dogs would come a runnin'. Also remember, when you're tired, angry, or frustrated, you send negative energy to your dog, which of course is not good. But I've never heard anyone blow anger through a whistle, the sound just gets more exciting. As long as you're going out, swing by the market and pick up some good old American cheese. Okay. You're back with a whistle and you say you've already got cheese in the fridge. We're ready to go.

Here's how to start. Tonight, cut up three small (dime-sized) pieces of cheese and grab the whistle. Walk over to your dog, wake him up, and give him a couple of pats. He's up and kickin'? Good. Get down on one knee, and trill, three quick toots, on the whistle. Don't blast it! Trill it quickly and quietly so you don't scare your dog. When you blow the whistle your dog should be sitting a couple of feet in front of you. So trill (blow) the whistle, and immediately give a single piece cheese to pup, along with upbeat praise.

He doesn't need to move; all he need do is open his mouth and take the cheese. Wait about 20 seconds and repeat. Twenty seconds later, repeat.

Congratulations, you just completed lesson one. Give the cheese as quickly as you can after trilling the whistle. Repeat this exercise tomorrow morning and again in the evening. Repeat day 3 the same. Just remember, there is absolutely no distance involved. What you want is to have your dog associate the whistle with getting that small, but important, bit of cheese. Your dog hears the whistle, opens his mouth, gets the cheese and ecstatic praise from you. Period.

Now you're ready for phase two—distance. First, cut up two or three dozen of those little cheese pieces, place them in an empty plastic food container, and place it in the fridge. That way, you can simply take a piece of cheese from the fridge, close the door, put it on top of the fridge, and your dog will never associate the fridge opening with his getting cheese.

After 20-30 minutes, casually look over at your dog. He's lying perhaps 12 feet from you. Of course you are inside your home. Take your whistle and trill it. Hey, here comes your dog. Get down on one knee and, as soon as he gets to you, give him the cheese and "fracture" him with praise. DO NOT REPEAT THIS 3 TIMES as you did in phase one. Just a single time. That's enough. Do that twice a day, once in the morning and once in the afternoon or evening. If you keep repeating it, pup will get tired of it eventually, and that would not be good. By the way, he should never know when he's going to be called from now on. As he gets better at it, begin making it a hide-and-seek game. With my dogs I'd hide behind a door, or behind a sofa. I'd whistle downstairs from my office. Your dog should never know when they will be called.

After a couple of weeks, you may begin, if you wish, chaining a verbal task. Trill the whistle and immediately call "Here." When he comes, cheese and lots of praise. Do this for a week or two. Then, simply reverse the procedure. Say "Here" first, then follow immediately with trilling the whistle. Once again, cheese and tons of praise. By week 4, begin alternating your call. The first time you call, whistle. The next time use "Here." When he's coming to you like he's on railroad tracks, begin intermittent cheese, but continue with praise, but tone it down a bit. Sometimes he gets cheese, sometimes he doesn't. But he always gets praise.

Next, begin using it outside. If you've a fenced-in backyard, that makes for an ideal training platform. When you let him out first thing in the morning to pee and poop, as soon as he's through, trill the whistle. You should be standing at your doorway when you begin this. Oh, I forgot to mention this, which is important. When you begin the hide-and-seek game, increase the volume on the whistle, just don't blow your brains out. Remember also, coming when called has two parts. Part A is about the act of coming. Part B is about doing it NOW. Lots of dogs learn part A but never learn B. You want your dog to learn both. And please, never punish him if he doesn't come.

HEEL

We are going to save Heeling for the next chapter. And no jumping ahead.

DOWN

First of all, do you want "Down" to mean lie down or get down from the furniture or Aunt Sadie? You must not use the same word for both. Keep it simple. If, to your dog, down means to get down, then for the other down, use another verbal cue. Drop or flop would work nicely.

Down should mean to lie down. Single words for tasks work better than multiple words. And, contrary to popular belief, unless you're working more than one dog, you need not use your dog's name prior to giving him the task. He knows who you're talking to.

My technique for helping your dog to learn to lie down when told "Down" involves, in part, helping your dog learn to give to pressure. Horses need to learn to give to pressure, and so do dogs. Here is how I helped my own dogs to learn the task "Down," as well as several thousand clients' dogs. Attach your 6-ft lead to the buckle on your dog's buckle collar. Do not use a slip, commonly called a choke, collar. Just a plain buckle collar will be perfect. With your dog standing next to the chair you're now sitting in, simply bring the lead down to the floor and under the sole of your shoe, short enough so your dog's head is pulled down about three inches.

Now ignore your dog completely, and begin watching the Ohio State Buckeyes take on Michigan's Wolverines. Your dog may buck a bit, or may whine. Ignore it. If your dog lowers its head just enough to relieve the pressure while still standing, quietly reach down and take up the slack. Remember, ignore the dog. Keep the pressure there and, eventually, your dog will lie down, relieving the pressure completely. At that point, reach down and quietly pat him and tell him, "Good dog." Keep your shoe on the lead. If your dog begins to get up, he finds that he, once again, puts pressure on his neck, and he lies down again, after which you give him a little praise. Now let me see you do that. No need to hover over him with your eyes. Simply watch the TV but be aware of what your dog is doing. As soon as he lies down, give him some praise. Eventually, as soon as your dog begins to feel the pressure, he'll lie down. Why? Because it works, and he begins thinking, what a smart dog I am, and the faster I lie down, the faster I take the pressure off. Self-learning, with a bit of help from you, is extremely powerful.

I then progress to the next phase. With your dog standing, get down on one knee and face your dog, 90 degrees to him. Your right shoulder is now a little out in front of his nose, while your left hand holds the lead slack, a few inches under his jaw. Now tell your dog "Down," and immediately bring your right hand straight down to the floor, while your left hand (holding the lead) immediately goes straight down to the floor, putting some pressure on your dog's neck. Do not JERK the lead down, simply bring it down to the floor. Your dog will most probably lie down quickly, at which point you give him some praise. Your left hand, the lead hand, should drop immediately AFTER you say "Down," not at the same time. This is important as your dog should hear the cue (Down) just a bit before feeling the pressure. I suggest you repeat the procedure two more times. At the conclusion of the third time, I'd give a bit of quiet praise and then just watch TV for, perhaps, 30 minutes. At the end, get up from your chair, telling your dog "Break," and walk away holding the lead. Do this after each tasking session on Down. Eventually your dog will associate the word "Break" with getting up from the down position and releasing. You have now begun to help your dog to learn that the word (cue) Break means that he can release from the down position and, eventually, from the Stay task in general. One more point before moving on. After your dog is responding well to the Down task, when you cue him with Down and he responds with hand and voice cues, tell him "Stay" and sit with him lying next to you for, say, three minutes. Then, release him with the "Break" cue. Remember, if he releases without given the Break cue, there's no need to correct him. Simply bring him back to the spot where he was and repeat the exercise. Do that until he makes the smart decision to do it correctly. No pressure on you, and you have also extended the Stay to not only when he's sitting, but lying down as well. Good job. Time to move on.

Chapter 7

Simple Reinforcement: Farther Along The Path

Make the wrong thing difficult and the right thing easy.
~RAY HUNT, HORSEMAN

ongratulations! You have accomplished quite a bit with your dog since I've last seen you. He's sitting, coming to you, staying, and lying down when told to. He even does it in the presence of low-level distractions. We're now going to do some simple reinforcement for what he's learned by using a Mendota British slip lead, or what I call an avoidance lead. I will further show you how to use this lead to help your dog learn to heel properly. We will be following a principle of simple conditioning to help make all this work. The principle behind this form of conditioning is the following: Any behavior that results in the cessation of a negative stimulus tends to become reinforced. It is, technically, what is termed Negative Reinforcement. Now hold on there, don't go getting all freaked out, spilling your coffee all over yourself. For example, if you look out the window and it's pouring rain, you'll most likely put on a foul weather jacket before you go outside. Why? Of course, so you don't get soaked. But how did you learn to do that? Well, in the beginning, you went outside and got soaked. The rain, in that instance, is the negative stimulus. After you've done it that way a couple of times, if you're a normal human being, you throw on your foul weather gear to AVOID getting soaked. You've learned that when you put on the foul weather jacket, you avoid the rain. That's what Negative Reinforcement is all about. Any behavior (wearing foul weather gear) that results in the cessation of a negative stimulus (being rained on) tends to become reinforced. So why is it called Negative Reinforcement? Simply because it involves some form of Negative stimulus. Let me explain this further, before you fall asleep on me completely. Let's first look at Positive Reinforcement.

Postive Reinforcement

Cue	Appropriate Response	Reinforcement
"Sit"	Dog sits	"Atta boy"

Of course you already knew that. Now let's ... Hey, WAKE UP, I'm talkin' to you ... Thank you. Now let's look at Negative Reinforcement.

Negative Reinforcement

Cue	Negative Stimulus	Appropriate Response	Reinforcement
"Sit"	Slight neck pressure	Dog sits, ends pressure	"Atta boy"

Negative Reinforcement has absolutely nothing to do with punishment. Do not forget that. People tend to confuse the two, including, I might add, many professional dog trainers. Why do they confuse the two? Because it is confusing and, to further confuse us, many technical manuals on behavior tend to make proper understanding of negative reinforcement confusing as hell. In my book *Dog Tales,* I told about a little girl named Lizzie who was afflicted with severe mental problems. This was close to 30 years ago and I was working with the family's beautiful four-month-old yellow Labrador retriever. One afternoon a behaviorist with a master's degree was working with Lizzie while I was working with Mollie. After we had finished and were taking a break, we were introduced. She asked me, "Ray, how did you learn about negative reinforcement?"

"I know nothing about negative reinforcement," I answered. "I've read three or four manuals with descriptions of it, and I can't figure out what in the hell they're talking about and I've been working dogs for over 15 years."

"Well," she answered, "know it or not, you're using it to help Mollie to heel, and you're doing it perfectly." That wonderful young woman then proceeded to educate me about negative reinforcement, using the example of how to stay dry in the rain. You never know where you're gonna get an education.

Negative Reinforcement has two parts. The first part is called Escape conditioning because the dog escapes the negative stimulus by completing the act we want completed. The second part is called Avoidance conditioning simply because, after the dog understands fully how to escape the aversive (negative stimulus), he's graduated to the avoidance phase of learning. That simply means that after learning to complete the task with consistency and without delay, he learns to avoid the aversive all together. So escape conditioning simply means that a particular response terminates an unpleasant feeling. It's very powerful stuff, and when done correctly, it's fun. Actually, that's precisely how you helped your dog to lie down. You applied just enough pressure to make standing uncomfortable (difficult), and lying down comfortable (easy).

Reinforcing the Sit Task

Now let's get you and your dog started on reinforcing the Sit task. You need to purchase one learning aid before we begin. You will need a

Mendota (that's the brand name) British slip lead. I like the Mendota product because they are extremely well made with good materials. I have a couple that are at least 10 years old. I use them all the time, and I have never experienced so much as a loose stitch. You can order through Amazon. They come in two lengths and diameters. I prefer the ½-in diameter for all but very small dogs. The 3/8-in diameter is a better fit for them. They also come in two lengths, 4-ft and 6-ft. I suggest one of each. Oh, I see you've already got them. Well then, let's get going. If you're working your dog on your left side, you will want to put the slip on your dog correctly. Face your dog, holding the long end of the 4-ft slip (the end with the handle on it) in your left hand, and the loop part in your right hand. The slip lead should now look like the letter P in a horizontal position. Now slip it over his head and slide the leather tab (keeper) so that the loop gets smaller. Adjust the keeper so that there is approximately a one-inch slack in the loop. It should not be tight on your dog's neck. Ok, it looks fine. Okay, bring your dog around so that he is standing at your left side, just like he was when you were working the later stages of Sit in the previous chapter.

Now, hold the handle of the slip in your left hand, and tell him "Sit," at the same time bringing your right hand up just like you've been doing.

Now, before he has a chance to sit, bring your left hand up, putting some pressure on your dog's neck. Not a lot of pressure, and do not jerk it. Just slide it up, and hold it there all through the process of your dog going into the Sit position. As soon as he sits, instantly release the pressure and give your dog a little praise. Tell him "Sit" only once; do not repeat. Okay, he's sitting. Good job. Now release him with the "Break" word and walk him around for a few seconds, then stop, tell him "Sit," and repeat the process. I suggest you do five to six repetitions and then quit, twice a day.

Remember, not a lot of pressure, no pulling his front paws off the ground or jerking him around. Just enough pressure to make it a bit uncomfortable. And you must release the pressure as soon as he sits.

If he sits and the pressure continues, it will become confusing to your dog. This is pretty simple. The dog essentially teaches himself to sit both quickly and consistently and, when he does so, the pressure goes away and he gets praised. Proper timing on your part is very important. From the dog's perspective, you don't relieve the pressure, he does. Your dog is going to begin sitting faster and faster, until after a while you tell him "Sit," and he sits without any pressure on his neck. He has now graduated from escape conditioning to avoidance conditioning.

Congratulations to the both of you. Job well done!

Your next goal is to help him to learn "Sit" at a distance. At this point switch from the 4-ft slip to your 6-ft. Bring him into the backyard and let him wander around a bit, three to four feet away. Now tell him "Sit" and, once again, bring the lead up, putting the pressure back on him. The only difference between this stage and the first stage is the distance involved. As soon as he sits, release the pressure and give some praise. Then give him the Break word. Do a few more and then end the session. I prefer multiple, short sessions rather than a long "grinder." After a couple of these sessions, when he sits, drop the lead, tell him "Stay" and walk away 10 or 12 feet. Remember, at this stage always return to your dog at the end of a stay; do not call him to you. Eventually, when he's 15 feet or so away from you, you'll be able to tell him "Sit" with him wearing the slip lead and he'll sit facing you.

Reinforcing Down

We've already reinforced the Down task in the previous chapter. The only change you might make is to do some Down tasking with the 4-ft Mendota. Is this method effective? Let me tell you a story.

Boston's Big Dig downtown highway modernization plan was in its infancy, the cold, rainy season was in full swing, and Red Sox fans were eagerly suiting up for another season, raring to go with the highest of expectations. Springtime in Beantown and I was about to meet with my 1:00 p.m. appointment.

The sign on the chain-link fence hung at a weird angle, proclaiming, "This is a hard hat job site." Second trailer after the sign, Tony had told me, so I eased my truck around as many mud holes as possible while approaching his trailer. I picked what I hoped would be a safe parking spot, out of the path of 10-wheeled dump trucks and massive Cat front-end loaders prowling about the site. After locking the truck, I got into my goose down parka and started to walk across the mud toward the trailer. There was a Ford Pickup directly in my path, so I had to walk fairly close to it as I passed. As I passed by, about two feet from the passenger window, without warning I heard this tremendous growling and crash. I literally jumped about two feet and turned to see the truck rocking side to side, and an enormous Rottweiler, eyes blazing, teeth gleaming, his nose shoved against the glass. Now mind you, I'm very comfortable around dogs, but this big boy caught me totally by surprise, and I could feel a hot sensation at the back of my neck.

"I see you've already met Max. You're Ray, right?" said the heavily built man with the big grin under his hard hat, standing by the trailer door.

"You Tony?" I asked, still a tad shaken.

"That's me," the big man answered.

"That dog scared the hell out of me," I told him, as I reached out to shake his bear paw of a hand. "Yeah, I'm Ray."

We entered the construction trailer, and I set my briefcase down on the large table at one end, its tabletop cluttered with drafting materials, pencils, rulers, a light blue hard hat and what appeared to be Ray-Ban aviator sunglasses. Tony was a very nice guy, and he loved his Rotti. Max had just turned three, and, except for one minor problem, was a wonderful pet. Max was not big on being told to lie down. Tony had brought him to a trainer to solve the problem, but Max bit the trainer while he was trying to get him to Down, and the trainer refused to see Max again, declaring Max a "psycho dog." After hearing about the trainer's adventures with "psycho dog," I sorta figured that, just maybe, I had a challenge ahead of me. I asked Tony if Max had ever shown aggression toward him. "Oh yeah, but only when I give him the Down command,"

"Could you be more specific?" I asked.

"Well, it usually goes like this. I tell Max to sit, which he does. Then I tell him to lie down, and give him a hand signal, which he blows off. I give him the down command a second time, and he growls and shows his teeth. Now if I tell him a third time, he'll lunge and bite my hand."

Seeing the wedding ring on Tony's finger, I ask him, "What's Max like with your wife?"

"You mean Stella? She's scared shitless of Max."

Swell, I thought. This dog nails everybody, but he's consistent.

Tony went outside to the truck and returned with Max on a lead and prong collar. Max was huge, pushing around 130 plus with no fat. He gave me a cursory glance, ambled over to a far section of the trailer, and returned with a giant, mangled rawhide bone between his teeth. I removed a six-foot Mendota slip lead from my briefcase and handed it to Tony. "Put this on, and take off your rig." I told Tony. "I want to do a bit of heeling with him. Does he know to heel?"

"Well, when he was around six or eight months I took him to a group class, but he never learned to heel very well. He always kind of pulled, you know, out in front of me all the time."

"Tony, just watch for a few minutes, and let Max and me get to know each other a little bit. By the way, do you walk him on the left or right side?"

"It's kinda his choice," was the answer.

We stepped outside the trailer and, with Max sauntering over to my right side, I said in a quietly firm voice, "Heel." Off we went, with Max immediately taking the lead. I made a quick left turn and, halfway through, snapped the lead lightly but with a bit of firmness to it. Max turned immediately and I shot him a quick, "Good dog," as he caught up with me.

Max caught on very quickly and was soon lumbering along right next to me, with plenty of slack in the lead. "Hey, looks like Maxie knows who the boss is," offered Tony.

"We're just beginning to feel each other out, Tony," I answered.

After about 10 minutes of heeling, and three Sits, I had Tony do a bit and then we brought Max back inside the trailer. It was now time to begin working on Down, and I knew that getting tough with Max would, no doubt, have me in the emergency room at Boston's City Hospital very quickly. This is the kind of situation that can go south in a heartbeat.

Attempting to demonstrate dominance to a dog like Max can have serious consequences. "Tony," I began, "I'm gonna get Max to lie down; however, until he does, please don't say a word to him or even look at him directly, okay?"

"Gotcha," Tony replied.

Very casually, I allowed the slip lead to drop low enough so that I could, without making a big deal of it, place the sole of my boot over it. Then, very gently, I took up the slack, putting a bit of pressure on Max's neck. After a few seconds, Max lowered his head to ease the pressure, so I took up the slack some more, putting pressure back on his neck. This cat-and-mouse game continued until Max's head was bent down about 10 or 12 inches.

At this point I asked Tony, "You a Sox fan?"

"Not really. I'm from New Jersey. Baseball's not my game. I love the Giants. Hey, what's goin' on with Maxie?"

"Well, Tony, the ball's in his court now. He's free to sit there with his head hanging down or he can decide to take the pressure off by lying down. It's up to him."

"How long do you think that will take?"

"I don't know and don't care. But the only way he can ease off the pressure is by lying down."

"But you haven't told him Down yet."

"I know Tony. I don't want to use that word yet. It's a cue for him to become aggressive."

Well, 22 minutes later, Max decided to lie down. "Good dog," I said quietly. We did two more repetitions. The third time he lay down in just over 11 minutes. And I still had all my fingers. "Do what I did three to four times, once a day. If you can do it in the trailer, so much the better. And do some heeling with him every day as well. Do the heeling just as I showed you. I'll see you next week."

The following week we met again. Tony told me Max was lying down in well under one minute, with no growling. I told Tony we were going to add something today. I put the slip lead on him, took him outside, and heeled him around the job site for perhaps 10 minutes. He did it perfectly. Then we brought him inside, and let him rest for five minutes. Then I heeled him to the center of the trailer, and once again put the lead under my boot. Max went down right away. As soon as he did, I told him, "Drop." I told Tony I changed the cue from Down to Drop because I was concerned that Max had already associated the Down word with becoming a cue to his becoming aggressive. Tony was pleased. I told him to work with Max like that all week and I'd see him the following week.

The following week when I got to the trailer, Tony told me that Max was dropping like a stone whenever there was the slightest pressure on his neck. "He's doing so well that I started telling him 'Drop' as soon as I put pressure on him and he lies down right away. Did I screw things up?"

"Nope, you've done fine, Tony." That day I added one more twist. I had Max sit next to me, told him Drop and moved my hand down to the floor in from of him with no lead pressure. Max went right down. I gave him lots of praise and then had Tony do it. Tony was thrilled at Max's turnaround, and then asked if I could come to the house to work with Stella. "I tried to get her to work with Max but, Ray, you know, she's really scared of him."

The following week I worked with Stella. We started with heeling, and it took a lot of time, but Stella was doing nicely with Max by the end of the session. I gave Stella lots of praise, but I could tell she wasn't ready to work on Drop. She wanted me to come the following week, but I said let's do it in two weeks, which gave Stella two full weeks to go on heeling walks with the big guy. The heeling, I reasoned, should give Stella more confidence when it came time to work on Drop. Our final session went beautifully. Stella demonstrated Quiet Firmness beautifully, telling Max to "Drop," and Max completed the task every time, without any pressure on the lead. "Hey, Tony, I'd behave myself around that new, confident wife of yours," I laughed as I headed out the door toward my truck.

HEEL

Okay, listen up. It would be easier to teach an elephant how to use a computer than it would be to help a person learn how to heel their dog by simply telling them how to do it. It's relatively easy to tell how to do it and virtually impossible for the person to be able to do it. Why? you ask. Can you master Tai Chi from a book, or become a good golfer from reading about the sport? Of course not. Well, it's the same with learning how to heel your dog. You need to have proper instruction. Heeling means that your dog is walking next to you, with a slack lead, or even no lead at all. The lead must be slack, and the dog must be right next to you, not out in front at all. Basically, all learning, four legs or two, begins with proper focus. If I'm teaching history to a classroom full of boys only at a Catholic high school, and 14 of those young men are focused on me and the 15th one is ogling a girl walking down the sidewalk, I can teach but he can't learn. Got it? Good. Heeling is, primarily, a focus drill.

I begin with this simple, but critical, point. Nothing helps establish a proper leader/follower role as much as heeling. When your dog is heeling properly, you are in the leader role. If your dog is not heeling properly, even if you've been working at it unsuccessfully, your dog is in the leader role.

Remember when I was engaged to work with Max? Remember the first thing I did? Correct. I worked him on heeling. Whenever I am asked to work with an aggressive dog, the first thing I do is work on heeling. I know I've already said it. Let me say it again. Heeling is the most critical task your dog needs to learn. On the other hand, if you could care less which of you is the leader, then skip this section. And I won't even know it. But your dog will.

Most owners don't take their dogs for a walk; their dogs take them for a drag. Everyone is familiar with this sight. Nanook of the North out in front, owner in tow. It doesn't have to be that way. The first step is to change your thinking. If you truly believe you can't get your dog to heel, then you're right. You will never be able to get your dog to heel. Change your thinking. Quiet Firmness.

I had a client with a hound of some variety that dragged his owners up and down the streets on walks. She loved people and would drag the wife over to people and then jump on them. I had worked with the owner and her hound for some time before the husband arrived home. He was a big, strong guy, and very nice. I suggested that he and I go outside and work on heeling like I did with his wife. He said to me, "Mr. McSoley, no disrespect meant, but my wife's the one with the issue. I walk her and when she starts to pull toward people I just shorten up on the leash so she can't pull. So I'm in control; it's Harriet with the problem."

I said, "Excuse me, Stephen, did you say you are in control when you walk her?"

"Right, I don't have a problem. I just tighten the lead so I can control her."

"You might not have a problem," I countered, "however, you're confusing control with restraint." We have control only when we get our dog to choose to walk next to us with slack lead. Dragging you around the block is no day at the beach for your dog either.

I heartily disagree with the age-old method of walking around the block, telling the dog to "Heel," and then jerking him back next to you time after time, while at the same time continuing to walk in the same direction. If you took a video of that scene, and then were able to slow the video down to slow motion, what you would actually see is that the dog doesn't come back to the walker, but rather the walker catches up to the dog. The dog is always, in that scenario, in the leader role. I have seen very few dogs learn to heel well with that method. All the mental pressure is on you, not the dog. I'm going to tell you how to change that.

Dogs are "into pressure" animals. What that means is that any sustained pressure in one direction causes the dog to move in the opposite direction. It's kinda like physics. That is why you witness the drag walk, described above. If you stopped one of those walkers and asked why you allow his or her dog to walk while damaging your rotator cuff, they would probably answer something like this: "Well, I went to obedience school, but they really never addressed heeling to any degree. Then I worked with a trainer and he wanted to use a prong collar, but I didn't like that approach. So we tried food and that helped somewhat, but that never worked when squirrels, rabbits, other dogs, or people were anywhere near. So I have given up. Wouldn't you think my dog would be smart enough to just back off the pressure? I mean, that's what I would do." Of course that's what you would do. Me too. But then, neither of us are dogs and that's what dogs do. Why? Well, first of all, it's not a matter of intelligence, but rather of reflex. It's called the Opposition Reflex. The harder you pull in one direction, the harder the dog pulls in the opposite direction. It's a self-fulfilling prophecy.

You can prove this to yourself. Have your dog sit and kneel next to him.

Make a fist and put some physical pressure into your dog's shoulder. Not a lot of pressure; it's not a strength test, guy. Or gal. Now release quickly. See? Your dog moved toward you. Do it again, and feel your dog pushing INTO you as you push with your fist. Then release.

Yep, he moves toward you. This little bit of understanding should help you grasp, to some degree, why the method I'm about to lay out for you is effective. It really does work.

Let's get started. Put the Mendota collar around your wrist, as you would around your dog's neck. Now, take the strap with your other hand and pull on it. Feel the pressure on the far side of your wrist. Pretend your wrist is your dog's neck. Never allow any sustained pressure on your dog's neck when helping him learn to heel. NEVER! Now keep the lead on your wrist as before, with slack. Now, as quickly as you can, snap and release the pressure. Feel how quickly the pressure releases. There is another reflex, the opposite of the Opposition Reflex. It's called the Avoidance Reflex. And you just experienced it on your wrist. Now I'm going to stand up and face you, about two feet away. I want you to take two fingers and snap the front of my neck. Do it! Ah, you saw me move my head back. I did so because of the Avoidance Reflex.

Now put the 6-ft Mendota on your dog. Make certain you have it on correctly, with the leather keeper adjusted so there's one or two inches of slack at your dog's neck, but not enough slack for him to back out of the collar. Give me the slip lead, and just watch. You said you would like her to walk on your left side, so that's what we'll do. I'm going to have her sit on my left side, and then I'm going to tell her "Heel" and step off with my left foot. When she shoots ahead of me, I'm going to let her go. That's her option and I respect that. But when she does, before the lead gets too tight, without saying a word, I'm going to change direction 180 degrees with a right turn, and when I'm about 90 degrees into the turn, I will snap the lead as quickly as I can in the direction I want her to go. I'll give her some praise as soon as she turns and looks at me, while she's catching up. I'll keep walking and when she shoots in front again, I'm going to repeat what I just did. If she wants to go out, I'll continue making right turns, every single time. She'll start to figure out that she can go out in front; however, when she does, I'm going to change direction on her. That's my option, and she needs to learn to respect that. Okay, I've made 13 right turns and notice that she is now walking beside me, looking up and FOCUSING on me. Heeling is, initially, a focusing drill. You'll remember how I spoke about the importance of focusing a few pages back. She's doing well and it has been a little over 15 minutes. Let's give her a 10-minute break.

Okay, break's over. Your turn, boss. Dog at your left side, left arm loosely at your side. Put the loop of the Mendota around your right wrist (so you don't lose the lead) and a couple of loops in your right hand. No! No! Don't ever wrap the lead around your wrist, loose loops instead. Now hold the lead in your left hand. That's the hand you'll snap with. Hold that hand comfortably by your side, like I did. Now say "Heel" and step off. And walk at your normal pace. You set the pace, not her. That's it, only next time just say "Heel," not "Come on, Sweetie." Good, you're doin' fine.

Watch it, she's getting out in front. No, don't ever yank her back and continue walking in the same direction. Make your turn to the right and give that quick snap. You'll get it. Now stop and start over. That's better. Now turn! Snap. Much better, and don't forget to give her some praise. Keep your left hand at your side. Don't bring it to your waist. Okay, begin again. All right, much better. Good, great turn and good snap. Just a bit quicker snap next time. Hey, that's it. Now you're beginning to look like a team. Are you relaxed? Your shoulders look pretty tight to me. Loosen your shoulders with a deep breath. Perfect. Praise your dog. You did?

Didn't hear you. My hearing's not good, courtesy of the Marine Corps.

Time for a break, for all of us. I know, good girl, a little warm out here today and you're workin' hard. In a bit we'll start on left turns. Left turns are a bit more difficult because there's a bit more involved. Drop your left hand to your side. Now snap your left hand and forearm straight back, like you're shaking paint from a paint brush. Jeez, Louise, that was truly awful. Come on. Shake it straight back. That's better. It's just a simple, quick snap straight back from your elbow. One more thing. Never break your wrist with the snap. Keep your wrist rigid. You fly fish? If you did you'd know what I mean about keeping your wrist straight.

Okay, let me show you a couple of left turns. We're heeling well, right?

She's drifting a bit in front so I'm gonna make a left turn. Watch. First thing I do is snap straight back just a fraction of a second before I begin my turn. See? Snap, turn. I'll do another if she drifts in front. Okay, watch.

Quick snap straight back, turn. Notice the snap is so quick it's over just as I begin the turn. Your turn. I want you to make a couple right turns first, just to warm up, then a left turn if she drifts. Great right turn; she turned right with you so no need to snap. There, that was a perfect right turn; no snap and she turned with you. And you remembered to give a bit of praise, but not so much that she loses proper focus. Now do some left turns. Make your turn if she drifts a bit. Now! That was horrible! You know what you did wrong? That's right. You began the turn without a snap and so you almost completely tripped over her. Do it again. There you go, much better. Make a few right and left turns and we'll call it quits. Excellent on both turns. Next time I see you, we'll work figure 8s. When your dog gets better, do your turns with no snaps.

Remember to always snap the lead in the direction you want your dog to go. If you heel your dog on the right side, first you need to reverse your Mendota. Another point. I never talked about what to do if your dog lags behind. When your dog is behind you, you want to encourage your dog to catch up. So little wrist snaps (break your wrist when you snap) and lots of encouragement. When your dog is in front you want to discourage.

Chapter 8

The Remote Collar (or e-collar as it's called): New Light On The Path

Cultivate a positive environment.
~Ray Hunt, Horseman

*S*omewhere,10,000 years ago, a man put a rope around his dog's neck, called him, and then yanked on the rope. The dog came to the man, the man praised the dog, and after many repetitions the dog, when called, came to the man without the use of the rope.

What was done with the dog that didn't learn to come by that method? If the rope didn't work, perhaps some ingenious ancient dog trainer used a crude slingshot. When the dog did not come, a pebble was let loose at the dog. The dog, feeling the sting of the pebble, turned around and ran to the trainer. The trainer praised the dog and gave him something to eat. After some repetitions, the dog came to the trainer without the use of the slingshot.

Today, thousands of years later, the modern dog trainer attaches a line to the dog's collar, calls the dog, and yanks quickly on the line. The dog comes to the trainer and the trainer praises the dog. What of the dog that does not "learn"? Some idealistic trainers believe that all dogs can be conditioned to come 100% of the time, no matter what they are interested in, by utilizing only positive reinforcement. Some dogs learn, some do not. My question to you, friend, is this: What has changed in 10,000 years of training dogs? Think long and hard on this, for I have. In 1974, I found a better way. I found a method through which I could help any dog learn to come when called, from any situation and under any set of circumstances. Furthermore, the dogs loved the method!

This chapter describes, in detail, the first major breakthrough in dog training in 10,000 years! Think about that. I've been training with the remote collar since 1974, 50 years, perhaps before you were born. I am going to explain what a remote trainer is and show you how to use it properly. The remote trainer has the ability to reinforce a command with 100% consistency, notwithstanding whether the dog is 20 feet away from you, or 400 yards from you. There has never been a training aid with the ability to do this before. With it, your dog will develop what I call a "third ear." This helps the dog to learn that no matter how interested or focused he is on something, his "third ear" remains focused on you, ready and eager to respond to your commands.

Perhaps the biggest advantage a trainer has with a remote trainer is simply that conflict and confrontation between the dog and you stop. When I discovered this aspect of remote collar training, a whole new world opened up for me. I no longer had to wrestle or fight to try to force a dog to learn from me. The dog wanted to learn.

I did a lot of remote collar demonstrations through the years. People were always astonished at how comfortable the dogs were and how quickly they began to learn the principles involved in remote collar learning.

The following compliment is from Sasha:

My name is Sasha and I am a "collar dog." I am 17 months old, born of a purebred shepherd mother and a husky mix father. I was one of 11 pups, and was most successful in getting plenty to drink. My first trainer described me as very strong-minded and feisty. I went to puppy training and was crate-trained and housebroken earlier. I grew rapidly and became a strong, happy 80-lb dog.

From the choke collar, I went to a pinch collar and still lunged in joy and friendship at dogs and strangers, and pulled to chase rabbits and squirrels. It was hard for my owner who was some 70 years young. We walk three to four miles seven days a week, from 5:30 am. to 6:30 am. There are no exceptions—ice storms, rain, sleet, and even hurricanes. Now I walk perfectly without the leash.

My first trainer left me when I was 10 months old. Mr. Ray McSoley came to my rescue. He felt I had potential but had never in my life been off a leash, even in the house. Within days, I stopped jumping on people, walked well at the heel, passed cats, rabbits, wild turkeys, dogs, and people with no trouble at all. I could be "free" in the house and then in the yard. I still have a few things to accomplish, but my owner now has a dog she can enjoy and be proud of.

Thank you, Ray.

SASHA, OWNED BY DRS. RICHARD AND MARION ELLIOTT, PLYMOUTH, MASSACHUSETTS

As soon as I mention electric dog collars to most of my clients, they think it's a form of torture. The previous sentence opened Chapter 5 of my first book, *Dog Tales*, published in 1988. Back then, my editor called to tell me she did not want to include that chapter in my book because she thought the use of remote electric collars was cruel. "That's precisely why it's going in the book," I countered. "For 20 years, the electric collar has been whispered about and kept in the closet. Jamie, I am going to blow open the closet door."

That chapter was short. Three pages, to be precise. Later, many people told me it took a lot of guts to do that chapter. I never looked at it that way; when you truly believe in something, speaking about it doesn't take guts.

Originally, it was my intent to title this chapter, "The Remote Trainer: A Path Toward Perfection." Deliberating on that theme, however, brought me back to reality, for while the remote collar is the finest training aid ever invented, the word "perfection" is descriptive more of the unattainable in dog training rather than that which is attainable. Remember, God has yet to create the perfect dog, and I rather doubt that that particular form of creation is on His short list. Using the collar, however, can help your dog and you achieve more than you ever thought possible.

After Dr. Elliott began using the collar with her dog (the one mentioned above), she told me, "The collar has helped Sasha become the dog I've always wanted and never thought I'd have." The good doctor had discovered the collar is more than a tool—it's an instrument.

Not only is it an instrument, but today's remote is such a finely tuned instrument that I believe we are merely scratching the surface when we speak of its capabilities. As a result, I am first and foremost a collar person. Even so, the more I use and learn with it, and appreciate it, the more I know that it has to be used properly—it's not a shortcut. The collar is not a device to be used strictly to punish (correct) inappropriate behaviors. Believe me, it is not "the great equalizer" in dog training.

Not all trainers are collar people. Some trainers use the remote trainer (also referred to as an e-collar) as I do. Others employ the slip training (choke) collar, while still others employ the prong collar. Some trainers swear by the Halti/Gentle Leader aids, while others are Clicker training aficionados.

Not all professionals who use the remote trainers are using it correctly—some are really good with it, many are not. Some have no idea how to properly employ the collar. What makes this group truly dangerous is that they feel they DO know how to use it, and have no reservations about "helping" a novice get started with it. They don't know what they don't know. Take the following example: some time ago, I was having breakfast at a restaurant in Waltham, a small city some 20 miles west of Boston. I was reading the sports section of the *Boston Herald*, when I heard a voice ask, "Do you train dogs?"

Looking up from my paper with what I'm certain was a look of astonishment on my face, I answered, "Yes. What, are you psychic?"

"No," replied the young man in jeans and a dark-green, long-sleeved chamois shirt. "I noticed your hat."

Sure enough, it was one of those rare days when in lieu of one of my cowboy hats, I had worn my white baseball cap with the black Tri-Tronics logo embroidered on it. We exchanged introductions, as he settled into the booth facing me.

"I train upland dogs, mostly Springers, in the western part of the state."

"You use the collar?" I asked him.

"Yeah, but I'm gonna have to send mine back to Tri-Tronics. Something's wrong with it."

"What model do you have and how old is the unit?"

"It's a 200 Lite and is just under a year"

"A 200 Lite? Geez, those things are near bomb proof. What's the problem?"

"Well," he said, "when I hold the button on continuous stimulation, the thing shuts off after eight seconds."

I stared at this young fellow, hardly believing what I was hearing. "It's intended to turn off at about eight seconds, son. It's a safety feature built into the unit."

"Oh yeah? How come they do that?" he asked me.

To protect dogs from jerks like you, I thought, but ignored his question and countered with one of my own. "Why are you holding the button down that long? How are you using the collar?"

We talked awhile, and I would like to think I set him straight on how NOT to use a remote trainer. The scary thing about that guy is that he's training other people's dogs that way, and telling them that's the proper way to use the collar. Hey folks, it's not the car, it's the driver.

One summer, Tri-Tronics asked me if I could do four seminars at the Astro World Series of Dogs, an absolutely wonderful event held each year in Houston, Texas. That year, 14,000 canines and their handlers competed in breed conformation, obedience, agility, fly ball, and freestyle dancing. I had an opportunity to watch some of the competition and I really enjoyed myself.

Sunday morning a woman had volunteered her German short-haired pointer to me for the demonstration. There was a crowd of about 50 extremely interested people surrounding the ring in which we were working. That little female shorthair was having the time of her life as I demonstrated the basics of reinforcing the command COMING WHEN CALLED with the remote trainer. Her little stub of a tail was vibrating back and forth, and she was enjoying being the center of attention.

Suddenly a tall, stern-looking woman marched over to me, announced that she was the breeder, and that she was removing the dog from the ring. I said nothing as she took off the remote trainer collar, handed it to me, hooked up the dog to her collar and lead and dragged the dog away. As she disappeared into the crowd, I looked at the dog's owner still standing among the spectators with a look of embarrassment on her face. She then turned away and left as well.

I said to the stunned audience, "Well, it looks as though we've lost our demo dog," when an older gentleman with an Airedale offered his dog instead, challenging me loud enough for all to hear. "If you can get Hondo to heel, I'll buy you dinner tonight." Well, nine minutes later Hondo was heeling next to my right leg like he was glued there. I then proceeded to continue with the rest of the 45-minute seminar, discussing the remote trainer and answering questions from these interested folks. The reason I mention that scene is because, unfortunately, there are still dog people who misunderstand the remote trainer. They're not stupid or dumb, but they are ignorant; they just don't know about its great value.

Later, I was telling Fred Cohen, a local Tri-Tronics dealer in Houston, about what had happened and he said to me, "Forget it, Ray. There will always be those who stand and watch the world pass them by." By the way, the dinner was great!

About a year ago I gave an evening seminar on the remote trainer. At the end of it, a middle-aged woman, a dog trainer, approached me and said she enjoyed my presentation immensely, and that what I had said had changed her mind somewhat. "How do you mean, some-what?" I asked.

"Well, I can see the benefit of the collar when used by someone like yourself, but not for the average dog owner," she explained.

"Oh, why is that?" I asked.

"Because your timing has to be right on," she answered.

"You mean that proper timing isn't important with the slip collar?" I asked.

"Well, no," she responded. "Good timing is important whenever you're training. It's just that it seems that proper timing is more im-portant with the electronic collar."

"Proper timing is critical with any training device, ma'am. Poor timing in any dog training situation is counterproductive. The truth is that it's more difficult to be timely with choke or prong collars than with the remote trainer," I told her.

"Perhaps you've got something there," she went on. "It's just that the remote trainer seems so impersonal."

"You're right, and that's part of the beauty of it. The collar's only im-personal in that it removes conflict and confrontation between owner and dog—the dog actually learns how to train himself and does not associate the stimulation with anything that you do. That's one of the values of the dog's learning with the remote trainer."

I don't know whether I converted her that evening—mere words don't make a believer out of everyone. If, however, I have an opportunity to demonstrate the remote with a dog that has never learned this path, the dog's response is much more convincing. When people see with their own eyes how effective the collar is, and also how open the dogs are to learning with it, they better understand the potential of this system. I show clients how the collar works with their own dogs during my visits, and used to demonstrate its effectiveness in remote collar group classes that I ran years ago. Around 1980, when I still ran group training classes, a husband and wife had a really nice three-year-old vizsla that they just could not get to heel with a slip collar. He was always out in front. During the final class I suggested that they stay after so I could show them how easily their dog could learn to heel using the remote collar. I told the others that they were free to stay and watch the demonstration. Their dog learned the concept in about eight minutes, with not the slightest bit of pressure on the slip lead. Their dog was heeling right by my side, right past the other dogs, looking up at me, tail wagging. Talk about convincing! Every person in that hall was astounded.

What makes the remote collar so effective, and why do the dogs learn so quickly? Several reasons. Timing and consistency, plus the ability to "reach out" to the dog at any distance—instantly. The ability for the dog to modify and reinforce his own behavior without relating it to the owner.

And, in my opinion, the big underlying reason is what I call the purity of the learning environment. This is what I mean by that. The collar allows the dog to focus on what he is being asked to do without any yelling or yanking on the lead by its owner. That sullies the learning environment and distracts the dog from learning. It's not that you can't get your dog to learn using those methods, it's just that there's a better way for both you and pup. When you use the collar properly, nothing gets in the way of the learning process. Instead, the learning process becomes enhanced with the use of the collar. The moment an

owner begins using the collar correctly, both conflict and confrontation are no longer factors in the training. With our guidance, the dog
begins teaching itself, and that, my friend, is what it's all about. Your
idea has become his idea.

The Mind of the Owner

If you have a low patience level, a remote trainer is probably not a
proper path for you. If you cannot develop Quiet Firmness, this path
is not for you. Most dog owners can, in my experience, learn it, and so
they can learn to handle a collar adequately. You just need to be honest
with yourself.

The Path

When a program involving the use of the collar is implemented,
both dog and owner embark on an entirely different, and unique,
learning path. When properly traveled, this path makes, once again,
training fun for both. My yellow Lab, Kitt, for example, came running
to me whenever she heard the snaps open the carrying case for the
collar. Kitt literally loved collar work. Why? you ask. For two simple
reasons. One, I never hurt her with it, and two, she was always learning
how to "beat the system." In other words, she taught herself that the
smart thing to do, when she heard the word "Here," was to return to
my side from wherever she was. Former client Sandy Cain's Labrador
would sit and wag her tail whenever the collar was put on her, and
Ed Callitri's big Rottweiler, Buca, runs to Ed and literally pokes his
massive head into the collar strap while Ed holds it in a circle for him.

This is the way collar training should be. But how do you get there
with your dog? You must begin with the proper mental attitude. You
always begin with Quiet Firmness. I tell my clients, hold in your mind
two simple concepts. First, what is it that you want your dog to learn
and, second, how best can you help pup to learn it? Holding these
concepts places us in a thoughtful, proper mindset. Remember what

I said earlier; training should be fun. When it's fun for us, it's fun for pup. If it isn't fun for us, it surely won't be fun for pup. When you imagine yourself as a coach helping your dog to learn, with a huge emphasis on HELPING, that helps to get you in a positive mindset. That is part of your dog-owner responsibility, to set the proper tone for each teaching session.

I'll be walking you through the steps on how to use the collar properly for both reinforcing appropriate (positive) behavior as well as how to implement it to discourage inappropriate behaviors. But, before you begin helping your dog to learn with the collar, it's necessary for you to understand just what a remote trainer is, what it does, and how it does it.

The Purpose Behind Low-Level Electrical Stimulation

The purpose of electrical stimulation should never be to inflict pain. Pain excites panic, both counterproductive states of being. A feeling of discomfort is, obviously, necessary; however, there is a large gap between discomfort and pain. On a cold New England morning, when I get in my Jeep, the seat is cold enough to be uncomfortable, but not painful. If you're beginning to reinforce coming when called with your dog, you need to use a level that is uncomfortable, but a level below his pain threshold.

Then, when you call him with the proper level, your dog will feel the discomfort but will also be able to focus on you and begin to come. Conversely, if you use a level that is too high, he will lose focus on you and on the given task, and will instead focus 100% on his neck, thinking, "Hey, my neck is in jeopardy." As a result, his flight instinct may very well take over as well as his defense reflex. Excessively high levels are, therefore, not merely nonproductive, but counterproductive. Common sense is a very important part of using the collar.

Types of Stimulation - Continuous and Momentary

Remote collars vary in the form of electrical stimulation they send to your dog. Continuous stimulation means that your dog receives stimulation as long as you are pressing the button on the transmitter (remote collars should always have an automatic emergency cancellation after approximately eight seconds). If you press the button for one second, your dog receives one second of stimulation. Press for three seconds, your dog receives three seconds. Remember, with continuous stimulation, a duration of one second is a long, long, long time. Momentary stimulation, or nick as it is sometimes called, incorporates a preset time of duration. Because different manufacturers set different durations of momentary intensity with their respective models, I am going to limit my discussion to Garmin, the system I use. Garmin purchased Tri-Tronics several years ago, and continues to use some Tri-Tronics intelligence. I have used the Garmin Sport Pro model since 2014 or '15 and have found it to be user-friendly, reliable, and pretty close to bulletproof. There are other very good systems available. There are also, unfortunately, a few really bad ones out there.

When you press the momentary button, you merely activate stimulation for a pre-determined time of duration. Momentary stimulation on my Sport Pro, for example, lasts 100 milliseconds, 1/10th of a second. When you hear an experienced collar trainer talking about "nicking" his or her dog, they are referring to momentary stimulation. These two different forms of stimulation are used for different training situations.

Stimulation Intensity

Remote trainers, in today's market, are designed with what is called variable intensity. Back in 1978, Tri-Tronics pioneered and incorporated this concept of variable intensity or the ability to adjust the level of electrical intensity received by your dog. Prior to that, the remote collar consisted of a single level of high intensity. That was the system I learned with because it was the only system available. Because the level was very high, one's timing needed to be precisely perfect. It was not easy. Today's collars have little resemblance to those early units. They are more compact, lighter, more user-friendly, use far better batteries, the list goes on. Today's units allow you to "fine tune" the intensity level to your dog's physiological and psychological thresholds. Levels that are either too high or too low are counterproductive to success. You must establish and then use the proper intensity level.

Establishing Proper Intensity With the Client

The first thing that I do with a client whose dog we are going to train using the remote is to have the client feel the collar. Let me tell you a story. Several years ago I had a very nice client with a Scottish deerhound who would, given the opportunity, chase a deer. After working with five different trainers, the woman called me. When I recommended we work with the collar to reinforce her dog's not coming, Susan agreed, but I sensed reluctance. I took the system from my briefcase, turned it on and inquired, "Have you ever felt one of these?"

"No, but I know how it feels," she answered.

I put the collar on the palm of my hand, saying, "If you put the collar on your palm like I'm doing, you will get a very good idea how different levels feel."

"No, I'm not going to feel it." she said, firmly. I put the collar and transmitter back in my briefcase, reached for my hat and stood up. "Are you leaving?"

"Yep," I answered. "If you won't feel it, you won't use it, and if you won't use it, you're wasting both your time and mine."

"Why are you so darn insistent on my feeling it?"

"Because the only reason you won't feel it is because you're convinced it will hurt, and no client I know wants to hurt their dog. So, you won't use it."

"All right, give me the damn thing." So she held it against her palm, and I began by pressing level 1, moving up through levels 2 and 3 with no response from Susan. When I pressed level 4, she dropped the collar immediately as she jerked her hand back.

"You felt level 4, was it painful?"

"No, it wasn't painful, but I didn't enjoy it. And you're not going to tell me that Oscar will feel that level."

"I have no idea what level Oscar will feel, but Oscar will let me know what level is right for him."

Well, I began working Oscar on the collar, and after several minutes, when Susan would call "Come," Oscar began to turn around very quickly and return to her. After a few more minutes I told Susan we'd give Oscar about a 10-15-minute break.

"That was impressive, Ray," Susan said to me. "How high did you have to go?"

I showed her the transmitter with the intensity level right where she could read it. "Level 3," I said, showing her.

Susan was astounded. "I can't believe it. His level was actually lower than mine." And that is exactly the way I first introduce it to the dog.

Establishing Proper Intensity with Your Dog

To discover the proper intensity is a simple process, provided you know how to interpret correctly your dog's reactions. When I'm working with a client's dog, I put the e-collar on the dog's neck next to his buckle collar. The dog wears both collars for ten minutes or so before I begin training. After that period of time, I begin the process by putting a lead on the dog, but attaching it to the dog's regular buckle collar, not to the e-collar. I then take him outside and allow him to walk around a bit. Then, with the lead slack, no tension on the buckle collar, and with the remote collar set at the lowest level of intensity, I press the momentary stimulation button. I'm looking for some minor reaction from the dog that tells me he feels the stimulation. He may look straight down at the ground, or he may twist his head from side to side. He might cock one or both ears. He may have a quizzical look upon his face. If I get no response whatever, I then increase the level and repeat the procedure. I'll do this until I get a response from the dog. The dog lets me know what the proper intensity is for him. The leash is held slack while doing this, or if the leash cannot be held slack, I take the leash off the dog inside the house and establish base intensity level for him without a leash. You see, leash pressure on the collar may interfere with the electrical stimulation pressure, resulting in a false reading. Say nothing to your dog during this procedure.

The ability to change the level of intensity both easily and quickly for me is a very important feature, since different situations may require different levels of stimulation.

Collar Range

The range or distance the electrical stimulation travels can be a critical factor when using the e-collar. There's nothing worse, or potentially dangerous to the dog, than running out of range. Dogs have been killed because they ran out of range of the e-collar, did not respond to being called, and were hit by a moving vehicle. Collar manufacturers will tell you the maximum range for each model they have. The advertised range, however, may vary from the effective range. Different types of interference directly affect the range of a unit. An e-collar with an advertised range of one mile may give you a mile in an Ohio cut cornfield; however heavy brush, big canyons, or tall buildings can drastically reduce an e-collar's effective range. Depending on your use of the collar, it is perhaps wisest to purchase a unit with at least a range of half a mile if you are going to do extensive training outside. That way, if you are operating in heavy cover or with other objects cutting the range, you will still be able to reach your dog. Some situations call for greater range limits. There are brands that manufacture units with a range of one mile, and one with an honest range of two miles. A good rule of thumb would be to purchase a collar with a range greater than you will ever need. Remember, though, you are never going to use the collar if you cannot see your dog, right? Good, I thought not.

Another marvelous feature of the more advanced models is their ability to receive at greater distance with no external antenna attached to the collar. The receiver is the part that your dog wears around his neck. Earlier, with the longer-range models, an external antenna was mandatory, which at times created a bit of a stir among the uninformed. I have a client in London and when the locals saw the dog running around Hyde Park, a little boy exclaimed, "Mama, look at the doggie with the cell phone sticking out of his ear!"

Other Features

Certain features go hand in hand with quality. The receiver should be waterproof, not just water-resistant. Some manufacturers claim their e-collars are waterproof, so it's good to check out those claims. I prefer American-made e-collars. An e-collar manufactured in the United States should offer quicker turnaround service when necessary. Remember, a remote trainer will help your dog to learn only when it's on him. If the e-collar is in its case in the closet back home because its broken, or if it's away to be serviced and the turnaround time is unreasonably long, that e-collar's not doing you any good. Check out the service. Check out the warranty. An e-collar is not inexpensive, and should therefore last you many years. I have a Garmin Sport Pro that is six years old and is still operating fine on the original batteries. Please don't skimp on quality.

Some units use rechargeable batteries and some still use replaceable, although rechargeable batteries are so good nowadays that I recommend going that route. Size does matter to some people and some systems are smaller, and less conspicuous, than others. Because I have Labrador retrievers, quality overrides size; however, if I had a mini-breed, I'd still be looking for quality, but in a smaller package.

Many systems these days incorporate all sorts of bells and whistles. Some are worthwhile, others aren't. Tone and vibration are included in a majority of the better systems. I'll get into that more later on, when we start the actual training. Some e-collars feature a rising stimulation which automatically rises. Personally, I don't recommend it. I believe it can lead to undisciplined dog handler use. The fundamental premise to successful e-collar work is to use the lowest level of stimulation necessary.

Remember, your dog really is the one determining the proper level. Watch your dog and you'll both be working with the proper level.

There also are multiple dog units, allowing a single handler to control two or more dogs with a single transmitter. I've used them for years and they work very well. One last thought, an important one, before I forget. You should definitely check out how convenient it is to change intensity levels as well as how easy it is to switch from continuous to momentary stimulation, and vice versa, as well. The system I use also allows me to change intensity levels without taking my eyes off the dog, an important feature if you work your dog in fields or woods, where taking your eyes off your dog to change a level might result in your losing your dog.

USING THE REMOTE COLLAR TO REINFORCE APPROPRIATE BEHAVIOR

First Steps on the Path

I begin using the e-collar to reinforce what I call a Positive Action Task.

Examples of this would include: Heeling, Sit, Coming When Called. Why do I begin this way? Simple. Learning to do the correct behavior quickly and consistently increases your dog's self-confidence. It also helps to reinforce your role as chairman of the board (leader) in your dog's mind.

We're now ready to begin reinforcing those tasks your dog already knows and responds to most of the time. We want him to respond appropriately 100% of the time. You've charged the system, right? Of course you did.

Place the e-collar around your dog's neck with the "can" (the box containing the electronics) at the throat, where gravity would pull it. Snug it up. It should be snug enough so that if you hold the can and move it side to side it should not slide easily. The contact points must be in constant contact with the skin. I place the collar strap right behind your dog's ears—that's the narrowest part of his neck. Make certain you've turned on the system. E-collars seem to work better when they're turned on (a little Midwest humor). Oh, one quick tip. While holding the "can" in one hand, I hold the dog's skin at his throat below the collar. I hold the skin and work the collar up and down the neck, just a little, which helps settle the contact point through the fur and onto the skin. Works for me.

Reinforcing the Coming When Called Task

I love Dover, Massachusetts. A small town, it borders the town in which I live. Both are fairly typical New England, but Dover still has a "horsey element," so there still are some wonderful open fields where I have run my Labs for 60 years. I pray those fields will be there another 50 years. Of course there are absolutely magnificent and stately horse farms there. Somewhere around 12 years ago, I received a call from a woman who said her name was Bea. Her very good friend had used my services for her dog and things had worked out well. Bea lived in Dover and said that she had this hound, Moses, who was three years old and well trained.

Seems this "well trained" dog had been off the lead three times in three years and had run off, chasing deer all three times. He'd be gone two to three hours and Bea was beside herself with worry, fearing he would be hit by a car some day during a chase. I told her that solving the problem shouldn't be that difficult, and that I worked with precisely that sort of not coming when called all the time. So we set a time for me to go out and meet with both her and Moses.

It was toward the end of August when I turned off Farm Road and entered the long drive leading to the main house. Bea had instructed me to look for the barn and park there because her residence was above the stable. I knocked on the door a couple of times, and Bea came down and introduced both herself and Moses, a large, good-looking hound attached to a 6-ft lead. Bea ran the stable for her employer, took care of the horses, and did chores around the estate. I liked her from the get-go. When we got upstairs to her apartment, she told me once again how well trained Moses was. I asked her to please give me a demonstration and put him through his paces. Moses was very well trained, with one exception. The minute he was off lead he was gone. It's funny how things work. Here's a young woman with a really well-trained dog, living on 73 acres of, essentially, pastureland, and she can't let him run.

We talked about Moses for a bit, and Bea said she was wondering if a shock collar might help. It did, after all, do wonders for her friend's dog. After explaining that the remote was no longer a shock collar per se, I stepped outside for a minute, returned with my remote, and proceeded to explain to Bea how I used the collar and why it was so effective.

"Can we start this afternoon with Moses?" Bea asked hopefully.

"You bet," I answered, and 30 minutes later we were outside and I began showing her how to work Moses on the collar.

Moses responded very well during the initial session; we set up three additional appointments, and Bea told me that she would order a system. By the fourth session, I decided it was time to work Moses off the check cord that I'd been using. There were some very large Juniper bushes on the property, and Bea, Moses, and I were walking toward one when Bea said to me, "You know, Ray, if Moses spots a rabbit in one of the Junipers, he'll be gone." She no sooner had spoken when, sure enough, old Mr. Cottontail hopped across the path in front of us and darted into an enormous Juniper—with Moses in hot pursuit. In a millisecond, I lost sight of them both, guessed where they would exit, and ran toward that side. Sure enough, both had already shot out of the Juniper and were heading straight for one of the large open fields, which was bordered on one side by a three-foot stone wall.

I yelled to Bea, "Call your dog!"

Bea responded instantly, "Moses, here!" bumping him with the remote at the same time. Moses, about 30 yards ahead, slowed, then turned back toward Bea, still running straight out. When he reached Bea, she exploded with both relief and praise for Moses. His tail was wagging as fast as it would go, even though he looked back wistfully toward the stone wall and the rabbit that had cleared it just moments before.

About a month later, I received a late evening phone call. It was Bea. "So sorry to call so late, Ray, but I had to give you the news."

"What news?" I asked, concern in my voice.

"Well, I had Moses out behind the main house this evening, just as the last of the sunset was passing. Suddenly, I spotted two deer in the apple orchard, and Moses saw them at the same time. He took after them. I was wearing my fall parka, which was zipped up, with my transmitter tucked in the inside pocket, and I remembered your telling me to always have the transmitter in my hand. With no time to fumble for it, I hollered 'Here' to Moses. Ray, he turned on a dime and ran back to me. I never in a million years really thought he'd come back in that situation, and I never used the transmitter. The collar really has worked a miracle for Moses and me, and it might have saved his life tonight. I just thought you'd want to know."

And I thought that you'd like to know as well.

Okay. You read about how using the collar properly helped Moses to come when called when faced with his toughest distractions. So let's get going. I see you have a 26-ft Flexi (brand) lead. That's superior to the 16-ft version which is too short. I actually like the Flexi

Lead better that then the old 25-ft polypropylene check cord I used for years. They're still good in that they're slippery and float so they slip through heavy brush as well as float on water. But make certain you're wearing leather work gloves. Polypro will burn hands like aged wood if you're trying to slow down a hard-running retriever. So beware. I see you've got the remote on Chase and you've established a starting intensity level like I recommended. And the collar's turned on. Let's go outside and get started. Okay, we're outside, on this side street where traffic is practically nil, and distractions are low. If you had an underground canine fence system such as DogWatch, you would not want to begin there. Why? Simply because you'd be applying the low-level stimulation inside an area your dog has always considered safe. Down the road, when Chase fully understands coming and is completely familiar with the system, you may extend training to your fenced-in backyard.

Now, allow Chase to mosey on out in front of you, free reigning on the Flexi Lead.

When he's 15-20 feet in front and FACING AWAY from you, stop walking, call "Here" at the same time you press the Momentary button. Do not call and then press. As soon as Chase turns toward you, begin praising him all the way back. Give lots of praise; help him out. Okay, call him. Great! You did great! You called and pressed correctly and he turned, a little slowly, but that's fine. And your praise was great. Let's walk a little bit and repeat. Okay, he's walking toward those shrubs over there. He's getting out a little far—call! Okay, I think you called first and then pressed. He didn't turn when you called, but did so after you pressed. Remember, do both at the same time. We'll do four more and then call the session over. Remember to move about; don't keep standing in the same place while repeating the exercise. Keep moving to a different location. That helps Chase learn that no matter where you are and he hears you call him, the smart thing to do is come. If he didn't turn when you called him, help him turn with some pressure on the lead. Not yanking, quiet pulling. We worked him for just about 12 minutes. That's enough for Chase. He has a lot of things to process: getting used to stimulation, turning when he hears you call ... forget about what other things he had on his mind, lots of stuff. You do too. You have to get comfortable using the collar, getting your timing perfect, not letting him see the transmitter, not feeling sorry for Chase; after all, you're helping him. So you both have mental stuff to get used to.

He may begin to get used to the level you're at and stop responding to it. If that happens, just go up a notch on the intensity. Tomorrow, when you do the exercise, move to a new area. You need eventually to work in six to seven different areas for Chase.

After you get to the point when Chase is turning as soon as he hears you call and he feels the stimulation, then you may begin a session with him off the Flexi Lead. Once off the Flexi, he may think he's completely free (which he is) and may decide to explore. Allow him to get out a ways, about 20 yards (60 feet) is good. When you call and he comes, give lots of praise.

Remember, he needs to be facing away from you still, at this point. Also, begin letting him roam a bit before you call. If you call every time he moves out, he can learn never to leave your side. So let him roam, smell things, enjoy himself. And coming to you when called should become the high point of his day. Eventually you're going to begin calling with no stimulation. When he responds, he will have graduated from Escape Conditioning to Avoidance Conditioning. He now knows that when he responds quickly to "Here," he no longer receives stimulation. He says to himself, "Hey, what a smart dog I am. I'm so smart I've learned how to beat the system." Which is exactly what you want him to think. You've helped him to teach himself that coming quickly and consistently is the wise thing to do. And think about this. You helped him learn to come when called without ever correcting him. Not a single time.

A few tips from an old dog man. You may find that, in the beginning, your dog may not react to momentary stimulation. That's okay;

you have a couple of options to help him. You may need to increase intensity one notch; however, before you do that consider the following. If you're using a system like the Garmin Sport Pro, which recycles quickly, you can bump him twice with the momentary stimulation, very quickly, or you may choose continuous stimulation. If you choose continuous, you must release the button the split second you see your dog turn toward you. If you hold too long after he turns, he will think that turning toward you still doesn't stop the stimulation, and he may turn to run away. Not good. And not his fault. So, take your time and use your common sense. Using continuous with a "green" dog (untrained to collar work), I hold the button down only as long as it takes me to call "Here."

Years ago, back in the late '70s and '80s, there was a method used by many trainers who believed, in order to reinforce a dog's recall with the remote, the stimulation should be applied not only until the dog turned back toward the trainer, but should continue until the animal REACHED the trainer. There is no need for me to attempt to explain the logic behind that method. I will simply say that approach is not only unnecessary, but also abusive. Do not even think of doing it. If you find that your dog does well on a short continuous button, that's fine. You will, however, find that down the road your dog will do perfectly well with momentary stimulation. Personally, I switch a client's dog to momentary as soon as I am able to. I'm a strong advocate of momentary stimulation. It's 100% consistent and the client seems more comfortable using it.

A major trap many handlers fall into is not using the collar long enough in the beginning. They use it for a few days, find it works magic, so they stop using it. The reason is that they felt guilty using it in the first place. If you're using your e-collar properly, using the proper level, why would you feel guilty? I've switched thousands of clients from using the prong (sometimes called a pinch) collar to using the remote, and some of them felt guilty in the beginning; however, they never felt guilty using the prong collar. Go figure. So, continue to use the remote even though your dog begins to come both quickly and consistently. After a week to 10 days, providing that you're training daily, that your dog is responding well, that you're becoming comfortable and competent using the system, and that the astrological arrangement of the galaxy is properly aligned (just kidding), you can begin phase 2.

This second phase, calling without the Flexi line or check cord, will let you know quickly how well you have done the initial work. I like my clients to begin this phase with their dog in their backyard. Let him loose in the yard, go to the back door, call, and press the button. When he comes give him a big praise and bring him in. Once is enough. You needn't do it multiple times. If he doesn't respond correctly, repeat the call. If he doesn't respond, increase the intensity a single level and call once more. If he still fails to respond, simply go back to the check cord for a bit. If you don't have a yard, bring your dog to an area where you have already worked him on the collar. Make certain the collar is on your dog and is turned on. If he comes when you call, give him big praise and walk around a bit. Let him explore without getting out too far and call again. You might call him three or four times at the most. Then hook him up and bring him home. And congratulate yourself on a job well done.

You now have pup coming freely (no line attached) but you're still pressing the button when you call. Phase 3 involves calling with no button. Do what we did in phase 2 except that you do it without pressing the button. Okay, we're in the field. Let pup run. Okay, he's been loose for about two minutes. He's now about 40 feet ahead of you. So, stop walking. Now, simply call him but do not press the button. Call him firmly but remain positively upbeat.

Okay, look at him beating it back to you! Lots of praise for him. No, more praise. That's it. Now, let him run again and have some fun. We'll call him a few (perhaps four) more times before we hook him up and call it a morning.

Now, when you're out and distractions show up, if you call him and he doesn't respond, go up a level. Always remember, excitability reduces sensitivity! If you're running for your life somewhere and get stung by a hornet, you're not going to feel the sting nearly as much as if you get stung on a street corner waiting for the light to change. It's the same with your dog.

Whenever your dog goes outside, have the collar on him. You don't want to condition a "collar-wise" dog. Collar wise conditioning happens when the dog wears the collar only when he's being trained. When the collar's not on him he does what he wants to do. When you drive to the post office, put the collar on him. Go for a simple walk, put the collar on him. When he's in the yard he should be wearing the collar. Do that and eventually, when you go to put the collar on him he begins to wag his tail because he knows he's going out. Yes, believe me, that WILL happen.

Reinforcing the Heel Task

The trip to Queens, the city of New York's largest borough, takes a little over three hours from Boston, provided you push the posted speed limits a bit. It was early December and I was responding to a call for some help with two resident therapy dogs in a nursing home. Casey, a Golden retriever, and Mollie, a pit bull, had begun pulling their handlers down the streets in pursuit of neighborhood canines.

It was a bit after eleven in the morning when we paid the toll after crossing the Throgs Neck Bridge and proceeded to thread our way into the never-ending stream of traffic bound for who knows where. My wife Mary, then a proud postgraduate of the Boston Art of Driving Institute, flawlessly zigged and zagged our car through the traffic, while I barked directions from my navigator's seat, a map of the city of New York on my lap.

Ten minutes later we pulled into the parking lot at the address I'd been given, parked, and proceeded to walk through the automatic opening doors of Ozanam Hall. As we approached the information desk, a neatly dressed security person looked up at me and in a pleasant voice asked, "Good morning, may I help you?"

"We're here to see Sister Philip Ann," I answered.

Shortly a tall, thin, middle-aged nun approached, attired in a Carmelite habit. "I'm Sister Philip," she said, smiling. "And you must be Mary and Ray. Come on, grab your bags and I'll show you where you'll be staying."

I liked her immediately. But then, I also liked my senior drill instructor, Sergeant Raffel, when I was in the Marine Corps. We were going to be staying in a beautiful, white two-bedroom house next to the nursing home. After making ourselves right at home, we returned to Ozanam and, as we turned the corner into the lobby, there were both Mollie and Casey, lying quietly on the floor, quietly greeting people as they entered from outside. When Mary and I arrived, both dogs were in Sister Philip's office, so they were not on hand to be our official greeters.

It was such a treat to watch the faces of the visitors light up as they entered the lobby and saw the dogs there. All of them acknowledged the dogs before inquiring at the desk about their friend or family member, but the children most of all. Casey and Mollie provided a homelike feel at Ozanam, adding a few degrees of warmth to this sunny, yet cold December afternoon.

Sister, Mary, and I went to her office where she outlined the dogs' issues. The dogs were both walked several times each day, and it had become increasingly difficult, and yes, even dangerous to do so. This section of Queens was very clean, with trees providing shade during the summer, towering above well-kept homes with small, yet pleasing yards. Because the yards were small, the dog owners wanted to get the most out of their individual space. Those with larger dogs fenced their yard, running mostly chain-link fencing, quite literally, along the edge of the sidewalk, and therein lay the problem. The nuns walked the dogs along the sidewalk, doing their level best. Attempting to walk the dogs in the street would have been to invite a serious accident.

So, here we have a nun attempting to walk her dogs past a section of fence when suddenly a couple of angry dogs arrive at their own side of the fence, literally a foot away. They're defending their "turf," barking and snarling at the Ozanam dogs. And Mollie and Casey are now responding by pulling on their leashes and trying to get to the other dogs. During these unfortunate encounters, the dogs' leashes become tangled and, on more than one occasion, the nun walking the dogs has been pulled off her feet, ending up on the sidewalk with cuts and bruises and, in more than one incident, broken bones.

I told Sister Philip Ann that I would begin working on reinforcing Heeling, first with Mollie and then with Casey. I outlined my program for her, telling her that I would reinforce both dogs' heeling using the remote collar, explaining to her how it worked and the mechanics involved in using it to reinforce heeling.

I began with Mollie, putting the remote collar on her, next to her metal "choke" collar, and established a level of intensity that resulted in her giving a quick, mild head shake. We went outside, I told her, "Heel," and we walked up and down the sidewalk for a couple of minutes. Both dogs had been previously "obedience" trained and knew what heel meant. When I said, "Heel," she walked right next to me with a nice slack lead. I needed to snap the metal slip collar only a couple of times to get her heeling perfectly. Her previous trainer had, quite obviously, done a very good job, using the metal (choke) slip collar.

Then it was time to begin to reinforce her heeling with distractions, using the remote collar. It took just a short distance before the first dog emerged on the other side of his fence, snarling and barking. Mollie began to respond, at which time I turned to the right 180 degrees, saying "Heel," and tapping the momentary remote button. Mollie turned immediately to catch up to me so I gave her a quiet "Good girl." I turned again to repeat the process. I did this a few times until Mollie completely ignored the other dog's challenging attitude. Then I brought her back to Ozanam. The entire process took less than 20 minutes. Once back at Ozanam it was time for Casey. I began the same way, first establishing a level of intensity that Casey would feel, which was nowhere near painful, but rather uncomfortable. Outside, Casey did as well as Mollie and, surprisingly, learned a bit faster than Mollie.

I told Sister Philip how both dogs did, and why it was important to begin the collar work without her being there; I wanted to limit distractions to other dogs, and I felt Sister's presence would make it more difficult for the dogs to learn from me. There would be plenty of time later for distractions once the dogs were more comfortable and familiar with the new technique. "Tomorrow," I told her, "I'll get you involved." Before leaving her office I asked Sister if she knew someplace I could get breakfast as Mary and I had driven all over the neighborhood that morning without finding a single breakfast eatery. Sister told me that the nuns had breakfast on the 4th floor from 7:30 to 8:30 and that, if eating breakfast with a few nuns wouldn't bother me, it would be fine for me to take part in the buffet breakfast. I thanked Sister and left. I need my morning breakfast!

That evening, Sister Philip treated Mary and me to a lovely dinner at a well-known New York restaurant on Long Island. The conversation was spirited throughout dinner and, early on, was mostly about dogs, but Sister also entertained and enlightened us with some wonderful stories about the incredible work her Carmelite order does for the elderly. Later in the evening after we had dropped Sister back at Ozanam, I said to Mary, "How about a nightcap?" Mary agreed and we drove off to find a local hangout, both of us feeling like a couple of high schoolers about ready to break our curfew. Those nuns are such natural disciplinarians!

The following morning found me showered, dressed, and taking the elevator to the 4th floor for breakfast. I arrived in the dining room a few minutes past 7:30, and the buffet was already set but the room was empty. Perfect. I filled my plate with scrambled eggs and bacon, poured myself a cup of hot coffee, grabbed a chair at a large round table, and sat down. I had just helped myself to a mouthful of eggs when the door opened and a couple of nuns entered—wearing bathrobes! The look of astonishment on their faces matched mine. I jumped to a standing position and, through my eggs, exclaimed, "Good morning, sisters," and then began laughing. And then one of the nuns began to laugh and I realized, fortunately, that I had met her the day before and she recognized me. She quickly told her companion and both began laughing. I asked them to please join me and, shortly, a small herd of nuns appeared, you guessed it, in bathrobes. Soon we were all sitting at this table, laughing and talking. It was one of the best breakfasts I've ever had.

Later that morning I worked with both Mollie and Casey together, along with Sister Philip and two other sisters. I gradually increased the level of distractions, helping both dogs to deal well with other dogs snarling, barking, and jumping up at their fence. Both dogs did exceptionally well, actually heeling past the dogs without barking at them, much less breaking the heel to lunge and become tangled in their leads. Two more short sessions that afternoon left both Mollie and Casey exhausted. I left a remote system that I had brought with me for Sister Philip.

Early in the evening I packed the car, and we said our "thank yous" and goodbye to Sister Philip, Mollie, and Casey, and headed back to Boston. We had just crossed into Connecticut on interstate 95 when we came upon a car in the breakdown lane. As we passed I saw a woman's face through the window so I pulled over and backed up close to her car. I got out and walked back to the car to find TWO NUNS sitting in it! The driver lowered her window and I found out they had a flat. I also learned they were from none other than Ozanam Hall! Well, I took care of their flat and they went on their way. We once again started toward Boston but both agreed we should stop for pizza at Peppi's, a college hangout in New Haven, where their enormous pizza oven is still fired by coal. We not only had a wonderful pizza but had the honor of meeting and speaking with the owner. If you're ever in New Haven, include Peppi's on your bucket list.

We arrived back home a bit before midnight with me feeling that, once again, the remote trainer had been assigned a most difficult task and had accomplished it perfectly.

Okay, let's take your dog out and begin working on heel. He's now coming like he's on railroad tracks when you call him, so let's begin helping to reinforce his heel, that is to walk next to you with a SLACK lead. That's right, I said a slack lead, no more pulling.

So, you helped him learn to heel on your left side, so that's the side we'll be working on. If it was the right side, then we'd begin reinforcing the right side. It's up to the owner to decide on which side they want their dog to heel. Okay, let's get started. What's your dog's name again? Bud? That it? Oh, short for Budweiser. Good name. Let's go.

That's it, have Bud sit on your left side. Now, tell him "Heel" and step right off. No, you don't need to use his name first; he knows who you're talkin' to. Good, you're doing fine. Now look, he's drifting out in front. Make a right turn and when you're 90 degrees into the turn, tell him "Heel" and press the momentary button at the same time. Okay, turn now. Good, almost perfect. There, he's drifting in front, make another right turn. Okay, he turned, but he didn't turn when you said "Heel," and you pressed the button after you turned, and that's when Bud turned. Let's walk until he strays in front again. There he goes, make your turn. Perfect! You did everything right and Bud did it perfectly. Now he's walking next to you the way he should, with the lead slack. Remember to praise Bud as soon as he turns when you do. He needs the praise; he ain't no cinder block on the end of the lead. He's a living, thinking, feeling animal. So don't forget to praise him when he gets it right. All right, take a short break. Listen while I tell you how to make a left turn with a left-side-heeling dog. Right turns are easier because you're turning AWAY from the dog. On a left turn you're turning TOWARD (into) the dog, which makes it just a bit more difficult, so listen. You're holding the transmitter in your right hand. You're going to step off with Heel. If Bud pokes his head ahead of you, say "Heel" and at the same pull back slightly and gently with the lead while pressing the continuous button, holding it down only until you turn in front of Bud. Come off the button and slack the lead as you continue making the left turn.

Think about what I just said. Take your time, I'll wait. Okay, watch me do a couple of turns. (Talking to Bud): "Sit." "Good dog." "Heel." See how well he's doing. (I kick a stick out in front). Okay, there he goes out in front. "Heel." I pull back slightly on lead while pressing and holding the continuous button just until I cross in front of Bud. See, he slowed way down as I pulled back bait on the lead, told him Heel and pressed the continuous button until I crossed in front of him. Now you try it. Good, needs a bit of polish but you both did it well. The left turn on a left-side-heeling dog takes practice to get your timing down. After doing it that way for a while, you'll be able to say, "Heel," press the button at the same time and begin your left turn, no more using the lead to help. That remains slack throughout the process.

It's actually a good idea to do some dry runs that involve practicing the left turn without Bud. You walk, say "Heel," and slide your left hand back, pressing the continuous button with your right hand, holding the button down till you've turned 90 degrees, which puts you in front of the dog. Immediately come off the button and praise Bud. Eventually, you'll be able to heel Bud around with no lead. Yes, you can! Remember, practice holding the continuous button down ONLY AS LONG AS IT TAKES YOU TO SAY THE WORD HEEL - PERHAPS A QUARTER OF A SECOND.

Reinforcing Going to Place

Please go to the section in Chapter 9 titled Going to Place to have pup learn about Place before reading this section.

NOTE: Many clients of mine use the collar for coming and heeling only. I'm perfectly comfortable with that. You may even decide not to use the remote at all. Once again I'm fine with that.

Before attempting to reinforce this task, your dog must thoroughly understand what the task is. Therefore, go to Chapter 9 and read the section "Going to Place." After your dog understands this task and goes to his place when you tell him, without putting any pressure on the lead to help him, you may proceed to the reinforcement phase.

Use the same "target" you used to teach PLACE. With the remote collar on him and the lead attached, have Bud sit about three feet from the target, with him facing it. Tell him "Place," pressing the continuous button, holding the button down until his front paws reach the target. As he steps onto the target, release the button and praise Bud as he goes into a sit. You may find that you need to refresh his memory by helping him with the lead as in Chapter 9. Praise him and, when you're ready, release him with the word "BREAK" or whatever word you use. Do not praise him after giving him the release word. The release is its own reward. Repeat this process four or five times and end the session. Practice this exercise daily until Bud proceeds to the target, turns and sits, and remains there until given the release.

Once Bud's at this point, begin doing it without the lead. Always remember, use the lowest stimulation level that is effective in helping Bud to learn, and never go above that level. Eventually, tell Bud "Place" and he will execute with no lead and no stimulation.

By now you're working as a team and having fun doing it. The e-collar, properly used, removes the conflict and confrontation between owner and dog, doesn't it? It puts the fun back into training.

Reinforcing the Sit Task

Sit, with my Labs, has always meant two things. First, it means to sit. Second, it means to remain sitting until told to do something else, whatever that something else might be.

Put the slip lead on Bud. Now, as you learned in the previous chapter, tell him Heel and walk perhaps 15-20 feet. At that point stop, say SIT and immediately pull, gently, straight up with the slip, holding until Bud sits, releasing the slight pressure immediately. After maybe 10-15 seconds, release Bud using your release word. Repeat the entire exercise two or three more times. Now, repeat the exercise and right after saying Sit, as you pull up the slip lead, push the continuous stimulation button, holding until Bud sits, then release both lead and button immediately, and praise Bud. Do three or four repetitions and end the session. If he breaks the sit before being told, simply repeat the "Sit" and the button. The button MUST be released the second Bud sits.

Soon, you'll be able to advance to using only momentary stimulation, and eventually, no stimulation at all. Gradually, begin distance sitting if you'd like Bud to do that. I begin by having the dog standing away from me wearing the slip lead. He may be three to four feet away from me. I give "Sit" and press continuous until he sits. Gradually I do it at increasing distance. Take your time with this, don't confuse the dog by moving too far away too soon. Take your time. Help the dog. Eventually your dog learns not only to sit when you ask him, but to remain seated (Stay) until given your release word.

Reinforcing the Down Task

I have never felt the need to reinforce this task with my own dogs; however, I have been asked by hundreds of clients to help them get their dog to lie down—reliably. Personally, I've found that reinforcing the down with the slip collar results, eventually, in a dog completing the down reliably. If, however, you wish to collar reinforce down, here is how to do it. With the slip collar on your dog, have him sit. Then, as in the previous chapter, tell him "DOWN," and follow immediately with sustained pressure on the lead till he lies down. If you've done your homework, when you give him "Down," he will lie down right away. To reinforce this with the remote, do the following:

Have your dog sit. Give him the hand signal and verbal "DOWN" as he begins to lie down, press the continuous button, holding it down until your dog is lying down. Release immediately!! Praise your dog. Do not overdo this exercise, three or four repetitions are enough, then end the session. It should not take long before a simple DOWN from you results in him lying down. Personally, I see no reason to reinforce Down with the collar, unless you're planning on using the Down at a long distance.

Using the Collar to End Inappropriate Behaviors

When I was five years old, for some unknown reason, I became fascinated with a lamp in our living room. I was told over and over to leave it alone, as I guess my parents were afraid I might try to pick it up, drop it, and break it. One day the bulb died and it was removed but, before they replaced it, I stuck my index finger into the empty light socket. I left the lamp alone after that.

The single, greatest advantage the remote trainer has over more widely used and accepted methods of correction/punishment is simplicity itself: THE DOG ASSOCIATES HIS BEHAVIOR WITH THE UNCOMFORTABLE STIMULATION. He doesn't associate the owner as responsible for his correction; rather he himself assumes that role. He self-corrects. Allow me to illustrate that fact for you by explaining how it is used to end the problem of a dog stealing food from the counter.

Scooter, my clients' six-year-old female yellow Labrador, was a charmer.

Everyone who knew Scoot, as her owners called her, adored her. The first time I saw Scoot she reminded me of Kitt, a yellow Lab by her own right. The only difference between the Scoot and Kitt was 20 pounds. If Scoot jettisoned those pounds she could pass as Kitt's identical twin. Tonnage aside, the only issue with Scoot was simply this: food on a counter was open season for Scoot, with no annual license fee nor bag limit. Leave food on a counter and it soon vanished, not into the air but rather into Scoot's tummy. Her owners had tried solving the problem themselves and, when nothing they tried helped, they invested, over time, in three separate trainers. They even sent her away to boot camp for two weeks. She was returned in the afternoon, in plenty of time to inhale half a pound of bacon the following morning. "Any eggs or toast?" I queried, thinking my Midwest sense of humor might lighten things up a bit. In return I was rewarded with ice-cold glares from both Jane and William, Scoot's caregivers. After listening to a litany of edibles stolen from counters throughout the years, the real reason for enlisting me to help centered around that year's Thanksgiving, two weeks prior to my arrival. Apparently Scoot got a serious hankering for poultry, grabbing the Thanksgiving Big Bird as it sat on a serving platter on the kitchen island. Jane had poured herself a glass of wine and had gone to the living room to join their 12 guests for a couple of minutes when suddenly came the deadly sound of a serving platter crashing to the floor. The vegetarian Thanksgiving meal was served sometime later.

William simply told me, "Scoot's out of here." Jane began crying.

"If you put food out on the counter now," I asked calmly, "might Scoot go for it?"

"Of course she'll go for it, and then you'll grab her and shake the daylights out of her, I suppose," said William, "like the other trainers and I have all done many times, and it won't make a damn bit of difference."

"She does it a lot when we're out of the kitchen," Jane said to me.

"I can't stop Scoot from food stealing—" I began when William interrupted.

"Well, at least you're honest," he huffed.

"But I can help Scoot stop herself," I continued.

I told them about the remote collar and Jane told me they'd tried one a couple of years ago but it had little effect; she still stole. After they had told me how they used it, I was certain I could help. I asked Jane to put something Scoot really liked on the counter, but to push toward the rear so it would take Scoot a little while to reach it. I put my collar on Scoot, quietly tapped it at increasing intensity until I saw her ears twitch. Then I turned it up two more levels. With food on the counter I suggested we all go into the next room. In the room I placed myself where it was difficult for Scoot to see me but I could see her if she jumped for the food. Sure enough, before a minute had passed, she jumped up to get the food. Because it was out of immediate reach, she couldn't snatch it and get down before I could apply the stimulation. I used a short continuous stimulation which stopped her from trying to reach the food but she remained with her front paws on the counter. I gave two more taps and she jumped down. All this time I hadn't done a single thing. Jane was about to say something to Scoot, so I pressed my index finger to my lips and when she saw me she remained quiet. Minutes later Scoot jumped up again. This time she jumped off quickly as soon as she felt the stimulation. She did not jump again, but came into our room and lay down.

"Unbelievable," said William. "If I hadn't witnessed it I would not have believed it."

"And you didn't say a thing," added Jane.

It took three sessions but Scoot never stole food after I was finished.

By the way, did you know that jumping up on people is the number one behavior complaint, nationally, from dog owners? It's true. Know why? The answer is simple.

Because it can be an extremely difficult problem to solve. But, unknown to most, it can also be rather simple to resolve. Difficult, because almost every form of correction involves you, the owner, personally getting involved in whatever form you choose. Knee the dog in the chest, squirt water at him, turn your back, hit him, yell at him, step on his hind paws; and yes, there are one, maybe two, friends of yours who actually enjoy your dog jumping on them. The list is endless. They all have one thing in common; they all involve you, the owner, intervening. And that creates conflict and confrontation between you and your dog. And that is absolutely the worst possible result. So, do you really want to solve jumping up both effectively and quickly? If the answer is yes, then get a good quality remote trainer (e-collar).

Jumping up on People

When you use a remote trainer to solve this problem, you no longer try to give your dog this message, "Don't you dare jump on Aunt Sophie." With an e-collar, you simply think, "So you want to jump on Aunt Sophie? Go right ahead; it's your choice." And, when your dog does jump, you simply tap the button on your remote, AND YOU SAY NOTHING.

I use momentary stimulation for almost all corrections. Why? Simply because that's all that's necessary, that's why. Momentary stimulation is 100% consistent, which is another sound reason for using that mode. A Garmin Sport Pro uses momentary stimulation lasting 100 milliseconds. That's 1/10 of a second. And it's 1/10th of a second every time the button is pressed, not less, not more, 1/10th of a second. Perfect consistency whether you use it or your wife uses it.

The steps in correcting jumping up are as follows:

First, always begin using the lowest setting. When your dog jumps, simply tap the transmitter. Remember, say nothing. If you say something then you bring yourself into the correction and that's the last thing you want to do. If he gets off, DO NOT PRAISE HIM! He's not doing the right thing by getting off; he shouldn't have been jumping, so he's ending the inappropriate behavior. We don't praise for ending an inappropriate behavior; we praise for your dog's appropriate behavior. And that's not semantics; it's understanding simple principles of conditioning and learning. Now, if your dog does not get off, simply go up one level of intensity. At some point your dog will get off. Stay at that level because it works. If he yelps, drop down one level. We want the level to be uncomfortable, never painful. You think that you set the level. Well, think about that. You see, we don't set the level, the dog does, because he tells us what level is effective. He does that by getting off. It becomes his decision to get off and eventually not to jump at all. When it's the dog's decision, that is far more effective than it being our decision. When your dog no longer jumps, then you can have him sit when, let's say, you come home from that long day at the office. You come in, tell him "Sit," and when he sits, then he gets praise.

How long might this take? It varies. I've solved jumping problems almost immediately. On the other hand, I've had clients who told me it took two weeks before their dog stopped jumping completely. What about age, you ask? Well, last year I worked with a 10-year-old Irish setter who had been jumping on everyone for almost his whole life. You guessed it—he no longer jumps.

Jumping on Counters and Tables

Use the previous technique, but with one possible exception. Your dog may only jump on the counter when you are out of the kitchen. That's because he was punished by you in the kitchen. When he counter jumped, you yelled at him or used some other silly technique always involving you. If you're in the kitchen he won't jump. If you're somewhere other than the kitchen, he knows he has a green light to jump. So, if that's where you are at this point, it's okay. Don't despair. Set him up with the food, remembering to keep the food back from the edge of the counter for reasons I've already explained. Prior to this you've already planned your strategy. You went into an adjoining room and picked a spot where you could spot him, but it was hard for him to see you. You may need to use a mirror for this. I've done it with clients by going outside and spying through a window. If you're close to your neighbor it might be a good idea to mention to her what you're going to do. Just so you don't end up being arrested by the local police for being a peeping Tom. I once set up a client's dog, then went outside to the window I had picked out, only to find that the sun was reflecting off the window glass directly in my face. I couldn't see a thing. As I said, plan ahead.

Pica - Ingesting Inedible Objects

Monty was one handsome German shepherd dog; even the long scar on his belly couldn't affect his good looks. Plus, he had a pleasant, outgoing demeanor to match. Everyone who knew Monty fell in love with him. Unfortunately, Monty ate rocks. Had already had two operations to remove them and, after the second, while still at the vet hospital, he attempted a third while being walked by one of the vet techs. Poor Monty, three trainers had already tried solving the problem. None of their techniques were effective. The third had remarked, "There is no solution for this dog." Then their vet recommended they call me as a "last resort." His owners told me about Monty's problem over the phone and inquired if I could help. "You bet," I answered simply.

After arriving at their home, I told them about the remote and its proper use, and I had them feel a couple of intensity levels. I had them take Monty for about a 15-minute walk while I scouted the area looking for rocks.

Holding a towel in my hand to keep my scent off them, I selected two rocks about two inches in diameter and placed them on the bricks next to the fireplace. I sat in one of the chairs and told them to let Monty loose. He came over to me and, after receiving a couple of pats, spied the rocks. As soon as he put his nose down I tapped him twice, quickly, with the transmitter. Monty jumped back like he was stung by a bee! He backed away about six feet and stared at the rocks. I made certain no one in the room laughed or said a word. After about two minutes, Monty cautiously approached the rocks. Once again, he put his nose down and, once again I tapped. He quickly jumped back. That was enough for Monty. His owners were astonished! Watching Monty walk away from the rocks and lie quietly in a corner was beyond their wildest dreams. They purchased a collar and set a follow-up appointment. I told them not to allow Monty anywhere near any rocks in the meantime, knowing how difficult that might be. During the follow-up appointment we worked outside. I had Monty in his backyard with no lead on him. I removed a rock from my pocket and tossed it on the ground about five feet away from Monty. He took off like a shot after it and as soon as his nose went down, I tapped him. That was enough for him. For the next hour Monty walked around his backyard, ignoring every rock I had laid out for him. I told them to take him to different places and to tap him whenever he bent down for a rock. I'm pleased to report that Monty won't even sniff, never mind pick up, a rock. Monty's owners told me the remote saved Monty's life.

Guarding Objects

Solving this problem is similar to solving pica problems, but with one difference. I allow the dog to take the inappropriate object and go off to his favorite lair. I approach in a nonchalant manner, stopping three to four feet from the dog. I tell him "Drop," and immediately tap the transmitter button with momentary stimulation. If he doesn't drop the object, I increase the intensity by one level and repeat. I do this until he drops the object. I do not attempt to pick it up nor do I offer praise. I wait a while to see if he will challenge me for control. If he walks away I quietly walk over and retrieve the object. If I start to walk over and he attempts to take the object, I simply repeat the "Drop" and tap. Eventually the dog will walk away, and I pick up the object, saying nothing.

I need to add something here. Before I work with the guarding, I will first take the dog outside and work him on Heeling for, perhaps 10 minutes. I need to establish myself in a leader role first, before even attempting to work on the dog's object guarding. You may need to enlist a professional dog man prior to your attempting this procedure. No one needs to get needlessly bitten in an effort to resolve a potentially dangerous problem. I have worked with a few thousand of these cases over the years and I understand full well that you need to establish some leadership first.

Taking Objects to Gain Attention

First, do not do this technique with puppies. Adult dogs only. The solution to this problem is similar to the one directly above. Your dog arrives with your slipper in his mouth. Simply tell him "drop" and tap. No praise after he drops it.

Digging

The digger is, usually, a bored dog. Do not put him outside for long time periods. It's like leaving a three-year-old in your backyard unattended. Simply not a good idea. Exceptions are some of the rodent-seeking terriers, such as the Jack Russell. Know the characteristics of the breed before you make your purchase. One more thing. Many dog owners put their dogs outside to allow them to get their exercise. Dogs do not self-exercise, so be a part of his exercise. Play fetch, etc.

Chasing Bikes, Squirrels

Holly and Ed McGruder live in a lovely home in Lincoln, Massachusetts, a lovely town about 20 miles west of Boston. Holly is a rose gardener, carefully tending to over 150 rose bushes. They also have a handsome Golden retriever, the love of Holly's life. I was called in to help, if I could, with a serious incident that had occurred the prior week. I arrived sometime during the afternoon, parked my Jeep under a gorgeous Japanese maple tree, took the path to their front door, rang the bell, and waited. A short time later Holly opened the door and I quickly introduced myself to Mrs. McGruder. "Call me Holly and please do come in," she answered pleasantly.

After we both were seated I took out my notepad and pen. Holly got up and left the room, returning shortly accompanied by a strikingly handsome retriever. Upon seeing me, he immediately ran over, tail wagging, and nuzzled up alongside my chair. "Ray, meet Gunner, our two-year-old Golden."

"He sure is a looker," I answered, giving Gunner a few scratches behind his ear. "So, tell me what's going on and how I can help."

I looked up at Holly and tears were beginning to run down her cheeks. "I think we may have to have Gunner put to sleep," she said, almost in a whisper.

"Why?" I asked.

"Gunner killed the neighbor's dog," she answered as she broke down sobbing.

I allowed her time to compose herself a bit, then said, "Tell me why."

And she told me the following story. When Gunner was a puppy, Holly would bring him outside while she attended to her gardening. There were several rabbits in the area, she said, and they would nibble the leaves of her precious roses. She would clap her hands and yell at them and they would run off—temporarily. So when Gunner got a little older, she would encourage him to chase away the rabbits. Gunner loved the game. As he grew older, as soon as he was outside, he would begin his hunt, searching for that white tail attached to his prey. He never caught any, she told me; he just chased them away from the roses, and Holly would praise him when he did.

One week ago, Holly said, their neighbors (close friends) were away for the day, and had hired a friend's teenaged daughter to dog sit for their one-year-old Maltese, Lu Lu. The neighbors lived next door, but the houses are far apart so I couldn't see their house. Early in the afternoon, Holly and Gunner walked down their very long, winding drive to get the day's mail. What Holly didn't know was that, shortly before, Lu Lu had shot past the young teenaged dog sitter as she opened the front door to take the mail from the mailman who had knocked on her door.

Holly and Gunner got the mail and were walking back up that long drive when, suddenly, Gunner spotted a white tail in the tall grass up ahead. Holly saw it as well and quickly realized it was their neighbor's Maltese. Gunner exploded after the little dog, with Holly pleading with Gunner to "Come." Gunner caught Lu Lu, shook her with several violent jerks, and shook the life from her.

I consoled Holly as best I could, and she got up, asking if I would join her in a cup of tea. I said yes, and while were waiting for the water to boil, Holly's husband, Ed, walked through the door. Holly introduced me as I began to stand to shake hands.

Ed ignored my extended hand, saying, "I know why you're here. I know Holly wants desperately to keep Gunner, but I will not have a dog killer in this house. I told her we have to put Gunner down, and that's my final decision."

I looked directly at Ed, and said, "Mr. McGruder, Gunner's your dog and it's your decision, not mine. I will tell you, though, in my opinion, Gunner is not a dog killer."

"Not a dog killer? He killed our neighbor's dog, for god's sake. What in hell would you call him?" He was yelling at me at this point.

I answered quietly, "I'd call Gunner a really nice dog, Mr. McGruder. You don't have a dog killer; what you've got is a dog that doesn't come when he's called." Ed simply stared, open-mouthed, as I continued. "Holly tried her best to get Gunner to come, but your dog has never learned to really come, to come 100% of the time. If he knew that, I would not be here now." After the smoke had cleared and the truth hit home, Ed quietly sat down and asked me if I could get Gunner to come under any circumstances. I told him I could and we set a day for me to begin working with Gunner. And Holly made three cups of tea.

Please, dear reader, help your dog to learn to come when called, all the time.

Ray conducting a remote collar clinic near Tucson, Arizona

Me trying hard to get in balance with a friend's horse in Arizona.
I've a ways to go.

Ray with Jake at a field trial in the late 1970s

Me taking a break working with the trainers and dogs Marianne and
Whitney at Best Friends Animal Sanctuary in Kanab, Utah

*My client heeling her two former aggressive dogs
toward each other on a beach in England.*

Ray with a former client's super confident great German Shepherd

Finn, a great teacher, associate and deep in wisdom at age 13,
a few months before he passed over the bar.

Me at age 7 with Smokey, my first Labrador friend

Ray and Whitney, the former three-time runaway

"Communication"

Me on the beach in England with the 2 dogs I saved,
no longer fighting with each other.

Section Two

Chapter 9

Aggression: Dogs On The Warpath

Instead of a hard tightness, try to find a soft firmness.
-RAY HUNT, HORSEMAN

I sat upright on the gurney, my legs dangling, my left wrist still oozing a steady drip, drip, drip of blood onto the once crisp white sheet. My mind was completely numb except for the dull, throbbing pain. Silently, I cursed myself, thinking, "How can I do my job with just one hand until this heals?"

Just then the green curtain was yanked aside, and a young male doctor and two nurses surrounded me. "Hello, Ray, I'm Dr. Jacobs," the doctor announced brightly. Spying my mangled wrist and forearm, he mused, "Well, well, what happened here?"

"Dog bite," I answered matter-of-factly.

"Hmm, I've seen lots of dog bites, but never one this serious."

Jacobs appraised me quickly from head to toe and, with the air of Sherlock Holmes about to nail his victim, queried, "So, what are you? A mailman?"

"Not hardly," I muttered without lifting my head.

"So, what is your occupation?"

Slowly, I raised my head, stared him straight in the eyes and answered, "I'm a dogman. I work with dogs."

"Well," my comical physician retorted, "perhaps you should pursue another line of work." Both nurses joined in as he laughed uproariously at his own joke.

I'll never forget Larz, a five-year-old male Kuvasz. Larz was big, about 110 pounds, with big teeth. Even Larz's house was big, set about 60 feet from the main road, the three acres enclosed by a six-foot wrought iron fence, separated only by a narrow, brick path leading to the imposing, massive front door. Larz resided in Gloucester, a town still known around the world for its rich fishing heritage. Her harbor is spectacular, and very large. Evan though it was close to 20 years ago, I recall a sunny yet cool late spring morning as I braked to a stop opposite the house. I heard the barking as I got out of my car, and I couldn't help but notice his polar bear cub size as he ran along the inside of the wrought iron fence, barking at my very presence parked across the road. As I crossed over to his side, the barking turned to snarling with bared teeth. "This must be the place," I muttered to myself, as I walked up the path to the front door, the big Kuzasz matching my every step, wishing, I was certain, that there was no fence between us,

The heavy brass door knocker announced my presence, if by chance the dog hadn't, and, in short order, a most pleasant, older woman labored to open the heavy wooden door. "Are you Mr. McSoley?" she asked, her high-pitched voice barely audible above the primitive sounds still erupting from my right.

"Yes, ma'am," I replied.

"Well, I'm Abbey Waters, and we're so glad you're finally here."

I'll just bet you are, I thought.

"Come inside and meet my husband, Dudley, Mr. McSoley. I believe he's in the Florida room."

After shaking hands with her husband, a short, somewhat overweight man with thinning grey hair and an apparent serious manner, I selected a pale-blue covered chair with arm rests, opened my briefcase, and removed my notepad and pen.

"Would you like me to bring Larz in now?" Mr. Waters asked. "Not quite yet," I answered. "I'd like to get a history first, and find out just how I can be of help."

Alternating back and forth, Abbey and Dudley told me about Larz. He had come from an out-of-state breeder as an eleven-week-old pup. They told me they were not looking for a guard dog, but rather a dog that would simply bark and let them know when people approached. "We read up on the breed's history and the Kuvasz seemed to be exactly what we were looking for," Dudley stated.

"Larzie is devoted to me; I really don't think he would allow anyone to hurt me. He doesn't even like it when Dudley tries to give me a hug," Abbey added.

Larz was largely an outside dog, growing up and maturing on the Waters's property. He quickly became too large and strong to be walked, so the fenced-in yard soon became both his home and territory. He slept inside the house at night, spending evenings with them in the Florida room. As a young pup he would greet both friends and strangers by jumping on them, and they were never successful at curbing that particular behavior. As a result, Larz was soon put outside whenever people came to the house. The iron fence ran along the edge of the sidewalk and it was not long before Larz began running up and back along the fence, barking continuously at anyone who ventured past.

"I'll bring Larz inside for you two to meet," said Dudley, as he suddenly rose from his chair, leaving the room. Sure enough, a few minutes later Dudley reappeared at the threshold of the room, both hands wrapped mightily around a thick leather guard dog lead, holding onto

Larz for all he was worth. As soon as the dog saw me, he exploded with rage, teeth bared, his body straining heavily against the heavy pronged collar pressed tightly around his neck. Dudley, at this point, was literally straddling the dog, yelling "No!" and yanking repeatedly upwards on the lead and collar.

"This is what our trainer told us to do to get him under control," Dudley yelled at me from across the room. The scene before me was utterly chaotic: dog in control, wanting me for lunch, Dudley hopelessly out of control, yanking furiously on the collar, the prongs clearly hurting the poor animal. Literally cupping my hands around my mouth so I could be heard above the racket, I yelled to Dudley, "Get Larz out of here!" realizing that it was only a short matter of time until the crazed dog dragged Dudley with him over to me, and at that point I would be in serious trouble. Beads of sweat appeared on Dudley's brow, his face crimson, his breathing ragged. The scene was seriously like something out of a horror movie.

Suddenly, Abbey got up from her chair. "I'll take Larzie," she said, beginning to walk toward him. "I'll lock him in the library." The two of them were able to get the dog turned around and Dudley quickly backed into the room, closing the sliding door until Abbey was safely down the hall. With the noise level back to normal, he reopened the door and dropped into his chair.

Immediately I had a very bad feeling in my gut. *You've not seen the last of Larz,* my sixth sense told me. No sooner had Dudley uttered the words, "There, that's better," when I heard the pleasant, little woman from the library begin yelling, "Larzie come back, Larzie come back."

I thought, *This is not good.* It wasn't good. Within seconds Larz blasted into the room, eyes blazing, heading straight for me. With no time to do anything to protect myself, I remained seated and calm, my arms resting on the arms of the chair. Larz and his 110 pounds charged into the side of my chair, his muzzle poking hard at my left arm, sniffing loudly. I stared straight ahead, saying and doing nothing. Larz then bit deeply into my left forearm, in three separate places.

When I did not respond, he stopped the attack, continuing to prod my mangled and bleeding arm, growling savagely, daring me to move or challenge him in any way.

Abbey appeared at the threshold. "Oh God, Dudley!" she screamed, tears welling in her eyes. "Get the dog!" Dudley sat, paralyzed. Finally, after what seemed forever, he got up, got Larz's lead (still attached to his collar), and pulled him away. Larz went along without protest, evidently pleased he had done his job. Dudley put Larz in the yard and I asked Mrs. Waters where the bathroom was so I could wash my arm with soap and water and assess the damage. There were several deep puncture wounds and numerous lacerations from the canine teeth; however, there appeared to be no serious muscle or artery damage and, despite a lot of pain, I assured them both I would survive.

Abbey was a dear and insisted on putting antiseptic on my wounds as well as bandaging my arm as best she could. They both insisted I go to the emergency room at the local hospital and wanted to drive me there, but I told them I could make the drive myself if they would write down directions. I stayed about another 30 minutes before leaving, discussing with them what to do with Larz. They realized there was no way they could safely keep him. "What should we do with him?" they asked. I recommended they contact the breeder, explain in detail what occurred, and ask if he/she would take him back. "What if the breeder won't?" Abbey inquired. I told them euthanasia was, in my opinion, the only other option for Larz, as this could never be allowed to happen again. I pointed out to them that Larz was way too much dog for them and that they could never achieve a leader/follower role with him. "Larz is a seriously high-risk dog to anyone but yourselves, and even you could possibly become a victim under the worst-case scenario," I told them.

They asked if I would consider working with him. I told them no, not because I was afraid but rather because I could not, in my heart, simply try to make them feel better by saying I'd take Larz on as a client. They then told me about the other trainer from three years ago. "He told us to use the prong collar to correct him."

"Well, we just saw how effective that was," I answered.

They called me two weeks later, thanking me for helping them with the decision and inquiring about my arm. The breeder had already come and gone, taking their beloved Larz with him.

I never heard from Abbey and Dudley Waters again.

Many people have an aggressive dog story. I've got 'em in spades. For 50 years I've been helping dogs and their owners deal with aggression. Dog/dog aggression, territorial aggression, fear aggression, dominance aggression, object-guarding aggression, aggression toward adults or toward children, dogs biting family members and fine with everyone else, predatory aggression—in short, been there, done that.

Aggression is the most serious behavior problem in a dog. The "ologist" experts tell us there are something like 15 distinct forms of aggression. Perhaps so. I can tell you this; when a client contacts me about his or her aggressive pet, they really aren't that concerned about hair-splitting the specific type. Their dog is aggressive to other dogs, toward humans, or both. Period.

The Secret Fundamental Reason For Aggression

I'm going to ask you a couple of questions. Do you know, fundamentally, what aggression is about? What is the basis for aggression? What is it that ignites the spark that, in a neurologically sound animal, sets off an explosion of aggression in a loving dog? Before reading any further, take a minute to see if you come up with the correct answer. No, do not read further. Think first. Okay, you've thought about it. I'll give you my answer in a minute or so. I want you to understand something. When I give a lecture on dog aggression and I ask that question, it's extremely rare that anyone gives me the correct answer. Why is that? I believe it's simply because we associate aggression with something on the surface rather than with what's going on UNDER the surface. So, I'm going to share my secret with you. I'm going to let you in on that secret, the secret that thousands of dog owners should know, yet unfortunately, don't.

The underlying, fundamental reason for aggression is—CONTROL. Think about it. It suddenly makes perfect sense, doesn't it? Control. And, in the dog/owner relationship, both dog and owner can't be in control. And that means that when your dog demonstrates aggressive behavior, he or she is either 1) attempting to gain control, or 2) simply reinforcing the control he or she already has. And that means that you, the owner, are not in control, and when an owner is not in control of his dog, chances are, at some point, we're going to have problems.

Another way of looking at it is to say that there is a responsibility problem. I know that might sound anthropomorphic, but it's true. For example, let's say your dog lunges at dogs approaching both you and your dog when you are walking it on a lead. When Maxine, your lovable dachshund, lunges at that approaching dog, there's a responsibility problem. Maxine is taking on the responsibility for dealing with that dog. Maxine needs to understand that dealing with that approaching dog is YOUR responsibility, not hers. Her job is to be responsible to you. Period. I'll talk more about that later in the chapter.

How Dogs Become Aggressive

Let's return to Larz for a minute to see if we can deduce what went wrong with him, and when it went wrong. He came from a reputable breeder. Clearly too much dog for the Waters, he never had proper socialization nor early and continual quality training so necessary for him to ever have a chance at working out with them. Jumping up on people can be an annoying problem with a small or medium-sized dog, but it can pave the way for major problems down the road if not corrected in a large, imposing breed such as the Kuvasz. Because of his jumping, his lifestyle took a dramatic turn. Rather than learning to integrate with people, he was isolated whenever anyone came to the house. The property was fenced in such a manner that the fencing had been installed right up to the edge of the sidewalk. This contributed to "barrier frustration," a condition that, by itself, can condition aggressive behavior in some dogs. And the Kuvasz as a breed is content to become the guardian, responsible for, rather than to, family. If we add all this up—no socialization, lack of early, qualified training, isolated from non-family humans early on, exposed to barrier frustration as well as spending long periods of time outside, answerable only to himself, inappropriate training later on, a guardian-type breed to begin with, and a couple who wanted a protector—we can easily understand how and why Larz ended up as he did. Now before all you Kuvasz breeders come hunting for my scalp, let me state that I am not saying to the readers to avoid choosing a Kuvasz, or that the breed is innately aggressive. I have seen aggression in practically every breed with which I have worked.

Aggressive behavior is either genetic, environmentally influenced or, in probably the majority of circumstances, some combination of the two. I have witnessed aggressive behavior toward humans in a puppy as young as six weeks of age. It's extremely rare but I have seen it. In that single instance I was brought in by the breeder, and actually witnessed the behavior. The breeder had been attempting to deal with the behavior for one week before consulting with me. We were successful in resolving the issue.

Aggressive behavior can be genetically linked. Aggressive dogs, when bred, have a good chance of siring and whelping aggressive offspring. It's pretty simple, folks.

On the other hand, there's the environmentally influenced aggressive dog. This is the dog that, given the proper surroundings, proper handling and training, matures into a wonderful companion animal. However, place that same dog in an environment in which the influences are all negative and, boom, you've got all the ingredients for a problem. Let's take a look at some of those influences.

Selecting the Wrong Dog

More on this in the chapter on puppies (Chapter 12). A rose is a rose does not apply to dogs. Line up 10 Labrador retrievers and 10 German shepherds, chances are that you will have dogs with superior retrieving skills among the Labs, and a greater propensity for territoriality and protection among the shepherds. Am I against a good German shepherd dog? My personal dogs have always been Labs because they suit my lifestyle; however, I have always maintained that a good German shepherd is a tough dog to best. The key is understanding what you're getting.

Abdicating Responsibility

Lack of proper training. Almost all of my clients respond thusly when I inquire about their dog's training: "Well, we took him to puppy school when he was just a puppy, and he did really well." I'm sorry, that's not getting your dog trained. That's like your child learning to ride her bike with training wheels—and never taking them off. She never really learns to ride properly. She merely gets the concept. Puppy stuff is pre-school.

You've got to continue. That's why I took both the time and the effort (and when you hunt and peck on the computer, that's effort) to write the earlier chapters, because I know from firsthand experience what happens when owners do not train their dogs. "But, Ray, you don't understand. I simply do not have the time." Bull!! People have the time; they just don't realize it.

In my earlier chapters I talked about making learning a lifestyle for your dog. If you truly don't have the time, get yourself a cat.

Socializing

This is the word everyone uses. "You've got to socialize your dog." But what, exactly, does that mean? It means different things to different people. I'll ask a client, "When your dog was young, four or five months, did you get him out and around a lot of people?"

"Oh yes," some will answer. "We took Dodger everywhere."

"And he enjoyed the attention and petting from strangers?"

"Oh well, they never petted him much. You see, he was always in the car with us."

These people think they were socializing their dog by taking him for a ride in the car. That's not socializing. When you socialize a dog, you get him out for walks. You take him places where he can interact with people, lots and lots of people. You let him run free (no lead) on trails where he can be greeted by people as well as other dogs, and run around with them. You let him experience going into water, burying his nose in snow, getting wet in the rain. You bring him into shops that don't object to having a young pup in their store. I have a good friend who's a bartender in a wonderful restaurant named the Brickhouse in Dedham, Mass. Finn, my 13-year-old yellow Labrador, has met thousands of people and dogs. When he was 13 weeks, I stopped by the "Brick" one late afternoon for a cold draft. Finn was in my Jeep in his crate. There was one couple at the bar and Lori, the bartender. She asked how I was and I told her about Finn. "I wish I could come out and meet him, Ray," she said sadly.

"Perhaps next time," I said, getting off the bar stool. "I'll be right back." Two minutes later I returned, Finn in my arms. I placed him up on the bar. Lori turned around, saw Finn and nearly fainted. He ran along the bar top to her and began licking her face. The couple began to laugh and Finn turned and ran across to them, getting petted and licking them in return.

Lori, with this incredibly beautiful smile on her face, braced me with her hands on her hips. "Ray, you get Finn out of here before Vinnie arrives and tosses you both out."

"Yes ma'am," I answered, saluting. "Here Finn." Finn ran back to me and I went out and crated him.

"Ray," Lori said as I climbed back on the bar stool, "do not even think of doing that again," and burst out laughing.

Socialize that new pup of yours.

Making Him/Her An Outside Dog

"But, Mr. McSoley, Deacon loves being outside." I don't care; it's not ideal for the vast majority of dogs. I'm not talking about not putting Spike out for short time periods. That's fine. I'm speaking of your dog spending hour upon hour outside by herself. An outside dog can become, within a relatively short time frame, the owner of the yard, answerable only to himself. Examine the real reason(s) you're putting Snyder outside. Are there inside issues that are "resolved" by having pup outside? William Campbell, author of *Behavior Problems in Dogs* (American Veterinary Publications, Inc., 1975) wrote about a couple who put their Saint Bernard out because he drooled all over the furniture inside. The good dog inside soon became an aggressive terror outside.

Barrier Frustration

I spoke previously about this issue with Larz. I've been preaching about this for years. I talked about it in my first book, *Dog Tales*, over 30 years ago, and now, thankfully, others are speaking about it. Your puppy is outside, behind the fence. The fence is installed close to the sidewalk. People walk past, and he watches them approach, then pass by. In the beginning the dog is friendly. All he wants is for the people to pat him and be nice to him. But, perhaps the neighbor children, on their way to school, taunt him, perhaps they drag a stick along the fence, or bark at him. This process (agitation) continues until, guess what, our dog no longer wants to be petted. The window for socialization has closed. He now wants to bite, to get at what he cannot reach due to the barrier. And it was never his fault.

Playing Socially Dominant Games

Playing tug-o-war, roughhousing, teaching the dog to chase squirrels (predatory aggression), etc.—all these games may, in some dogs, begin to condition aggressive tendencies. So why do owners play these games?

Because they don't know any better. As a general rule, there is almost a complete lack of understanding how and why dogs behave as they do.

Improper Training Methods

I'm not dumping on trainers; the vast majority of them do a fine job—even under, in many circumstances, difficult situations. However, there are some positively rotten ones out there. I know a few, and they sure as hell shouldn't be training dogs. They train by employing fear and intimidation, and that approach can end up doing irreparable harm to your dog. A poor trainer can, literally, ruin a potentially fine dog. Get some information on your trainer before you hand your dog over to him or her.

SEARCHING FOR CLUES: WHAT MAKES A DOG AGGRESSIVE

The People Factor

I had a client with two Shetland sheepdogs. One potential problem with many Shelties is severe nuisance barking as well as going after people when they enter, or go to leave, the house. They will "nip" at the visitor's ankles, much as they would "heel" sheep, nipping at the sheep's hocks, just lightly grabbing the trouser cuff, not the wearer's skin. But some of them take their job more seriously, grabbing the ankle itself. My client had the latter problem. They would hold the dogs' collars when friends entered, while the dogs attempted to pull away and go at the person. I asked them if they said anything while this behavior was ongoing. We pat them and tell them, "It's ok, it's all right." I asked them why they did that, "We want to let them know that it's all right."

"That what's all right," I asked. "Their behavior?"

"No, of course not. We want to reassure them that the situation is all right."

But that's not what the dog understands. He learns that when he barks, or attempts to go for the visitor, his behavior is rewarded. Rather than understanding that the situation is all right, he learns from his owner that his behavior is all right.

Don't do that.

Around 30 years ago, Dr. Stan Read, a veterinarian in Lexington, Massachusetts, where the "shot heard 'round the world" (in Concord) was fired at the beginning of our Revolutionary War, referred a lovely woman client of his to me. She had a female German shepherd named Duchess who had developed an eye condition requiring daily application of ointment in both eyes. This woman was referred to me because, after medicating Duchess for almost two years, she suddenly was no longer able to perform the daily task.

I arrived at her modest home one evening. Funny, I can no longer recall her name; I do recall, however, that the weather was cold, with snow flurries in the air. Funny how the memory works sometimes. She told me about the eye condition, and how she was able to treat the eyes for quite some time. "Now, Mr. McSoley, if she so much as sees the ointment tube, she will chase me from the room, and she has even bitten me on my rear."

I asked her if she would be kind enough to give me a demonstration, and she agreed. Leaving the kitchen, she returned after a couple of minutes holding the tube in her hand. I looked at Duchess, who had already spotted the tube. Let's call the woman Peg. Peg had taken perhaps three steps into the kitchen when Duchess growled, jumped up and ran at her, chasing her from the room and actually nipping Peg on her behind in the process.

"I get the picture," I told her, feeling a bit responsible and somewhat embarrassed as she, gingerly, sat down.

I was truly fascinated at this point. "When did the change begin?" I asked.

"A few months ago, she began to become increasingly more difficult. Now, for the past month, perhaps a little bit longer, it's been getting impossible. I now have to bring her to Dr. Read every day, and that's really difficult for me."

"How is she with Doc Read?" I asked.

"Oh, she's perfectly behaved there; they have no problem whatsoever. They can't understand the change in her either."

I asked Peg to explain to me how she would medicate Duchess. She explained that, in the beginning, she would have Duchess sit and she would put the ointment in her eyes with no difficulty. However, as time passed, she began to have Duchess get up on Peg's bed, lie down, and then she'd do the eyes. That progressed to Peg placing a small, white blanket on the bed, having Duchess lie on the blanket, whereupon Peg would then medicate. This process would take about 15 minutes.

Slowly, I began to understand the root cause of the problem. I told Peg that I'd see what I could do to help, that I certainly could not guarantee success, but that I would give it a try. I worked with Duchess before I left that evening, having her sit, and progressed to the point where I could hold the tube and Duchess would remain sitting.

I worked with Peg and Duchess on five consecutive Saturday mornings. When I arrived for the final session, I had Duchess do some heeling, and then I told Peg that I was going to medicate Duchess, and would she be kind enough to go for a drive for about 20 minutes. I did not explain that this was because I knew Peg would be nervous and that Duchess would immediately pick up Peg's nervousness and that, in turn, would make Duchess nervous. And when Duchess became nervous she would, no doubt, become aggressive.

I should in all honesty tell you that, after the initial session, I was not at all convinced that I could solve Peg's problems with Duchess, and that probably Peg was simply not going to be able to keep her. I awoke around 2:00 a.m. the following morning, thinking of how Peg had told me, with tears rolling down her face, how she loved Duchess and could not bear the thought of giving her up.

That thought came back to me as I looked at Duchess and with quiet firmness told her, "I'm going to medicate your eyes this morning, young lady, whether you want them done or not. Your mistress is in a real tizzy over your antics, and that is patently unfair of you." I already had the tube in my shirt pocket, got down on one knee and had Duchess sit. I removed the tube from my pocket. Duchess remained calm until I had the tube about six inches from her eyes, and at that point she began to show her teeth in a silent, warning snarl. I already had one hand on her leather collar, so I quickly dropped the tube, got my other other hand underneath her collar, locking both hands together under her jaw so she could not bite them. Quietly repeating, "Behave yourself" several times, and holding the collar firmly, she erupted, growling savagely, and trying her best to twist around so she could grab my wrists. We acted like two Sumo wrestlers for about a solid minute and then I began to feel her neck muscles soften, followed by a submissive sigh.

I removed one hand from her collar, reached and picked up the tube. I told her once again, almost in a whisper, "Behave yourself." I then calmly medicated the right eye, followed by the left. After completing the task, I put the tube back in my shirt pocket and gave Duchess a quiet "Good girl."

Not long after, Peg returned, with a cup of coffee for me (I think I was hoping for something a bit stronger). "Well, Peg, we got the eyes done. Now it's your turn."

"Did she give you any problems, Ray?"

"No worries, Peg," I lied.

I then had Peg medicate her dog's eyes, which she did, and from then on, she had no more problems. I told her to medicate Duchess in the kitchen only, no more on the bed rituals.

What can be learned from this? First, Peg had told me that she was never comfortable medicating Duchess. The tube had a long, metal nozzle, and she was highly afraid that Duchess would turn quick, stabbing herself in the eye and causing severe damage. As a result, Peg eventually devised this elaborate pattern surrounding the process. In other words, she began making an increasingly big deal out of a simple matter, and in the process made Duchess increasingly nervous. Because Peg was nervous, her anxiety played into Duchess's emotional state. Peg's anxiety was, ultimately, responsible for her dog's aggressiveness. Remember, with Doc Read she was perfectly behaved, because the doc was a good dog man as well as a good vet.

The solution? Peg got some professional help from me. How did I resolve the situation? First, I let Duchess understand, largely through "Heeling," that she was no longer chairman of the board. She was re-assigned to junior vice president. Once that was accomplished, she no longer needed to worry about the situation. As leader, it was my responsibility to handle the situation, not hers. She then was able to begin to relax, to give up CONTROL, which, as you now understand, is what aggression is about. Second, I also made it simpler for her, no more long, involved process. Third, I got the job done in a quiet but firm manner.

If you have an aggressive dog, I would strongly urge you to seek qualified, professional help, someone with experience who can deal with the problem in an objective manner. That person needs to have a calm, confident approach. And you have to be comfortable with him or her. By the time the problem gets to the point where you feel you can't do anything, you've become emotionally involved, with con-flict and confrontation as the result. And that's counterproductive. Remember, frustration is low-level anger. A good pro will be able to handle your emotionally charged situation with a calming, objective approach.

Emotion is one of the main reasons dealing with an aggressive problem is almost always beyond the scope of the owner. Emotion is one aspect of chi, your inner energy. For example, you're walking King down the sidewalk and someone with a dog begins to approach. You have had aggression problems with your dog in the past with dogs approaching, so you immediately become tense and stressed, and so you pull up on the lead. You have just transferred that negative chi to King, and he immediately realizes that you are no longer in control, which forces him to step in. So now he begins to pull and bark or growl at the approaching duo. You tighten the lead as much as you can, and cross the street if that's possible. If not, with King choking, you struggle past the other dog as best you can. You think you have gotten control by tightening the lead, but you've done the opposite.

I had clients, not long ago, with such a problem. It was our initial visit, and I had brought Finn, my trusty Lab, along with me. The clients live in Wayland, a very nice town some 30 minutes (except during the a.m. and p.m. commute) west of Boston. They have a simply gorgeous five-year-old female Briard named Marie that "goes off" on approaching dogs. She had recently been in her first dog fight, hence the shout out to me. When it first started, they had consulted with a couple of trainers. The first one had used food treats and a harness to resolve the problem, while the second had used the prong collar. Sue said she thought Marie was a bit better with the prong, but Sue hated using it. So Sue would do her best to avoid other dogs, walking Marie at 5:00 in the morning, and turning around and going away when she saw another dog.

I put her on my Mendota slip lead and took her out to do a bit of heeling. After 10 minutes I knew that the Mendota would not be helpful because by using the prong, they had conditioned Marie to develop what I call an "iron neck." She simply did not feel the Mendota. I suggested we go straight to the e-collar, and Sue, with some reluctance, agreed. We went out and began working on heeling. After perhaps 15 minutes, Sue was heeling Marie, and Marie was walking right next to Sue, tail up, clearly enjoying herself.

"Any better?" I asked.

"So much better," Sue answered. "She has never, ever, heeled like this."

We went back inside to give Marie a chance to process what I had just done. Sue made tea, and I had just taken my first sip when Ted, Sue's husband, breezed into the house. "Oh, Ted," said Sue as Ted strode past us. "I'd like you to meet Mr. McSoley, the gentleman I contacted to help us with Marie."

Ted ignored us both, removing his coat as he advanced on the refrigerator. Removing a glass from a nearby cabinet, he shoved it under the ice maker on the door of the fridge. Pouring himself either scotch or bourbon, he turned toward me and queried, "What's your first name once again?"

"It's Ray," Sue answered before I could.

"Well, Ray, here's the deal," said Ted, taking a sip of whatever was in the glass. "I don't have a problem with the dog. Sue has the problem."

"Does Marie lunge at dogs when they approach you on a walk?" I asked rather quietly.

"I don't give her that chance … Ray, is it?" Ted answered matter-of-factly. "I just wrap the leash around my hand, tighten up on it and drag her past the other dog." He continued, "You need to understand, Ray, Sue can't do that, doesn't have the strength, so she can't control Marie like I can."

"Please excuse me, Ted, what did you say about Sue?" I asked.

"I said she can't control the dog. I just wrap up the leash tight and I have good control."

"No," I courageously responded. "Ted, you don't have control" and before he could interrupt I added, "You're confusing control with restraint. Restraint you have, control you don't have." There was total silence in the room for at least five seconds before Ted walked into another room.

"Let's you and I go back out and see how Marie does when she sees Finn, my Lab."

"You've a dog in your Jeep?" she exclaimed.

"Yep," I answered. "He's got water and it's cool today. Let's see how they do."

Suddenly, Ted reappeared before I had a chance to stand up. "If anything happens between my dog and yours, you'd better not get any ideas about bringing a lawsuit. You got that?" Ted said, spitting the words out.

"No worries, mate," I cheerfully answered.

I went out to my Jeep, let Finn out to pee, and then had him jump back in. I went back inside and told Sue to go out to the Jeep and let Finn out. I told her his lead is on him and he heels on the left side. I told her to walk Finn up two driveways and remain there until I came out with Marie. Sue went out and I followed about five minutes later. I got to the street and called out to Sue to walk Finn right past us. She started walking toward us and, before I started toward them with Marie, I happened to glance back at the bay window. Ted was standing there, watching. When Sue got about 30 feet from us, Marie's ears cocked, her tail went up and she began to tense. She moved ahead of me and, as she did so, I turned to my left, away from Marie (Marie was heeling on my right side), told Marie "Heel," and tapped the collar. Marie turned immediately, returning to the heel position as I was halfway into my turn. I turned around completely and continued walking toward Sue and Finn. We passed each other about six feet apart. Marie never even looked at Finn. We repeated the pass once more; this time Sue had Marie and I had Finn. We passed each other perfectly. "Okay, let's wrap it up and go inside," I said.

When we got back inside, Sue and I once again sat down at her kitchen table, and I told her to get a Garmin (e-collar), their Sport Pro Model. It's what I use, and have been doing so for years. Marie walked around the kitchen for a bit, tail up and wagging, obviously proud of herself. I said to Sue, "Well, whadaya think?"

"I'm absolutely stunned," she answered, wearing a huge grin. "Marie normally would have gone right after Finn. I never would have dreamed this could happen, and they were so close to each other."

"We'll go back outside in about 10 minutes and take them both for a walk together. By the way, Sue, have you noticed where Marie is?" Marie was lying on the kitchen floor, right next to me. I reached down and gave her a quiet pat, and she gave me a couple of tail wags. About that time Ted came into the kitchen and pulled up a chair. "I saw your dog and Marie passing each other, and Marie appeared to be calm," he said to me.

"You have no idea, Ted," Sue interrupted. "You should have been there."

"Would you mind … Ray, right? … if I went outside with you two? I'd kind of like to see it firsthand."

"Sure," I answered. "We're going back out to walk together, so please join us."

Well, we went back out and this time we were going to walk together, around the block. We started off, Marie walking off Sue's right and me walking Finn on my left. As we walked down the street, looking at us from a helicopter, it was, right to left, Marie, Sue, me, and Finn. The dogs were separated by Sue and me. I had Ted follow us. After we had walked a couple hundred feet, I stepped behind and around Sue so I could now be on her right side. Because Finn heels on my left, that put both dogs about three feet apart from each other. We walked that way halfway around the block. Then I stopped and told Ted to "take the reins."

"What do I do?" he asked me, nervously.

"First, take three or four deep breaths, Ted. We're just goin' for a walk, so just relax," I told him. "You just heel Marie; I'll hold the transmitter. Just tell Marie to 'Heel' and start walking. Sue will do the same. I'll just walk behind you guys."

We finished the walk, and they both wanted to do the block a second time. We did, then went back into the kitchen and sat down. Sue got three bottles of cold water for us, and before I could unscrew the cap, Ted asked me, "Okay, Ray, where can I get one of those zappers?"

"It's not a zapper, Ted," I answered firmly. "I hate that word. It disrespects both the instrument and the work we do with it. Call it by its proper name, either a remote trainer or an e-collar."

"Sorry, Ray," Ted said. "Where can we get one?"

"I'll write it down for you," I answered. "I recommend getting one from a place that has parts for them and also performs maintenance if you ever need it. Also, if you have a question and can't reach me, you can contact them and they may be able to help. Collar Clinic (collarclinic.com) is one such place. There are others. Lion Country Supply (lcsupply.com) is another, as well as Cabelas and Bass Pro. They carry the Garmin Sport Pro. And Ted, there are some other good collar systems out there. Dogtra and Sport Dog are just two. But you have to be careful because there are, unfortunately, some poorly made systems as well, and they can be totally counterproductive to good training. I use Garmin not because I'm connected in any way with Garmin, but simply because I trust the product."

I told them to contact me when their system arrived and I would help get them comfortable using the system with Marie. They both thanked me for helping her. And five days later, when I returned to help them get started, Ted had remembered my name.

LEARNING TO CONTROL AGGRESSIVE BEHAVIOR

Dog/Dog Aggression

Dog-on-dog aggression is, unfortunately, in my experience, exploding in popularity. It accounts for over 50% of my clients at this juncture. Get into your car and drive around an area where you see people walking their dogs. How many do you see dragging their poor owners around? Put another way, how many dogs do you see walking, on a slack lead, next to their owner? Not many of the latter variety, that's for damn certain. And they're being walked (or I should say taking their owners for a drag) on all types and manner of rigs. You see them wearing nose bands (a hackamore on a horse); harnesses of every description; double leads (like reins on a horse), yep, double leads! I saw one just last week. And of course the famous Flex Lead of various lengths. Rarely do you see a dog being walked on a simple collar and lead, such as a British slip lead.

I have written earlier on the critical importance of helping your dog to heel. By heeling I mean simply that your dog walks next to you on a slack lead whenever he's performing the heel task. To help you understand how truly critically important the heeling task is, I really need to tell you about a few of those cases, how I solved them and got both dog(s) and their owners patched up and on with life.

Understand, dear reader, these stories are not about dogs getting into periodic dust ups, growling, snapping, and nipping at each other, with every so often a mild puncture or cut here and there. These following stories are about dogs involved in mortal combat, fully intent on inflicting deadly serious injuries to one another or to a strange, innocent dog.

Sibling Rivalry

Nine years ago, I was asked to come over to England to work with two dogs that were having extremely serious fights. My clients, Kate and Charles, have a summer home in the Caribbean, and while there, Kate had gone to the local animal shelter and seen the two dogs (then puppies), about five months old. They were male litter mates and former street dogs. Kate convinced her husband, Charles, that they had to adopt these two pups.

Charles, being the loving husband, agreed. They returned to England with both untrained pups in tow and, for the next month, both pups loved their new home, playing together, sleeping together, and loving each other as well as both Charles and Kate.

Then, at the end of that first month, they had their first fight. Charles, being a big, powerful, in-shape guy, broke up the fight. Then they had another, and another, each one increasing in intensity, with Charles continuing to break them apart. Eventually, due to injuries to both dogs, they were separated from each other 24/7. At one point they did have a well-known behaviorist from London come to assist in solving the problem. She tried working with the dogs but, unfortunately, that wound up with both dogs having their most serious, bloodletting fight, which Charles eventually was able to break up; however, Charles incurred injuries in the process. The behaviorist told them that there was no way they could ever get the dogs past the aggression, and the only solution was to get rid of (re-home) one of the dogs. With the dogs now about 70 pounds each and nearing one year of age, which dog do you part with? While considering this dilemma, a dear friend of Kate's suggested they contact me, and, within three days I was on a Virgin Atlantic flight to London.

Kate's directions told me which train to take and at which stop to get off, which I did. I was met by none other than Kate herself, a lovely, quietly confident woman who insisted on helping me toss my gear into the rear of the Range Rover. After a short ride we arrived at her home, and I was introduced to Charles, Kate's secretary, and Becky, the tall, attractive dog walker. Becky was there to walk the dogs and, due to the aggressiveness of both dogs, she told me she needed to walk the dogs one at a time. I told Becky I would like to accompany her on the walk and, after removing my Mendota British slip lead from my duffel and jamming it into the rear pocket of my Wrangler jeans, off we went. George, dog number one, heeled very poorly, so I substituted the standard collar/lead setup that he was wearing with my Mendota. During the walk I began working on heeling, and by the time we returned, about an hour later, George was heeling quite well. Zook was next. Same Mendota, same process getting Zook to heel, and by the time we returned to the house, an hour later, Zook was also heeling well. The dogs went back to their separate rooms, and I was ready for a long nap. There was, however, a wonderful, healthy lunch prepared, and I dug in, trying my best not to embarrass my hosts even while consuming way more than my share. After lunch, Charles walked me around the grounds, and the landscaping was truly breathtaking. He educated me as to the names of the different plants and flowers, literally overwhelming me with floral information. After a second, shorter, training session with both dogs, it was time for dinner. I watched as Charles began preparing a portion of the meal and, once again, patiently explained and educated me, this time on how to make a proper risotto. I'm the one being trained, I thought, as dinner was served.

The conversation centered largely around me, how I became a dog behaviorist without a degree, how I learned to work with dogs with problems as well as their owners, inquiring about my book, *Dog Tales,* about my dog travels, etc. They also wanted to know if I truly thought I could help both George and Zook. I answered honestly that I didn't know but that I was hopeful.

I remained busy the next three days, working with both on heeling, two or three times each day. Charles and I, both of us being early risers, would share tea, brewed by my gracious host, around 6:00 each morning. During tea on the morning of the fourth day, Charles said to me, "So, Ray, I see you working with the dogs, getting them to walk nicely by your side, but when are you going to start working on their aggression?"

I rolled his question around in my head for a bit, and then answered, "Charles, I understand. When are we going to let both dogs into the kitchen together, and when they get into a dustup, you grab one dog and I grab the other, we separate them, pound the snot out of both dogs, so they never even think about fighting with each other again." I looked across the table at Charles, and there he was, an enormous grin on his face while simply saying to me, "Exactly." After joining him in laughter, I explained to Charles that what I was endeavoring to do, by heeling, was to establish a strong leader/follower relationship. If I was successful in doing that, then the dogs would learn that I, not they, was responsible for their behavior, and their job in life was to be responsible to me. When I had finished, I looked over at Charles. He simply nodded. He understood. I shall never, ever, forget Charles, one of the most amazing men I have ever had the privilege of both meeting and spending time with.

By this time I was able to heel one dog on one side of me and the other dog on the opposite side. They were, at that point, walking together, separated only by me.

The morning of day 5 I succeeded in having Kate heel George on her left side and Becky heel Zook on her left side. The dogs were, at this point, heeling with Kate and Becky, with me walking about 30 feet behind. I was beginning to transfer leadership from me to my clients.

Day 6 arrived, for me, about 4:00 a.m. This would be a huge trial day for both dogs, as well as for me. This was the morning I would attempt to heel both dogs on my left side. They would no longer be safely separated by one of us; they would be side by side, literally rubbing against each other. Charles would not be with me, nor would Kate nor Becky. I would be alone.

If I hadn't prepared them sufficiently, establishing myself as a strong leader for both dogs, the morning could very well end in bloodshed and a failed attempt on my part to save both George and Zook.

As I recall, tea with Charles that morning was reserved. At one point, Charles asked if I wanted him there. I answered no. This had to be done alone. A second person there could interfere with the dogs being focused on me.

Immediately after breakfast, I took out the second Mendota from my duffel, and asked Kate to take it, hook up George and bring him outside. I hooked up Zook and did the same. I walked over to George, with Zook on my right side. Taking the lead from Kate, I asked her to go inside. I then turned toward the drive, said "Heel," and began walking, bringing Zook around from my right side to my left. Zook came around and, right away, quietly squeezed in between George and me. We walked that way for the better part of one hour. Neither dog appeared tense at any time during the walk. I was never the least bit tense because, as you have already read, if the owner is tense, then the dog will pick up that tension and become tense as well. And when you are tense you are not confident. So I never doubted that the dogs would do well. After the session I put the dogs away, one in one room, the other in the other room, just like they were whenever they weren't training with me.

Day 7 was pretty much a repeat of day 6, but I had both Kate, and then Becky, heeling both dogs together. And we trained them in different places, including a couple of long beaches. And we stopped for lunch at one beach, the three of us sitting at a table enjoying our lunch, while both dogs lay at our feet. We were indeed making enormous progress.

Day 8 began, for me, enjoying tea with Charles. Then Charles said, "Ray, you've made brilliant progress with the dogs, and I know you're scheduled to fly back home tomorrow. However, I'm wondering if we'll be able to just let both dogs loose before you leave, or whether you'll need more time with them."

I answered, "I really don't know, Charles. As you know, when I'm not working with them, they're still in separate rooms, except when someone takes them, one at a time, for exercise, one running loose while the other runs loose inside the huge enclosure you had built for them." Charles had an enormous area fenced with 8-ft solid wooden walls so the dogs, when out, could not see each other, which was very wise on Charles's part. We talked for about 10 minutes when, suddenly, I announced, "Let's let them out now."

Charles looked at me and asked, "You mean let them out loose together, right now?"

"You bet," I answered. "It's a beautiful British morning, let's do it."

"Right," was all he said, as he got up and opened the large doors to the outside. Then we let both dogs out of their rooms and directed them out the doors. Charles has 13 acres on the property so there was plenty of space for them to run. Both dogs blew through the doors together, quickly disappearing from view. We went back to drinking tea and musing about this and that when Charles said, "Ray, the dogs have been gone 40 minutes. Do you think they're all right?"

"Well, I don't really know," I answered, adding almost in a whisper, "I hope so."

Charles just looked at me.

About five minutes later, both dogs suddenly appeared at the doors, their tongues hanging down about a foot. I got up, went over, and let them in. Charles has an enormous, round, bean bag dog bed which both dogs got on, lying down next to one another, playfully chewing lightly on each other's necks. Within minutes they were asleep. They're no longer separated.

They've never fought since.

Jack and Helen Webster live in a large, renovated farmhouse on 12 acres of gorgeous land in central Massachusetts. And they are the proud owners of three lovely dogs; two Golden retrievers and a large—no, a very large—Great Dane. The retrievers names are Zip, the male, a six-year-old absolutely handsome animal, and Winnie, an equally beautiful seven-year-old female. The newcomer is Ebony, a just turned three-year-old Great Dane. Ebony, pure black, bends the scale at 180 pounds of solid muscle. The only thing I was told, over the phone, was that the Dane had recently been showing aggressive behavior toward Zip.

I pulled my Jeep off Mechanic Street and onto a gravel secondary road, bouncing over it for almost one mile exactly before following the directions given me, and turning left onto a dirt road which ended half a mile later in front of the large, white farmhouse, owned by my new client.

I got out of my Jeep, and began to walk toward the front door when a tall, trim, middle-aged man wearing black cowboy boots opened the front door and called out, "You Ray?"

"Yep," I answered, and we both walked forward, meeting halfway between the Jeep and the house, and firmly shook each other's hands.

We walked back toward the house, neither of us speaking while we walked up the granite steps and into the house. The two retrievers, lying far down the hallway, jumped up instantly upon seeing a stranger in the house, and ran to greet me in typical Golden behavior. "This is Zip," said Jack, giving Zip a couple of friendly thumps to the dog's ribs. "And that lovely specimen is Winnie," he said, stretching out his arm to reach the girl and tousle the crown of her head. Looking at me, Jack said "Ray, come into the library and let me tell you what's going on."

We walked through a couple of rooms; Jack opened a door and we both went inside. As we entered, I glanced off to my left in time to see a very large jet-black Dane stand up, give me a once-over and then trot over to me, leaning heavily into my left hip. "That's Ebony," Jack said, proudly, "our newest addition." Jack and I sat down in two soft brown leather chairs, and he began telling me why I was called. "Ebony turned three just three months age, and his behavior toward Zip has changed, somewhat dramatically," Jack stated. "They've had four fights so far, and Zip is now very cautious around the big guy."

"I can see why," I answered. "I'd be pretty cautious, too, if I were Zip." Looking over at Ebony, now lying near the large fireplace about 10 feet away, I said, "Tell me about the fights."

"Not a whole lot to tell, Ray. They're unpredictable, sometimes I see it coming, most of the time I don't. But they're getting worse, harder for me to separate them. I yell at 'em, and I've smacked Eb on his nose a couple of times. That seems to work for a while, but then there'll be another fight. They've been good the last few days. You mind if I bring Zip in? Normally, he'd be in here with me, but he's much more nervous now."

"Bring him in, if you're comfortable doing so."

Jack called Zip, and a minute later Zip came slowly into the room, glanced at Ebony, I noticed, then lay down next to Jack's couch, on the opposite side from the big guy. Jack reached down and started petting

Zip while telling me about the fights, and that he got my name from his veterinarian. He was talking to me for perhaps five minutes when suddenly, with no previous warning, Ebony charged Zip, leaping over Jack's legs, grabbing Zip at the back of his skull, and lifted him up, growling and shaking Zip's head violently back and forth. Both Jack and I reacted instantly. I grabbed Ebony's tail and lifted up as I backed away, while Jack had Zip's collar and pulled in the opposite direction. We got them apart quickly and, although Zip was bleeding a bit from a couple of punctures, physically he seemed all right. I now had the Dane by his metal slip collar and could see poor Zip, trembling big-time.

"Want me to put Ebony in the kitchen, Jack?" I asked.

"Yeah, please, if you don't mind," Jack answered, his voice shaking bit. After I came back in and closed the door, Jack said, "Well, now you've seen it. Think you can help?"

"I sure hope so," was all I could think to say. "I'd like to start in 5 or 10 minutes with Ebony." Then I added, "Jack, I noticed that Ebony is intact, any—"

"Let it go, Ray," Jack interrupted. "They both are. Neutering's off the table."

Swell, I thought. Solving the problem would be very difficult were the dogs neutered. With them both intact, my chances just dropped from difficult to damn near impossible.

I started with Ebony, telling Jack I would be using the remote collar to reinforce Ebony's heeling. It didn't take long for me to realize just how insecure and lacking in self-confidence he was. I mentioned this to Jack. "You're telling me that brute has no confidence and is insecure?" Jack asked incredulously.

"Size just doesn't matter in this case. Jack. Just look at the way he's locked in against me. Danes are 'leaners,' yes, but this behavior screams no confidence."

I reinforced heeling with Ebony, and did so with Zip as well. I also, with Ebony, reinforced her coming when called. I met Helen when

I came for the second session. I liked her from the get-go, and not simply because she insisted on not only making coffee but placing two homemade blueberry muffins in front of me.

After six sessions over six weeks, I was once again sitting in their kitchen, drinking coffee and enjoying breakfast number 2. Both Jack and Helen were there. "Well, today we let 'em both loose outside," I said cheerfully.

"You really think they'll be all right together?" Helen queried.

"No worries, mate," I answered. "Let's get to it. As John Wayne once said, 'Let's go, we're burnin' daylight.'"

And burn daylight we did. We collared up both dogs, Ebony on his remote and Zip on his red leather one. They called their dogs, including Winnie, and the six of us went out into the very large backyard. Winnie immediately went off by herself while Zip and Ebony walked around the yard slowly, keeping about 25 to 30 feet between them.

"You think this is going to work, Ray?" Jack asked quietly.

"You bet, Jack," I answered.

Suddenly, as if on a signal, Zip began to run around the side of the house toward the big, low grass front field, with Ebony running behind. Zip ran on ahead, perhaps 100 yards, a football field length. "Somebody better call Zip before he's in Vermont," I said.

Jack called Zip and he turned and began running back, heading straight for the three of us now standing in front of the front steps. Ebony was, I noticed, standing directly between Zip and us. This will be interesting, I thought to myself. Sure enough, when Zip got perhaps 20 feet in front of Ebony, Ebony ran toward Zip. Zip stopped and Ebony went up to him and began to place his massive head very slowly over Zip's neck. "Behave," I said in a voice firm enough for him to hear, and gave a quick, momentary tap on his remote collar. The big black dog jerked his head up and away from Zip, and the two of them began running, side by side, past us and back into the backyard. They ran around together, along with Winnie, for perhaps five minutes. I happened to look over at Jack just in time to see him send a frisbee in the direction of the dogs. The frisbee landed between Zip and Ebony. They both got to it about the same time and Zip bent his head down to pick it up. Zip came up with it and they both played tag for, perhaps, another five minutes. A bit later the six of us went back inside. All three dogs lay down in the kitchen, exhausted. "I'm all done here, people," I said. And I was.

They've never fought since.

Aggression When Lead Walking Your Dog

Imagine not being able to walk your dog on a lead past a dog approaching, that dog being lead walked as well. Imagine the amount of anxiety and stress that would be on you if that were your dog. Think about that. As the other dog gets closer, your dog begins dragging you toward the other dog, barking and snarling, teeth bared, leaving you terrified, attempting to drag your dog by the lead past the other dog and owner.

Permit me to tell you about just one such dog.

Heidi Weil resides in Weston, a well-to-do, lovely community a relatively short drive west of Boston. Heidi's picturesque home is situated atop a small hill just outside the town's center. An attractive, trim, middle-aged woman, she answered the bell on the first ring, alerted no doubt by her dog that I could hear barking. As I stepped inside, I was greeted first by the dog, a handsome German shepherd who proceeded to stop barking immediately, and quietly sniffed my hand as well as my briefcase hanging at my side. "I'm Ray McSoley," I said quietly.

"I knew you must be, judging by Spira's behavior toward you," the woman answered, an air of measured confidence accompanying her words. "I'm Heidi, Ray," she continued. "I'm pleased you could come. And that is Spira, whom you've already met. Please do come in so we can talk."

After seating ourselves in Heidi's thoughtfully laid-out kitchen, she began to fill me in as to why I was there. Spira was a five-year-old female, and for a little over the first three years was the love of Heidi's life. Every morning she would drive Spira to the Weston Res, a man-made dog heaven. There was sufficient parking for perhaps 18 cars on a section of dirt, safely away from the road and passing cars. When you and your dog crossed the road to the "Res" side, most dog owners removed their dogs' leads, and the dogs and their owners would walk the circular path around the large reservoir. A walk around the rock-lined, fenced-in Res might take the better part of an hour, while the dogs raced around with other dogs, getting their morning exercise. When Spira turned four, things took a dramatic, and yes, traumatic turnaround. Spira got into a few aggressive skirmishes with other dogs, and Heidi stopped bringing her.

She began lead walking Spira around the neighborhood. There were lots of dogs there, many of them contained in their yards by underground fence systems, and many of those systems had the underground fence installed quite close to the street. When Heidi and Spira would begin to walk past, many of the dogs would bark and rush out to the fence line. Spira would then bark in return and drag Heidi toward the dog, becoming increasingly aggressive. She would also display this aggressiveness toward all dogs being walked on leads as they approached. And, eventually, she attacked and badly injured a couple of dogs.

At that point, Heidi told me, she began working with a succession of both professional trainers as well as local behaviorists. There were six in all, with not even one of them able to make as much as a scintilla of progress with Spira. One of the behaviorists, known abroad as well as throughout the U.S. for his research with dogs and pharmaceuticals, gave Heidi the following advice: put Spira on Prozac, never let her off the lead, and when you walk her, have her wear a muzzle. Swell.

She did put Spira on Prozac, and kept her on a lead, but could not bring herself to put a muzzle on her beloved Spira when she walked her. And then she attacked and injured a dachshund. The dog's owner, a very kind gentleman, told Heidi to contact me.

I had been taking notes as Heidi was giving me Spira's history. At that point, I said to her, "I'll take my Labrador, Finn, out and go over the top of the hill, on the road, out of sight. Take Spira out on her collar and lead, and I'll walk Finn back this way, over the hilltop, and let's see what we've got." Heidi told me that she'd been working really hard on heeling, and that Spira seemed to be doing better. We did the set up and I came up and over the hilltop. Heidi was perhaps 100 feet away and, as soon as Spira saw Finn … well, to quote Heidi, "Spira raged." I put Finn back in the Jeep, and we went back inside.

"I'll do the best I can," I said. "I'm going to put Spira on my remote collar, and see if we can begin to reinforce the work you've done on heeling. If I'm able to make some progress, let's continue. However, Heidi, if I'm unable to make any progress, I'm pulling out."

And we started. By the end of that session, Spira was beginning to improve her heeling. By either the fourth or fifth session, Heidi was able to heel Spira past other dogs when walking her around the block.

We would meet on Thursdays, as I recall, and on this particular Thursday, Heidi prepared some tea as I sat down. During these sessions, when I'd arrive, Spira would quietly leave the kitchen and proceed to the far end of the hall, where she would lie quietly. This Thursday was no different.

"Well, Heidi, I see Spira's still in love with me." I laughed as I sipped my tea. Heidi laughed along with me. "It's nice to see you smiling, Heidi," I said.

"You know, Ray, I didn't have much to smile about before you began your work with her."

"Yeah, well, you know this is my last time here, Heidi. Spira has come along beautifully. You can walk around the entire neighborhood without worrying about passing dogs safely."

"Yes. Well, you know, Ray, Spira used to play with other dogs at the Res. I miss that so much."

"Excuse me?" I stammered. "How the heck long ago was that?"

"It's been a long time, Ray," she answered quietly.

"So now you'd like me to get her so she'll PLAY with dogs again?"

"I'd love that," she answered.

I finished my tea in one gulp and said, "Okay, what the hell, let's go to the Res." It's futile to argue with a strong-minded woman, guys. We collared up Spira with her remote collar and Heidi, smiling of course, loaded her into her car. I got in my Jeep and called out, "I'll follow you."

Arriving at the Res, I think I quickly counted about 10 vehicles. I unloaded Finn and slipped my Mendota on him. Heidi had parked a couple of spaces away and proceeded to unload Spira. We both heeled our dogs across the road and into a field smaller than a football field. We headed toward one of the trails, the woodsy one. We had walked about 100 feet when I reached down and let Finn off the lead. Looking over at Heidi I could tell she was nervous, so I called over, "Don't worry, they'll be fine." We then did the entire circle, but saw only about six dogs. I decided to handle Spira after I let Finn loose, and when the first loose dog began to approach, Spira made a quick lunge and I said, "Heel," and tapped her with the remote collar. Spira came back immediately and, after that, we made it around the reservoir without incident.

We went directly to the Res on my next visit, and shortly after letting Finn loose, I noticed that, while racing around, he would, as he ran in front of Spira, get closer each time. I was watching Spira and so I reached down and unleashed her as Finn was making another approach. Now free, Spira immediately ran directly at Finn, and the two of them began running around together.

"That's the first time I've seen Spira's tail up in years, Ray," Heidi said. "I can't believe what I'm seeing; they're doing so well together. How did you know they'd be okay?"

"Finn told me," I answered. "He's better at assessing dogs than I am, to be honest." We did the circle with both dogs loose. I figured Spira would be involved enough with Finn and so she would ignore other dogs, which she did. Finn was the first dog she played with since her aggression began.

We kept returning to the Res, and I began leaving Finn home. Spira, little by little, began approaching some dogs, and getting along with them.

Heidi and Spira were now on their own. My work was finished. They continued through that summer, spending some time in western Canada. Spira met increasing numbers of Canadian dogs, and once again resumed her play behavior with them, under Heidi's watchful, but now calm, presence.

In the fall, Heidi called me and wanted me to swing by with Finn, when I could do so. She said she wanted the two of them to be able to play together again. When I arrived at Heidi's home and rang the bell, I heard Spira barking, and when Heidi opened the door, we both stood in utter amazement as Spira, recognizing me, ran up and jumped up on me, wagging her tail and licking the side of my face. "Wow, she never jumps on people, Ray; I'm shocked," said Heidi. "Do you think it's her way of saying thank you?"

"You bet," I answered, scratching her neck.

Spira never fought with another dog again.

Dear Spira passed away, unexpectedly, a year ago. She was eight. I miss her.

I could tell you many more similar success stories. People need to understand how critically important the task of heeling is. I had a dream once that I was in Fenway Park. The stadium was filled to capacity with dog owners and their dogs. I was on second base, yelling, "Teach your dog to heel well."

Threshold Aggression

I see a fair amount of this. Threshold aggression is actually territorial aggression; however, it occurs only as the person is attempting to cross the threshold—that is to say, entering the house. There are degrees of aggression with this problem. Dogs who merely run to the door and bark to alert the owner pose no overt threat (although this behavior may well escalate into something more serious). Dogs who bark and indicate more threatening postures—perhaps showing teeth—could bite. Then there's the dog that will bite at the threshold; however, once the "victim" is inside and seated, comes over to be his best bud.

Dog owners, in my experience, deal with threshold aggression very poorly and, in most cases, contribute to its escalation. The doorbell rings and Peanuts goes, well, nuts. They yell at the poor animal, attempting to grab and then restrain the dog by the collar. In many instances, during all of this, some owners hold the dog by the collar, telling him, "It's okay. It's all right, sweetie." Remember, I spoke about this earlier.

I have employed three very different approaches when dealing with this particular problem. I call one method Going to Place. The second I call Switch Conditioning. Bill Campbell, who I believe came up with the idea, called it a Jolly Routine. The third I call Walk First.

Going to Place

Some years ago I visited a client with a big, rugged Chesapeake Bay retriever. Chester resided on a large, working farm in Rhode Island, just a few miles from the Connecticut border. Whenever anyone, excluding the owners, attempted to enter the big farmhouse, Chester would bite, usually on the thigh, basically telling them, "Behave yourself; you're entering my house." Once they were seated, provided they stayed, Chester would come over to them, drop a ball in their lap, ready for them to play with him.

When I arrived and knocked on the side door (the owner told me to come to the side door, as no one ever came to the front), a voice called out, "Come in." I entered, walking into a small, working mud room. I saw no one. Then a woman appeared at the top of a flight of stairs and said I could come up. When I arrived at the top of the stairs, there was Chester, seated next to the woman. I introduced myself, and she proceeded to release Chester, who walked over to me, wagging his tail in a friendly manner. We both sat in the kitchen and she laid out the issue. Once people were out of the mudroom and up the stairs, Chester posed no threat, just he was with me.

I found out that lots of people, especially some of the farmhands, would simply open the door and walk in, and get bitten. "Two things to do here," I said. "Number one, from now on no one—I mean no one—walks in unannounced. And number two, let's help Chester learn to go to his place, and his place should be at the top of the stairs. He's claimed the mudroom as his, but not the rest of the house." So that's what we did.

Chester stopped biting farmhands and visitors.

So, how do you get your dog to learn "Place"? The first thing you need to do is select an appropriate area. I like an area 10-12 feet away from the door, preferably against a wall, or a stairway, where the dog can see the door and the person entering can see the dog. Okay, you've got your spot. Next, place a dog bed or white towel/blanket on the spot; an area 3 feet by 3 feet is ideal. With my clients, I bring along my 2-foot by 3-foot plywood platform, raised on 2x4s and covered with a large, white towel.

Why white? you ask. Because white is the color dogs see best. Let's begin the training.

Put a 6-ft lead on Ace and bring her about three feet in front of the "target." She should be sitting on your left or right side, whichever is convenient for you. If she's on your right side, as you give her the cue "Place," step toward the target, extending your left arm and hand in that direction in front of Ace, using the lead to help. After she gets on the target, give her praise. If you want, have her sit as soon as she gets on the towel, then praise. If she doesn't do it, just help her with the lead. Remain upbeat, don't get frustrated and loud, that will simply confuse her, or she may think she's doing something wrong. Have her remain on the target for, say, 20 seconds. Praise her again and then release her. I use the word "Break" for a release word, simply because it's not a word they hear constantly, such as "Okay." Do not praise her for releasing! Praise her for remaining there. The release itself is her reward. Do five repetitions and then call it quits. You can do two sessions a day, or even three. Want homework? Fine. At the end of the first week, stand three feet from the target, tell her "place," and give her the hand signal, but you remain motionless. She must have the confidence to move past you and onto the towel herself.

As Ace gets better with this, begin to move back a bit, one foot at a time. Now you're telling her to place from four feet away, then five feet, until you're giving her the task from the door. When she's doing the four feet well, you can begin telling "place" and, when she gets there and sits, tell her "Stay" and walk to the door, open it, say something like, "Not today," and return, all the way, to Ace. Praise her, then release. If she breaks the stay on you, don't get angry or frustrated, simply repeat the exercise until she does it correctly. And remember, always end a session on a positive note.

Eventually, you will send Ace to her spot, open the door, reach around and ring the bell. If she breaks, repeat until she doesn't. Be firm, not loud, when you tell her Place. At some point, when she's doing well, begin having family members ring the bell or knock on the door from outside. They remain outside while you tell Ace to Place, and do the complete routine. You open the door while she's in Stay, and invite them in. Later on, have neighbors and friends help out. As with switch conditioning, it's best to begin with family. This requires Quiet Firmness, time, and patience. Lots of patience. This technique may take three to four weeks to become effective.

Edna was a client of mine a number of years ago. She lived in a quiet community at the edge of the suburbs, off the beaten path, as people say. Her husband worked for Sylvania, and would spend up to three months at a time on the Kwajalein Atoll, in the South Pacific. They had no children, so Edna would be alone when Frank was gone. They got a German shepherd and named him Alpha. He was going to be Edna's watchdog. They did not want a trained protection dog, figuring a barking German shepherd would be sufficient to discourage anyone with mischief on his or her mind. Well, Alpha took his name to heart. He bit his first intruder when he was 14 months old—the milkman. Edna and Frank were both horrified and very concerned. They talked with their vet, who recommended they contact me. I recall the first time I saw Alpha and Edna like it was this morning. I was able to get into the house, fending off Alpha with my canvas briefcase, with Edna straining to keep Alpha at bay, pulling back on the lead for all she was worth. Alpha was a beautiful specimen, tipping the scales at just over 100 pounds. After perhaps 30 minutes, Alpha had accepted me and, from then on, he never challenged me.

I suggested we help Alpha learn to go to his place. "Where do you suggest?" Edna asked. When you entered the house from the front door, you faced the staircase.

"I believe the staircase would be perfect," I answered. Halfway up there was a landing. "I think the landing is a perfect target, Edna. Let's get started and see just how smart this old boy really is."

Alpha was smart, I mean really smart, and he took to "Place" better and faster than any dog I've worked with. At the end of the second session, Edna would tell him Place and he would shoot up the stairs, sit and stay on the landing. Sometimes he would lie down there.

"Should I make him remain sitting, Ray?" she asked.

"Nah. I think he'll stay sitting when real people begin coming to the house and we're testing him."

Sure enough, when real people were added to the training, Alpha remained on high alert, sitting on the landing, and staring at the person entering, including me.

With my work finished with Alpha, I didn't give the big guy much thought. Then, about eight months later, I received a phone call from Edna. "Hi, Ray," she said, brightly. "I need to tell you about an incident two days ago. I had just finished morning coffee when there was a knock on the door. Alpha began barking and I had him Place on the landing. I opened the inside door, leaving the screen door closed and locked. There were two men looking at me. They were, I would guess, in their late twenties. The taller one told me they were hitchhiking from Pennsylvania to Boston, and could I get them each a glass of water? Ray, I didn't know what to do. I didn't want to slam the big door on them; however, I didn't want to leave the screen door to go get them the water. I just didn't trust them. And then, Ray, I remembered Alpha. I turned and looked, and he was just quietly sitting there. I turned back to the two men and told them, 'I'd be happy to get you the water, but if I open this door, my dog has been trained by my husband to attack, and I don't know the words to use to call him off. He was trained in German.' I stepped aside so they could see Alpha. Both men then looked up to see the big guy simply staring down at them. 'That's quite all right, ma'am,' the tall one said quickly. 'Really sorry to have bothered you.' Both men turned really fast and went back down the drive. Ray, thank you from the bottom of my heart."

"Edna," I answered, "thanks so much for calling. And give Alpha a couple of 'Atta boys' from me."

Sometimes the good guys win.

Switch Conditioning

In order for this method to have a prayer at being successful, both dog and owner must possess a good sense of humor. Additionally, the dog has to really love to retrieve. If he/she doesn't, forget it.

Each evening, for two or three minutes, get Lightning's favorite retrieving object— ball, frisbee, whatever. Walk over to the door most people use. Dogs tend, in my experience, to be more aggressive at the front door, rather than the back. This is because friends come to the back, while strangers and workmen tend to approach by the front. So, pick your door. Now, get him really excited, and toss/roll the object away from the door, down the hall, making a really huge deal out of it when he returns with the ball in his mouth. If you can employ the entire family to chip in with upbeat applause, so much the better. Don't take the object away right away, but allow him to enjoy being the center of attention for a couple of minutes.

Then, take the ball and do it two more times. At the end of the session, put the ball away. Do not leave it around for Lightning to chew or play with. From now on, that is a special object, used only for this game. Play this game each evening for a week or two.

The next step involves you ringing the doorbell just prior to tossing the object. Open the door, reach around and ring the bell, and immediately toss the ball, getting overwhelmingly excited as you do so. Do this two or three more times, then stop. Do this for a week. At the end of the second week, Lightning should be running happily after the ball after he hears the bell ring.

The final step involves people. Begin with family members. Have a family member outside ring the bell, but not enter. You, inside by the door, roll the ball away from the door, telling Lightning to fetch it up. When he chases the ball, quietly let the family member in. Make a huge deal out of this. Continue this over the next week, using different family members or friends the dog knows and likes. You're actually switch conditioning the dog from a territorial mood to a happy mood. Why does it work? Because the dog picks up your happy mood and he becomes happy rather than aggressive. He picks up your mood and copies it.

The final step involves both friends and strangers. Mix them up. Do the same routine and, if it works, you're on your way toward solving your threshold aggression problem. This method, when successful, is nice because it's easy to do and it's fun for everyone. And remember, a dog with a ball or frisbee in his mouth is perceived by the person entering the house as a happy, nonaggressive dog. Remember, your dog picks up on your mood. You're happy, she's happy. Your attitude's negative, her attitude's negative. So, a lot of it is up to you. Remain positive. You'll have a better dog plus you'll live longer.

Back around 1993-94 NBC had a televised show called *Monitor*, with a format similar to that of *20/20*. I was fortunate to be featured in one of their weekly segments, and they came up to my town, Westwood, Massachusetts, from New York and accompanied me on my travels to clients for two interesting, and tiring, days. It was a lot of fun working on a nationally televised show, and the crew they sent up was truly professional, and a lot of fun to work with.

One of my clients, Al, was living in Brookline, a town abutting Boston. He was a retired City of New York cop who had worked the streets of the south Bronx for 18 years. Believe me, this guy looked every bit as tough as he was. He was going to move with his wife to Syracuse, New York, and work with troubled teens as a social worker. He was in Brookline, going to school to earn his degree. I'll bet he'll do a wonderful job out there.

Anyway, this guy and his wife had a six-year-old female German shepherd dog named Katie. They got the dog while they were living in, as he said, "Joisey." They both were looking for a dog that would protect his wife at home while was on the job, but they only wanted her to bite "bad guys." The problem was, Katie took her job just a bit too seriously, and bit a few good guys. Well, when I saw them the first time, Katie took me for one of the bad guys. Snarling, teeth bared, tail elevated and swishing, hackles vertical, straining at the heavy collar and lead, had she not been restrained, I'd have been her next target.

After I was safely in their upstairs apartment for perhaps five minutes, Katie calmed down, came over to me, sniffed me up and down, then lay down between her owner and me. "What if I get up and walk around now?" I asked.

"She'll be fine," Al answered. "It's only when someone first comes through the door that she's a problem."

Well, I got up and walked around their apartment, then came back and sat down again with no problem. Then I spotted the tennis ball lying in a corner. "Katie like to retrieve?" I asked.

"She likes playing ball more than anything else. She'll kill for the tennis ball."

Laughing, I said, "Interesting word choice." Then I added, "I'm going to leave and return in about 10 minutes. When I ring the bell outside your door, I want you to get really excited, I mean really excited, and tell her to get the ball as you roll it away from the door and down the hallway toward the bedroom. If she goes after the ball, open the door right away."

"You want me to have her leash on when I do it, right?"

"Nope," I answered, "no lead. Just roll the ball down and lots of praise when she gets it."

"Jeez, Ray, I really don't think that's a good idea. I mean, she's really serious about people coming through the door."

I said, "If she won't get the ball, just don't open the door. See you in 10." I got up and left.

Ten minutes later I was back downstairs where the box with the apartment numbers and the corresponding bells were listed. I spotted #4 and pressed the button. The apartment upstairs exploded with Katie's barking. I climbed the stairs to unit #4 and rang the bell on that door. That just riled her all the more and I could barely hear my client tell her in a very excited voice, to "get the ball." A moment later the door opened and I walked in. Katie turned with the ball in her mouth, and charged me from a distance of perhaps 20 feet. She was definitely not a happy camper and she stopped, literally, six inches from me, growling, teeth bared—but she wouldn't let go of the ball.

Al was still talking very excitedly, and I stood very still. After perhaps 15 seconds, Katie turned away from me and began her victory prance around the apartment, holding the ball that was her prize. Slowly, I walked over to my chair and sat down. We let Katie keep the ball for perhaps five minutes. Then my client called Katie over, took the ball from her mouth, and put it in a cabinet. Katie came over to me, sniffed me once again, and was fine as I scratched her behind an ear. I worked with Katie for four sessions. Two of Al's neighbors played the game with me coaching them, and the landlord also joined us.

Well, Katie was on my appointment pad while *Monitor* was filming me, so I thought, "Why not?" After all, their producer had told me they wanted a typical day from me. Well, we filmed Katie that afternoon, doing her ball routine. Everyone, the sound guy, video guy, lighting guy did their job, filming from outside the doorway. I asked if any of the crew wanted to play my part. Strange, there were no takers! And Katie stopped biting visitors.

Walk First

This is, most definitely, an unusual approach when dealing with a threshold aggressive dog. I was sitting in my clients' kitchen during my first visit in beautiful Marblehead, a sailing mecca on Boston's North Shore. Their home was gorgeous, located on land that offered an exquisite view of Marblehead Harbor. Brad and his lovely wife Phyllis were, I guessed, in their early thirties, and both were avid sailors. Lucy, the dog, was a three-year-old female Bouvier des Flanders, and a happy member of the sailboat crew. Lucy tipped the scales at around 85 pounds. She was leashed as I entered their home, barking heavily but very little growling and not showing teeth. It took about 10 minutes for her to totally quiet down and cautiously approach. I ignored her completely until she finally put her very large head on my thigh. I then gave Lucy just a few quiet pats. "Wow," said Phyllis, "she likes you." "Lucky for me," I answered with a grin. "How can I be of help?" "Well, Lucy has become somewhat aggressive when people arrive at the door," offered Brad. "We're both a bit concerned that we've lost control, wouldn't you agree, Honey?" Phyllis answered simply by nodding her head. "What do you do when people arrive at the door?" I asked. "Well, you pretty much saw it," Brad answered. "Have you done much training with her?" I queried. "We had a really nice young man train with us for a couple of months, starting when she was about one," answered Phyllis. "He seemed to be a bit like you, you know, quiet, soft spoken, but firm with Lucy." Brad jumped in with "We'd be happy to show you, Ray, we can go into the backyard with her." "Lets do it," I answered, "The day is perfect for it." Phyllis got what looked to me like a Mendota slip lead and slipped it over Lucy's head. The three of us, plus Lucy, exited to the backyard, where Phyllis proceeded to put Lucy through her routine. The trainer had clearly done a very good job training Lucy. Her heeling was particularly impressive. "Well done, guys," I said, after Brad had shown me that he too could handle Lucy. After we went back inside and were, once again, seated around the huge kitchen island, an idea came to me. "I have a thought about this. I've never done anything quite like it; however, I think we should take full advantage of Lucy's prior training." I went on, "When people arrive at the door put the lead on Lucy and have her sit. Then tell the person arriving that you were just going to take Lucy down to your mailbox to check for mail. Invite the person to come along. You will heel Lucy down to the mailbox and, when you turn around to come back, give the lead to the visitor and have him or her heel Lucy back to the house. You and your guest enter first, then allow Lucy back inside. I betcha it will work. Let's try it with me." We did it with me. Lucy did some barking while heeling on the way to the mailbox, but ended the barking about halfway there. I heeled her back. She gave me a couple of, "what the hell is going on here" looks but did a great job. By the third trip down there was no barking. I asked Brad and Phyllis both to please keep in touch. I suggested that they begin with good friends to make it easier for Lucy early on. They did remain in touch. No more threshold aggression. Caution. This will not work with the majority of dog owners. Your dog first needs to be very well trained, which most dogs aren't. Second, I would not attempt this with a dog that has already bitten, or shows teeth.

Object Guarding

This can become a high-risk problem for dog owners. The dog that guards objects from its owner can quickly become a nightmare. It's one thing if they guard a particular toy of theirs. That can be annoying, but sometimes just throwing that toy away ends the issue. However, when a dog becomes aggressive to the point of biting the owner if he or she attempts to claim the object from their dog's jaws, it can quickly result in a trip to the local hospital's emergency room.

What is the solution? One method, currently in favor, is called Trade Off, and it goes like this. Your dog takes one of your favorite expensive Italian leather shoes. Your trainer recommends Trade Off. So you get a piece of chicken from the fridge, slowly approach your dog, offering the chicken in trade for the shoe. Bravo, it worked! For a while. Unfortunately, after a while, the chicken no longer works. Now what to do? I suppose Chateaubriand might be effective, but that can get pricey pretty fast, plus there's no guarantee that's going to continue to work. After all, what you're really doing is simply reinforcing the very behavior you're trying to extinguish.

Satan knows that, if he takes something and guards it from you, that act gets him precisely what he wants. Another tactic, often recommended, is ignoring the behavior. Ignore the behavior and the behavior will end, say many "experts." Really? Could have fooled me. If we're dealing with attention-demand barking and the owners have the patience to ignore that particular behavior 100%, the barking will eventually stop. But ignoring one type of behavior, namely attention-demand barking, doesn't mean you can apply that to your dog guarding an object. The dog may simply take the object to reinforce the CONTROL he has over you. Plus, when your dog takes something of value, or something that could be harmful to your dog, such as your prescription eye glasses, do you continue to ignore that? No, you attempt to take it back, and that will end up with you in your local emergency room. There is, however, a simple, straightforward approach that always works. I say that, having worked with a few thousand object guarding dogs. Storytelling time.

Myron Jacobson lived with his wife, Louise, and their teenaged daughter, Sophie, in a contemporary home in the lovely town of Needham, a relatively short drive from my town. Louise called me in tears one evening, telling me she got my name from her vet and could we set up a time for me to come over as they were having an ongoing problem with their Standard Poodle, Onyx. I agreed and we set up a day and time.

I arrived at the appointed hour, and was invited into the Jacobson's living room, where Myron and Louise selected a chair for me. "We need your help with our dog," said Myron. "He's a two-year-old Standard Poodle, and the son of a bitch steals our daughter's stuffies and destroys them. She has a large collection up in her room and she's very angry and disappointed with our dog."

"What's a stuffy?" I inquired innocently.

They both stared at me as though I had just rolled off a turnip truck headed for market. "It's a stuffed animal," said Louise, as though she didn't think I was serious. "Hers are mostly Steiffs. They're rather expensive."

"I see," I said. "Why don't you just keep her door closed?"

"We do, for the most part, but there are times when Sophie forgets," said Myron. "She's just a kid."

"That's unfair, Myron," said Louise. "We forget as well."

I jumped in with, "What happens when you take them away?"

"That's the problem. We can't take them away, although I think I'm getting better at it," said Myron.

"Getting better at it how?" I asked.

"Well, when Sophie comes home from school," said Myron, "at some point the door is open, and Onyx—that's the dog's name—sneaks in, grabs a stuffy, and goes under the piano there, and God help you if you go under there and try to get the stuffy back. That damned dog will attack you."

"So, what do you do then?" I queried.

"Well," answered Myron, "I have these welders' gloves, and Onyx and I fight for a while. It's a daily fight, usually in the evening. I'm not gonna let that goddamned dog get the better of me."

I looked over at Louise and, with a straight face, asked quietly, "Do you have welders' gloves as well?"

"Indeed I do not," Louise answered icily.

"Well," I said calmly, "I can solve the problem."

"This I want to witness," declared Myron.

"By the way, where is Onyx?" I inquired.

They both looked at each other. "He's locked in our bedroom," said Louise. "He's being punished."

"Could you let him out, please?" I asked. "I'd like to start working on the problem."

I reached into my bag and retrieved my remote collar system while Louise traipsed upstairs to release Onyx from Alcatraz. A minute later this handsome, jet black, large Standard Poodle came bounding down the stairs, spotted me, and immediately raced over and happily jumped up on me.

"Get down!" yelled Myron. Onyx ignored Myron, so I quickly stood up and Onyx quickly got off me.

"That's a handsome guy you've got there, Myron," I stated. "Did you happen to get him from a breeder on the North Shore?"

"How did you know?" Myron asked, clearly astonished.

"I know her Poodles, Myron," I answered. "She breeds nothing but the best."

Louise had reentered the room. "Here's the deal," I said. "You can't solve Onyx's problem. He needs to solve the problem himself. It's kind of like the four-year-old who is always going near the hot stove. You've told him 'hot stove' 50 times, and he still sticks his hand out toward the burner. One day he does make contact and, guess what, he never does that again. So that's what we'll do with Onyx. I'll use the remote collar, and when I tell him 'Leave it,' I'll simply tap him with the remote, and he'll drop the stuffy."

"What if he doesn't drop it?" inquired Louise. "He's very stubborn, and I don't want you getting bitten."

"He won't bite me," I assured Louise. I had them both feel the collar to get an idea how it felt. I always do that with a client. If they don't feel it then they have no idea what it feels like, and they'll probably think it must cause pain to the dog, which it shouldn't.

I put the collar on Onyx, and after about 15 minutes, I asked Louise if she'd be kind enough to open her daughter's bedroom door. After Louise came back down it took perhaps 10 minutes for Onyx to go upstairs. A minute later he came back downstairs and went under the Steinway.

"Watch," I said and got up and approached the piano. Onyx fixed me with a steady stare. I stood right next to the piano, looking at Onyx, who by now was growling, and with the transmitter behind me, said in a calm but firm voice, "Leave it," and tapped the collar at level one. No reaction from Onyx. I repeated "Leave it" and raised the level to 2. No response. Nor was there any at level 3. I repeated "Leave it," at level 4 and Onyx immediately shook his head and dropped the stuffy, but remained lying down, with the stuffy between his paws. A minute later he again picked up the stuffy. "Leave it."

I repeated once more, tapping level 4. Immediately Onyx spat out the stuffy, and jumped up, banging his head on the piano's soundboard. He ran out from under and into the kitchen. I calmly reached down and picked up the stuffy, handing it to Myron. "Beats welders' gloves," I said.

Neither one of them could believe what they just witnessed. "That's it?" exclaimed Myron. "You just press a button?"

"Pretty much, Myron. You see, we're leaving the choice up to him. It's his decision. We just help him make the better one."

"Simply amazing," chimed in Sophie. "I could do it."

"That would make it consistent," I said.

They ordered a remote collar and I returned one more time to show them how to use it properly.

AGGRESSION OFF THE LEAD

Establishing "Sense of Presence"

Tony Iannello lives in the North End of Boston. When I moved to New England from Ohio, way back in 1960, the North End was perhaps 90% Italian. Hundreds of people were born there, lived their entire lives there, and passed away there. And, yep, people spoke Italian there.

The North End has changed some. There is still a heavy percentage of Italians living there, but there are young, non-Italians moving in. Back in the '60s, if I went there for an evening out, you could sense you were being watched. There was practically no crime reported in the North End. First, there was pretty much no crime to speak of and, second, the residents took care of their own. So, if you behaved yourself, it was a wonderful place to go for an Italian dinner. It was truly close to being in Italy. I loved the North End. I do still. With over 100 restaurants, large, small, and tiny, all serving up authentic Italian food, what's not to like?

Back to business. Tony had a three-year-old male English Springer Spaniel that he would walk with down to the harbor. There's a lovely park there where the North End dog owners bring their dogs to run around with the other dogs in the morning. I was sitting in Tony's small but lovely apartment, and he was telling me about the problem he was having with Gunner.

"So, Ray, I get down to the park, and I let Gunner off the leash. So, off he goes to run around with the other dogs down there. Everything goes fine and then, boom, the son of a bitch will get into it with another dog."

"Ever any injuries?" I inquire.

"No. No injuries. But Gunner's getting a rep, you know what I mean, Ray? I run out and break it up, and I grab Gunner, pick him up by the scruff of his neck, and yell at him, but it doesn't work. A couple of the guys have said stuff to me about him. You know what I mean?"

"Yep," I answer. "I do know."

"But here's the crazy thing, Ray. If Gunner's close to me, you know, like within 15 feet, he'll play nice with dogs all day, never gets in a fight. I can't figure it out. I mean, what the heck is that about, huh? You tell me."

"Here's my guess, Tony. When Gunner was young, I'm guessing you did a lot of training with him, right?"

"Right," he answered. "I worked on training him with the leash, every day, for his first year. I taught him to sit, stay, lie down, come, walk good on the leash, no jumpin', all that stuff. And he's really good. I mean it, he's good."

"How good is his coming when you call him?"

"Like I say, Ray, he's good."

"What about when he's at the park, he's 50 to 60 feet from you, and he gets grumpy with a dog?"

"He don't listen then, Ray. He won't come at all."

"Tony, here's the deal. There's what I call Sense of Presence. When he's close to you, you're his leader, you know, so 15 feet close to you, he never fights. But, when he's 50 feet from you, you've never established Sense of Presence, so he does what he wants. He's no longer responsible to you. *Capisce?*"

"*Capisce?*" Tony says, looking right at me. "*Capisce?* Ray, you got the map of Ireland on your face. *Capisce* my ass, Ray."

And I looked back at him and we both burst out laughing. "So, Tony, let's reinforce Gunner's coming with the remote collar. When we're finished, Gunner will come to you no matter what he's doing."

"You mean if he's in the middle of a fight, he'll come?"

"When we're done with his coming when called, he'll be like he is when he's within 15 feet of you, no more fighting, because you've extended a Sense of Presence to him no matter where he is."

So, that's what we did. And guess what, dear reader, no more fights. *Capisce?*

When You've Traveled the Extra Mile

Sometimes it doesn't work. When dealing with an aggressive dog, always do your level best to resolve the problem; after all, you owe that to your dog. On the other hand if you've done everything possible, and I mean everything, and nothing is helping, it might be in everyone's best interest, including the dog's, to euthanize the poor animal. The most difficult part of my profession is when I need to tell a client that his dog, in my opinion, should be euthanized. It rarely happens and so, when it does, I feel a great deal of empathy for that dog because somewhere a human failed him. It could have been an irresponsible breeder or a bad trainer. It could have been the owner who had no clue how to bring up a dog. It could be something no one will ever understand. Allow me to tell you about one such dog.

I remember Bofie, a four-year-old Bernese mountain dog, like it was yesterday. Bofie would at times become extremely aggressive when in the back seat of his owner's car as well as Jim's golf cart. Jim was an internationally respected arborist while Betty was equally respected as a master gardener. Professionals from around the world would come to their estate to walk among their 30 acres to purchase rare plants and view the many unusual, majestic trees. I spoke with both Jim and Betty at great length but I could never uncover a reason for his random need for control. He was, in general, a well-trained, loving dog. I agreed to work with Bofie. I began with Heeling, a task he had never mastered. That task progressed very well. Inside of three weeks he was heeling perfectly. I reinforced the other basic tasks as well. I then helped him learn "Out" which meant get out of the car or off the golf cart. The training took a total of four months.

One Sunday night after I'd been out on my boat with my wife Mary and the kids, I got a call from Jim. Bofie had gone into their car early Saturday morning and wouldn't come out. I drove over immediately. When I got near the car Bofie began snarling viciously. I opened the rear car door cautiously and told Bofie, "Out." Bofie didn't move and continued to snarl and show teeth. I tried "Out" once more and Bofie suddenly leaped out, biting me badly on the upper leg as he did. As soon as he landed he sat, wagging his tail and licking my hand as though nothing had happened.

I put my lead on him and tied him to the back-steps rail while I went in to talk with Betty and Jim. I told them that Bofie had a dark side to his personality, something that triggered that vicious need for control. I told them I could not get inside that dark side. My biggest fear was that Bofie would be sitting in the passenger seat on the golf cart at some point and some innocent visitor would go over to give him a pat. As soon as the person reached out, Bofie would explode, sending him or her to the hospital with serious injuries. I told them it would happen; it was simply a matter of when. Bofie needed to be euthanized.

Reluctantly they both agreed, asking me if I could take him to their veterinarian. Of course I said I would. I returned the following morning. It seemed like a long ride to Angell Memorial Animal Hospital, even though it was no more than half an hour. Bofie rode beside me, and as could be expected, was calm throughout, making it that much harder to do what I knew in my heart needed to be done. Bofie stared out the passenger-side window most of the way, the small brass bell that hung from his green nylon collar clanging gently. At the clinic I brought Bofie into the side room where I would see patients with behavior problems, and went to get the doctor. I returned a few minutes later with Dr. Dean Vicksman, a good friend.

I put my right hand on Bofie's head to keep him still and with my left hand I scratched him behind his ears. Dr. Vicksman inserted the needle into Bofie's right front foreleg and after a few seconds Bofie began to lie down and I slowly helped him to the floor. I continued to pat him as he gradually lost consciousness. Moments later Bofie passed on. Dr. Vicksman quietly put his hand in mine while I took off Bofie's collar and bell that would never clang again. I knew Betty and Jim would want to keep it as a gentle reminder of a troubled yet wonderful dog. You bet I still think of him.

Many years ago, after recommending to a client for the first time in my practice that he euthanize his Springer spaniel, I called a psychologist friend of mine that evening to discuss my feelings. I told Michael how difficult a decision it was for the family. "Of course it's a difficult decision, Ray," he told me. "It's supposed to be. But that doesn't mean it's not the correct decision."

Through all these years I have never forgotten those words. There are, literally, millions of wonderful dogs out there. Please don't allow yourself, because of guilt, to become shackled to a high-risk, dangerously aggressive dog. We get a dog to help us enrich our lives. A dog is someone to love and care for; that is our responsibility. The dog's responsibility is to adapt to our lifestyle and to live in harmony with us.

It is a wonderful gift from God that the vast majority of them do just that.

Sometimes it is possible to rehome a difficult dog. If that works for you then I'm all for it. But please do not try to pass on a seriously troubled, highly aggressive dog to an unsuspecting potential owner. There is always a person who is willing to take on such a dog. The problem is that, in my experience, that person feels the reason for the dog's aggression is that it never received the necessary love it needs, and they believe they are the only person capable of providing the dog that necessary love. Such a person is dangerously wrong. One last thing. There are true no-kill rescue places. Best Friends Animal Sanctuary (Society) is one such place in Kanab, Utah. It is run by angels. I know because I've been there. A couple more rescues are Freedom Rescue in Houston, Texas, Grammy Rose in Acton, Maine, and Buddy Dog is another, located in Sudbury, Massachusetts. There are many others as well.

Chapter 10

House-Training: The Path To The Outhouse

*It's amazing what you can learn once you've
already learned all there is to learn.*
~ RAY HUNT, HORSEMAN

*T*wo weeks ago I met with a client in Boston. A lovely young couple—we'll call them Nicole and Tom, and their 12-week-old Bernese mountain dog that we shall name Rolex; after all, the Bernese hails, originally, from Switzerland. Rolex was peeing and pooping at will, so to speak, on their bare floors and carpets. Newspapers were spread out at one end of the hardwood floor hallway, and another two days' worth of *The Boston Globe* was spread out in the kitchen. They would take Rolex out just about every hour, and sometimes he would relieve himself outside and other times he wouldn't. Nevertheless, he certainly wasn't shy about going inside. At times he would use the papers; at other times he'd use the floor. At the end of their rope, they called their vet, who suggested they call me.

Ugh! House-training. The mere mention of the word conjures up mental images of gallons of disinfectant, paper towels by the carton, and time after time of trying to catch the Canine Culprit "in the act" so we can rub the little bugger's nose in it, just one more time, so he'll finally get it.

Oh, come on, time to lighten up. That's not what house-training is all about. Were YOU potty trained in a month? Didn't think so. Nicole and Tom, like so many dog owners, simply did not understand the necessary process.

Years ago, I saw close to 100 house-training problems each year. Now, thankfully, I see perhaps 10% of that. Why the change? Several reasons. For one thing, dog owners now understand better the value of a proper dog crate and how, when utilized properly, it can help the pup learn the house-training process much more easily. Also, there are several well-written books devoted to raising puppy the correct way, and those books describe the house-training method in a clear, concise manner.

Furthermore, more owners are enrolling their pups in puppy classes, so more solid information is being dispensed. Additionally, there are probably, and hopefully, far fewer puppy mills and pet shops around today than there were a number of years ago. In short, we have a more educated dog owner.

There are, however, factors that affect the ease with which the house-training process is accomplished, and many owners know nothing about those factors. For example, in his wonderful book *Canine Behavior* (Charles C. Thomas, 1965), author Dr. Michael W. Fox writes, "Traumatic experience or lack of experience (isolation) or training during a critical period may make it difficult to establish a particular pattern later in life. Bed wetting in children is a good example of this. At a certain age, the child is easily toilet trained, but if this critical or sensitive time is missed, training is more difficult. House-training a puppy follows a similar pattern." Therefore, the puppy's age when we begin the process can be pivotal regarding our degree of success.

When one of my yellow Labs, Kitt, had her litter of seven, I began the process quite early. My whelping box had a divider, splitting the box into two "rooms." Early on, the divider was in place, with towels on the floor in the room where Kitt and her brood lived. And mom cleaned up what messes I didn't get to. At a little over four weeks, I removed two of the three slats separating the rooms. The newly opened room I covered first with newspaper, then wood shavings on top. One by one, the exploring pups climbed over the low slat and explored the area. And, yes, they would pee and poop there, on their own. While they were being weaned, I would put their food in the original room (hope I'm not confusing you) and soon, the pups began sleeping along with eating in that room, but would crawl into the other room to pee and poop. The pups were beginning to learn house-training: don't pee and poop where you eat and sleep. This was not my idea. A very wise Lab breeder taught me this. Wise, indeed. Those pups house-trained very quickly when they left to live with their new, happy owners. In other words, if the breeder keeps the whelping box clean, pups begin to learn the process of house-training at a very early age. If, however, the litter is kept in unclean conditions, and therefore they eat, sleep, and eliminate in the same area, that environmental influence will eventually overcome the natural instinct to be clean.

Some breeds, historically, have a more difficult time learning the process. I've been hearing for years, "Ray, I think small breeds are more difficult to house-train than large breeds." If that is true, and I'm not at all convinced that it is, although I do see more house-soiling issues with small breeds than larger ones, might it be not genetically but rather environmentally influenced? The majority of small dog breeds that I do see with house-soiling issues are perceived by their owners as lap dogs. Those dogs tend to be spoiled, overindulged pets. William Campbell *(Behavior Problems in Dogs,* American Veterinary

Publications,1976) nicknamed them "affectionate parasites." Ouch, Bill! I'll discuss the lap dog house-soiling problem a bit later.

Let's first discuss the normal process in house-training a young pup. Now, understand that house-training is one of the first "tasks" your pup will learn from you, and that task will be, for that pup, either a positive or negative experience. And that, my friend, is up to you. Yes, you.

Contrary to some beliefs, pups do not house-train themselves. Even though Kitt's pups had a leg up from early puppyhood, they nevertheless needed guidance from their new owners, in a completely new environment. Because of that, it is a process that needs to be built on mutual trust and respect, rather than fear and intimidation. We help pup learn the fundamentals by rewarding them when they eliminate in the proper place rather than punishing them for eliminating in the wrong place. If you train with that premise foremost in your mind, and you follow my guidelines, things should progress smoothly.

Do you now see one of the problems, potentially, with the puppy mill or pet shop dog? Do not get a pup from a pet shop. I am currently working with clients and their beagle, whom they got from a pet shop at 16 weeks of age. This dog was eliminating throughout the house, including in his dog crate. Why? Because that's what the pup learned to do in the pet shop, to live and to eliminate in the same case in the storefront window. What a lovely beginning for a pup! Two strikes against him and a low fast ball on the way by the time he spent his first night with his new, naive but loving owners.

Understand, please, that more than anything else, your dog wants to please you and, given the proper cues, will perform the appropriate behavior. What many owners fail to comprehend is that their dog isn't soiling the house because he's angry, spiteful, stubborn, or stupid. He simply doesn't understand. There are three distinctly different types of house-training dilemmas, depending upon the dog. I've classified them as the naive dog, the insecure dog, and the submissive excitable dog. Although the behavior of pooping and peeing in the house are the same in all cases, the root causes of the problem differ.

House-training the Naive Dog

Let's discuss this dog type first. Puppies are included in this category, so, if you've got a puppy, the following program applies to you as well. The owner hasn't conditioned the pup to understand that eliminating outside is appropriate and that peeing and pooping inside the house is not. By my definition, the dog who goes outside only is house-trained; the one that goes inside, or both inside and outside, is not. It's 100% outside, or your dog is not house-trained. The following steps, then, are for training the naive dog.

- Think that you're training the dog from day one

- Establish the proper area outside

- Use key phrase along with properly timed praise

- Set up a strict feeding schedule and going-outside schedule

- Utilize proper confinement techniques

- Establish a proper sleeping area

- Keep a daily chart

- Use an odor neutralizer and properly clean a soiled area

- Structure your dog on a daily basis

- Check with your veterinarian

- Take lots of patience pills

- Correct effectively and sparingly

Let's go through each one of the above.

Think you're training from day one.

No matter what has happened so far, it's best for you to mentally wipe the slate clean in terms of anger, frustration, and guilt (best for your dog as well). Give both of you a break and begin training with a positive attitude.

Establish a proper area outside.

Where do you want pup to go? That's where you take the dog. I suggest, if possible, the backyard. If you've a woodsy area behind the backyard, so much the better. Don't fixate on a specific area initially. Make it easy for your dog to learn that the main objective is for the dog to do his business outside, no matter where. After a while you can work on getting him to go in your area.

Use a key phrase and proper praise.

A key phrase can be a great asset in house-training. I used to recommend "Hurry up!" I now suggest "Do it," as it is a phrase used less around the house. Do not use a praise phrase, such as "Good dog."

Here's how using a key phrase works. Whenever I took Kitt outside for her to eliminate, as soon as she began to either pee or poop, I'd say, all the while she was going, "Do it. Do it." As soon as she finished I'd tell her, "Good girl," and bring her back into the house. What I was doing was conditioning Kitt to understand the primary reason for going out in the backyard was to eliminate, and also to learn, eventually, that when she heard that key phrase, she was to eliminate. Also, when pup first goes outside in the morning, bring him back in as soon as he goes. If you're going to give him exercise, have him back inside for five minutes before taking him out again. That way, he understands that the first thing he does is eliminate, and later on he'll go outside for exercise. Your dog will begin to go quickly, wherever he is, because, down the line, he will have learned to associate that key phrase with eliminating. There were many times when Kitt was with me for the day in the truck and I'd be racing from client to client, and I'd only have a few minutes in between to stop and let her pee. I'd tell her "Do it," and she'd go right away, with no sniffing for five minutes to locate that perfect spot.

Set up a strict feeding and going-outside schedule.

What goes in comes out. If you feed Honey one day at 8:00 a.m. and the next day at 10:30, don't expect her to defecate on any type of regular schedule. When your puppies are completely house-trained and you wish to feed on a self-feeding basis, have at it. Until then, however, keep to the schedule. For example, for three feedings a day, you might:

7:00 a.m. - 7:30 a.m. Pick up dish after 30 minutes.

1:00 p.m. - 1:30 p.m. Pick up dish after 30 minutes.

6:00 p.m. - 6:30 p.m. Pick up dish after 30 minutes.

Keep to this on weekends as well. Be consistent.

Utilize appropriate proper confinement techniques.

I always use a crate to help me house-train my own pups. It's foolish to allow your pup to run helter-skelter through your house if he has no sense of where to eliminate. If you use a crate, be fair to pup. Don't expect him to live in his crate for excessively long time periods.

Now, how do you use the crate to assist in the house-training? It's simple. House-training should consist of three distinct parts: outside time, supervised free time, and crate or other confinement time. Let's say between 7:00 a.m. and 9:00 a.m., pup doesn't eliminate in the house. We know this because we've been keeping our chart current (you'll read about the chart in a bit). However, any time after 9:00 a.m. can be a problem unless pup's taken out. As pup grows older, though, we don't want to get into a pattern of taking him out every two hours. So, how do you go about increasing the time gaps between trips outside? Easy, we use the crate. Rather than taking pup out at 9:00 a.m., keep him in the crate until 10:00. Take him out at 10:00 a.m. and after he goes, you may give him what I call free time. What's "free time"? you ask. Well, when you bring him back in, give him time to run around loose, UNDER YOUR WATCHFUL EYE. In other words, do not allow him to run loose throughout the house. If you're in the kitchen, allow him to be in the kitchen with you.

If the next time you would normally take him out is 11:00 a.m., crate him at 11:00 and take him out at noon. If he goes, give him free time. After a number of days, his system will have adjusted to the new schedule. When that time is reached, rather than taking him out at 10:00 a.m., crate him till 11:00. In other words, you use the crate to continue to push back his crate time and to increase his free time. Eventually, you take him out at 7:00 a.m. and, after bringing him back inside, he gets free time until noon. How long that takes to accomplish depends upon the particular dog, the environment, the owner's daily schedule, etc. What works for one owner may not work for you. It's pretty simple; you just keep moving the crate time back. What if you take pup out and he doesn't go? Simple. After a reasonable time, bring him back in and crate him for 30 minutes. Then, take him out again. You do this until he goes outside; then, reward him with free time.

Establish a proper sleeping area.

When house-training, I recommend that a client have their dog sleep in their bedroom, in the crate. That's what I do, for the first week to 10 days. Remember, I usually get a new pup between 9 -10 weeks of age. After that, I hook pup up to a 20-in. line attached to the foot of my bed, on the blanket that was in his crate. He'll do fine. Honest, he will. And he will be out of the crate, which is a good thing. If he cries, ignore him, unless it's at a time you would normally take him out. He'll survive, and so will you.

A chart tells what, when, and where pup did his pee and poop. Keep a physical chart. Do not even think of keeping a mental chart. They don't work. You got that, partner? Mental charts do not work. The chart, when kept properly, may help point out a particular time problem. Here's a sample chart:

Daily Chart

Day	What	When	Where	Comments
Monday	Pooped/peed	7:15 a.m.	Yard	
Monday	Peed	9:30 a.m.	Yard	
Monday	Peed	11:30 a.m.	Kitchen	Out at 11 a.m., didn't pee
Monday	Peed/pooped	2:30 p.m.	Yard	

And so forth. The chart will tell you if things are getting better, worse, or remaining the same.

Use an odor neutralizer and clean a soiled area properly.

There are a host of neutralizers in today's marketplace—some work while others just arrive well packaged to appeal to the consumer. For many years, clients of mine have praised Nature's Miracle, so I pass that testimonial on to you. An alternative is a mixture of 1/4 plain old white vinegar to 3/4 room temperature water. You may find club soda (no scotch) does the trick for your dog. I have used the latter for many years with good results. You want the product to neutralize the pH factor in the urine.

When you find a spot, first blot up the urine as much as possible so the rug is as dry as possible. Second, saturate the area with the neutralizer. Third, after leaving it down for a couple of minutes, blot it up as dry as you can. A commercial cleaning salesman once told me that covering the area with a white cloth before blotting it up makes the process much more effective. It keeps the chemicals from prematurely being released from the carpet. NEVER, I repeat, NEVER, use ammonia. Ammonia is urea. Have you ever smelled a baby's diaper after peeing? It smells of ammonia. I put that in my first book and I repeat it here.

Also, do not clean a soiled area with pup present. Why? Two reasons. (1) You are not the maid, dutifully cleaning up after pup and, (2) you really do not want to make a big deal out of the process.

Structure your dog daily.

You know the reasons by now. An unstructured dog will make any place his toilet area, because no limits or authority has been established. You will recall in the beginning of this chapter I briefly mentioned the "lap dog." These are dogs with little to no structure in their lives. They are pets viewed anthropomorphically by their overindulgent, unknowing owners.

Many of these dogs pee throughout the house (insecure), bite their owners to impose their will, and, in general, become four-legged tyrants. Is it any wonder they are never successfully house-trained?

Check with your veterinarian.

All the behavior modification programs in the world are not worth a penny if pup has a physical problem that contributes to his/her eliminating in the home. When in doubt, check in with your vet FIRST.

Invest in patience pills.

This is pretty self-explanatory. Helping pup learn to go outside and not inside requires some time. Don't go into a blue funk when some friend of yours tells you HIS dog was totally house-trained in a mere three days. None of mine were and I'm pretty good at it. Just stick with it, help pup learn what it's all about, and have fun with it. By house-training your pup with patience, you're improving the relationship, and that should be fun!

Correct effectively and sparingly.

Anything beyond a quietly firm "No" is counterproductive. Pups do not become house-trained by being punished for going in the inappropriate area. They learn by following the guidelines I've set for you. If you see him eliminating inside the house, anything beyond "No" is simply wrong. Getting angry and taking it out on your pup may make you feel better for a minute or two, but it sure as hell won't help your dog.

House-training the Insecure Dog

Insecure dogs lack self-confidence. Adult dogs that leg lift in the home do so for one simple reason: they're insecure. Why does a male dog (and some females) lift his leg when he pees? He does it to mark territory as his. He places his individual "brand" on a certain hydrant. That tells other dogs, "This is my territory." That's what dogs do. It's in their DNA. When the insecure dog does it, however, he does so to make himself feel more secure, to feel safer. On the other hand, though, the place where a dog should feel most secure would be his home, where he lives. That being the case, why then should he feel a need to mark it as his? It's already his territory. If he's insecure, however, he continually feels the need to mark it, to make it his, to help him deal with his insecurity. If he then gets punished for it, he becomes more insecure and then needs to mark it again, so the problem becomes worse. Marking becomes a sort of false security blanket for that dog. On top of that, deep inside, he's not content. What to do?

1. Stop punishing him. It makes him increasingly more insecure.

2. Begin structuring daily. Have him Sit before he gets attention. Heel him on walks, and do not allow him to mark every tree, bush, shrub, fence post, etc., along the walk. Allow him to pee on property surrounding yours, period.

3. Stop all overindulgences. End coddling the dog.

4. Keep a chart.

5. If he's an intact male, neuter him; however, do not expect this alone to make an enormous difference.

6. Achieve a strong leader/follower role with him. He'll begin feeling better about himself because he's receiving praise for suc-

ceeding. By setting limits and reducing his sense of responsibili-ty, you begin to help him feel less worried about himself.

Helping the Submissive/Highly Excitable Urinator

When I have clients whose dogs exhibit this annoying behavior, this is what I advise them. When you return home, ignore your dog completely, including eye contact. No voice, no touch, no speaking. Ignore him until he calms down, which may take several minutes. Then, when you're in another room, stand quietly, facing away from the dog. When he comes over, reach down and stroke under his jaw for a few seconds. That's enough. Do not touch anywhere near the crown of his head. You must have everyone else do the same. If you follow this simple technique, you should see improvement in three to four weeks, perhaps sooner. It would be a good idea to enlist the assistance of a reputable, experienced professional to assist. In most cases, your veterinarian is a good source for referring such a person. Don't simply listen to Aunt Sophie or other "experts."

Chapter 11

Problems: Bumps Along The Path

I just keep trying to fix it up for them so they can find their way.
~Ray Hunt, Horseman

*R*ay Hunt, as well as some others like him, was able to teach his riding pupils so much about riding correctly because Ray, through years of hard and painful work, had learned the language the horse speaks. Ray said, "I've been trying my whole life and I'm still working at it." Man, am I ever thankful he said that! I've been trying for 50 years and I'm sure still working at it.

You see, a relationship between a dog and his human companion is a series of hills. You work at it until you reach the summit, pass up and over, and you both go on your way, until you reach the next hill. And so on. Many dog owners eventually reach a hill they find they are unable to move beyond. At that point they need a bit of help, sort of a leg up, but they don't realize it. They believe they can solve the issue by themselves. And that's where the going gets mucky. Attempting to solve a problem when you don't know what you're doing can wind up in a battle of wills and a strained relationship at both ends. If it's not fun for you, you see, it's not fun for pup either. Believe me when I tell you this. What I know I learned from doing it on my own, and dear friend, that's the hard way for both of you. I did it that way not because I was stubborn, but rather way back then I didn't know anyone who could set me straight. So I made a lot of mistakes along the way—probably more than you'll ever make. Hopefully, you can learn something from my errors.

I can tell you from experience that when you get stuck you need to hire a good professional to help get you unstuck. Don't let that issue become a mountain way too high for both you and pup.

There are lots of bumps along the path. Most of them are, with a little professional assistance, relatively easy to resolve. Others take more time and greater expertise. You'll be reading about some common and some not so common problems, and how I deal with them.

Correction vs. Reaction

When dealing with certain inappropriate behaviors, it becomes necessary to let the dog know his behavior is unacceptable, and doing so may involve correction. I deal with clients every day who have been "correcting" their dogs for days, weeks, months and even years, with no success whatsoever. How can that be? you ask. Many times, the answer is a simple one: rather than actually correcting their dog, owners more often than not are merely reacting to the animal. Allow me to attempt to explain how correction works and why, in so many cases, it doesn't.

Many years ago, when I was in the Marine Corps, did Corporal McSoley tell Colonel O'Brien that, in my opinion, he was doing less than an adequate job in running the battalion? I guess not. Why? Simply because the colonel is going to take it as a direct challenge to his authority. If, on the other hand, he calls me into his office and chews me out, ending with "Are we clear on that, corporal?" I answer, "Aye, aye, sir." You see, correction flows only from the top down, never from the bottom up. If your dog doesn't look upon you as the leader, then he's the leader. Any attempt at correction on your part is taken by the dog as a challenge to his rank. A client will tell me, "Ray, I correct Smokey but my correction is not effective." That, my friend, is an oxymoron. Ineffective correction is no correction; at best it's non-productive and at its worst can be counterproductive.

I visited a new client some years ago who had a highly wired gorgeous Irish setter. The dog was just over three years at the time and had been jumping on Tom, his owner, as well as everyone else for a majority of those years.

"Clancy jumps on me daily," Tom explained. "But I don't let him get away with it. I correct him every time he does. I'm very consistent about it."

"Let me get this straight, Tom. Clancy's been jumping on you daily for three years. If he jumps on you only once a day that's over 1,000 jumps. You're sitting there telling me you don't let him get away with it? You've corrected him at least 1,000 times. Tom, that's not correction, that's merely reacting to his behavior."

It's correction only if it works. We convince ourselves we're correcting Clancy when in fact it's not correction at all. We may even feel good about what we did, thinking, *Clancy didn't get away with that one*. But, truth is, he did get away with that one, and the one after that, and the one after that, and the.. .... Most dog owners, when they attempt to correct, do not focus properly—not merely their visual focus but their mind's focus as well. We're correcting our dog but we're thinking about the briefcase we left at the office, or our child that was bullied last week, or the meatloaf in the oven. If you're not 100% focused on your dog when correcting him, your correction will be ineffective and, therefore, no correction. You either get serious about it or you don't. I do not care what else is going on in my life, when I correct I push aside whatever else is going on in my mind so that I can focus 100% on my dog. And what am I thinking? I'm thinking, *This is the last time you are going to do that.*

There are two things I need to get across with correction. The first is obvious: I want that behavior to end. The second is this: I want my dog to be calmer at the end of the correction than he was before I did the correction. The calmer he becomes, the more he can focus on the correction. I also do not rush a correction. A correction may involve 20 or 30 seconds; however, when it's over, it's over. No grudges here. No trying to make the dog feel bad by not speaking to him for the next two days.

I'm also totally comfortable in my mind when I correct. I'm not uncomfortable making corrections. I have absolutely no problem correcting my dogs. After all, what is the purpose of correction? To end the particular behavior. And what happens when that behavior is extinguished? The relationship improves. So when you correct, both properly and fairly, and without the least bit of anger, you are helping establish a healthier bond. You're helping him learn. Why feel guilty about that?

One additional point here. NEVER PRAISE YOUR DOG AFTER A CORRECTION. Now I know a whole bunch of trainers just jumped up and said that they always tell their clients to praise right after correction. But why would you do such a thing? Let's say your dog, Juno, just jumped on the counter to snatch half your bagel. You tell him "Off" in a normal but firm voice. Juno gets off the counter and as he hits the floor you say to him, "Good boy, Juno." You do that to praise him for doing the right thing, getting off the counter. But did he really do the right thing—or rather did he simply end the inappropriate behavior because he never should have been on the counter in the first place? I submit it's the latter. Furthermore, from the dog's perspective, if he gets rewarded for getting off the counter, then he needs to get back on the counter first. So, at 4:00 p.m. on Monday you correct him but then praise him after. The following day, Tuesday, what's a sure-fire

way for him to get a "Good boy, Juno" at 4:00 p.m.? Simple. By jumping on the counter. So don't reward after correcting. It makes no sense.

How do I correct? I really do not use the word No. For jumping
up I use "Off." For taking things he shouldn't, I use the phrase "Leave
it." For excessive barking, it's "Quiet." There are times when I use my
fingers. For excessive barking I may go to the dog, put two fingers
on his collar, pull up just a bit so he's looking at me, and then I say
"Quiet." I hold that position, looking down at him. I might repeat the
"Quiet" a second time while continuing to hold. I might hold 20 or
30 seconds, long enough for him to soften, to relax. When I release, I
release sloooowly, perhaps five seconds. I do not get loud, nor overly
physical. Remember, however, to do this effectively you must first be
the leader (chairman of the board), and your dog must understand
that clearly. Do not attempt to use that technique to gain the leader
role. That is most important. Remember, mutual trust and respect. So,
just to review. When I use that method to correct, I'm employing five
elements: 1) holding the collar with my fingers under his jaw; 2) eye
contact; 3) verbal, letting him know in a normal, firm voice; 4) a slow
release of the collar only after the dog has relaxed his body, and 5) my
100% commitment to the correction. Remember that this is very firm
correction and must be used judiciously! Now let's talk about some
bumps.

Jumping Up

Did you know that 80% of dogs jump on people? So, if you have a
jumping issue, you're part of a large group. This problem almost always begins very early. Pup jumps up and everyone laughs. They even
like it when he does it; however, they like it less when he's still jumping
up at six months and 50 pounds and even less when at one year and 70
pounds. Never allow your dog to engage in a behavior that, down the
road, you are not going to want him to do.

Everyone has a cure for the jumper. There are dozens of techniques.

The majority of them aren't even worth trying. In my last book, *Dog Tales,* I related a story about a Golden retriever that jumped on his owner whenever he entered the house. The owner was single and lived with his mother. Jumping was only an issue with him. What I recommended was, upon entering the house, he ignore his dog completely, proceed to the kitchen, and turn on the gas burner underneath a two-quart saucepan filled with a specified amount of water. He was to continue to ignore the dog until the water boiled and the lid rattled, which took somewhere between five and six minutes. At that point he could tell his dog to "Sit" and pat him quietly. By taking this amount of time it allowed his dog to unwind enough so that he could listen to his owner. This procedure helped the dog to acknowledge his owner to be in the leader role at that point, rather than the other way around. Within three weeks' time, my client could enter the house, his dog would whirl in a circle two or three times, then run into the kitchen and sit by the stove. Did it work for other people entering the house? Of course not; however, that was never a problem for my client. It would be for most dog owners.

I have, throughout these many years, worked with thousands of clients whose dogs jumped on people. Do you want to know the best and simplest method for solving this vexing problem? Use the remote collar (e-collar). See Chapter 8 on how to use the remote collar for a jumper.

Equipment needed:
1 quality e-collar

Car Problems

Shannon was a gorgeous five-year-old female German shepherd dog. Michelle, her owner, was very responsible. She had done a marvelous job training Shannon, which showed as soon as I entered their lovely home in Sharon, Massachusetts. We both sat down at Michelle's kitchen table and, with Shannon's head resting on my thigh, I inquired, "Michelle, why am I here?"

She began to tell me about the issue. When Shannon was riding in Michelle's Ford Explorer, she would unleash an uncontrollable torrent of barking whenever an automobile would pass. I told Michelle I would like to witness this and so the three of us went outside to their car. The middle seat was folded down and a number of blankets lay on top, giving Shannon freedom for everything except the front seat. It was a late autumn evening, dark except for the large moon beginning to rise.

"Ray, you'll be able to witness her behavior after about a mile, when we reach I-95 southbound," Michelle said.

Commuter traffic was still moderately heavy on South Main Street as we headed off toward the interstate. I turned my head to see that the dog was already on high alert, staring at the approaching headlights. As the first car began to pass, Shannon lunged at the car, barking her brains out, her muzzle just inches away from the back of Michelle's head. I started to say something to Michelle, but Shannon's barking was so loud that Michelle could not have heard me if I was using a bullhorn. Finally, after perhaps the twelfth automobile had rolled by, I tapped Michelle lightly on her shoulder. She jumped and looked over at me. I quickly drew my index finger across my throat and jerked my thumb in the direction of her home. Michelle nodded and, after turning down a side street and turning around, we began heading back toward the state of tranquility. Neither of us said a word as we exited the Explorer. Michelle took Shannon's lead and we went back inside her house. I sat down again in the kitchen and looked over at Michelle. She was standing, looking at me with tears streaming down her cheeks. "I knew you wouldn't be able to help, Ray. You're the third professional I've had. The first one, a woman, brought along a spray bottle with cold water and all that did was get me soaked. The second one, a young man, climbed in the back with her and yelled no and yanked as hard as he could on her prong collar. That didn't work either."

"Be kinda difficult for you to do that and drive at the same time," I conjectured, attempting to inject a bit of humor into the atmosphere. "Michelle," I said, "get a Kleenex and then let's get started on the problem."

I reached into my briefcase and removed what groomers call a tub choker. It's the 30/36-in. plastic-coated cable that hangs from the ceiling over the groomer's wash tub. I said, "Let's go out and see what we can hook this to in your SUV." I located a ring in the floor, one on each side behind the driver and passenger seats. I selected the 30" cable, the shorter of the two. The ring in the floor was large enough for the snap on the tub choker to pass through the ring. I passed it through and then passed it through the ring on the other end of the tub choker, thus securing the choker to the floor, with the end with the snap on it ready to snap onto Shannon's collar.

I suggested we go back out and drive around a bit. Michelle put Shannon in the back and I hooked up the snap to the collar, giving Shannon enough room to stand but making standing difficult. "Let's go for a drive," I said. Off we went, driving back down Main Street and onto the interstate, Shannon barking at every car. After about 20 minutes, there was less barking. I turned around and Shannon was lying down. As a car would pass she would bark, but the excitable lunging had stopped. I told Michelle to head back to the house. As Michelle was bringing Shannon inside, I went to my Jeep and took out a Garmin Bark Limiter. When I got inside the house, Michelle was smiling.

"Ray, that is so much better," she said. "I cannot thank you enough."

I told Michelle that I wasn't quite finished. I showed her the bark collar and said that Shannon needed to learn to control her barking—not just lie down in the back, but learn to RELAX while lying down in the back. I put the Garmin on Shannon, with the device on the lowest setting, and off we went for the third time. After driving down the interstate two exits and then driving back north, Shannon was still barking at cars. I removed the collar, increased the stimulation by one level, and reattached it. We headed south again, and after perhaps a little less than 10 minutes, the barking ceased. I told Michelle to keep driving until we reached Rhode Island, about 20 minutes away. The cabin in the Ford remained quiet. We then headed back to Sharon. Inside the house I went over everything, explaining how the collar worked and how to adjust it on Shannon's neck. I explained the different levels of stimulation and told her to keep it on level 2. Michelle gave me a hug as I was leaving. I got down on one knee, called Shannon over to give her a pat, and she gave me a quick lick on my face. She never barked in Michelle's car after that.

Equipment needed:

1 Groomer's tub choker

1 Garmin Bark Limiter

Note: If you are not in the car, release the snap on the choker. NEVER have your dog hooked up to it if you are not in the car! Your dog may not need the tub choker. Just the bark limiter might be all you need.

Guarding Objects (Resource Guarding)

This can be an extremely serious problem. Thousands of dog owners end up in emergency rooms because they attempted to deal with this problem themselves. Please refer to Chapter 8. I always use the remote collar with this problem. The dog should never see the transmitter, the part you hold in your hand. You should put the collar on your dog first thing in the morning and remove it just before going to bed in the evening. There are some dogs that, if ignored, will eventually simply drop and walk away from the object. The problem comes when they take something that cannot be ignored. Eyeglasses are just one example. So that is why I use the remote. It's safe, humane, effective, and it ends conflict and confrontation between you and your dog.

North Attleboro is a town off Interstate 95 located a few miles north of the Rhode Island line. I had an appointment there with a client and his three-year-old male Rottweiler named Spartan. I pulled up to an older Cape-style home surrounded by absolutely gorgeous landscaping. I knocked on the light blue front door and was rewarded with barking that could probably have been heard back in Providence, Rhode Island. The door opened and I was welcomed by 125 pounds of Rotti, his enormous front paws almost shoving me off the top step.

"Sparty, get the hell off!" the large, fit man standing behind yelled to the dog. Spartan got off, allowing me to enter and introduce myself. The large man simply introduced himself as Nate. "It's actually Nathaniel, an old family name. I much prefer Nate."

"Nate's fine with me" I answered, following up with "Nice dog." Nate led the way to his small, immaculate office and pointed to one of the two chairs. We both sat down and I opened the conversation with "So, Nate, Spartan's jumping is the issue?"

"Oh, hell no, I don't care about that." He then placed his right hand on the desk and I saw the large bandage peeking out from the cuff of the dark green chamois shirt.

"That from the dog?" I asked, pointing to the bandage.

Nate unbuttoned the cuff and rolled up his sleeve. The bandage went halfway to his elbow. "This is what concerns me," he answered, showing off his wrapped arm. "I got this from Spartan last Tuesday."

"Stitches?" I queried.

"A few" came the answer.

Nate then filled me in on Spartan. He was never any kind of problem until 10 days ago. Nate was watching the college football national championship game when he noticed Spartan chewing on something.

Looking closer he saw it was a boat shoe. He told me he got up and told the dog to drop it. Spartan then took the shoe into the kitchen and lay down. Nate said he approached Spartan and reached for the shoe. Spartan let out a growl from deep inside but Nate was able to grab the shoe and pull it away. He then smacked Spartan on the nose with the shoe telling Spartan, "Bad dog," several times.

"How'd ya get bitten?" I asked.

Three evenings later Nate was in the same chair reading *The Wall Street Journal*. He said he took off his reading glasses, put them in the case and put the case on the small table by the chair. He then got up and went to the bathroom. When he came back out he saw Spartan lying on the kitchen floor with the eyeglass case between his paws. Nate yelled at him to "Drop it" and Spartan responded with bared teeth and a very serious growl. Nate said to me, "I can't have that bullshit from my dog" and he walked over and reached to take the glasses. That's when Spartan lunged and bit him on the arm.

"Did you get your glasses back?"

"Hell no. I grabbed my coat and my car keys and took off for the emergency room."

Then he said to me with deep sincerity, "Ray, I really love this dog, but I'm afraid I can't keep him." He said the ER doc told him his dog could have bitten him and cut an artery and the doc really scared him.

"Nate, we can solve the problem," I told him. "Did you recover your glasses?"

Nate said that oddly enough the glasses and case were not destroyed. "We can get him to drop it when you tell him to," I added. I went on to explain how I accomplish it with the remote collar. Nate told me he was willing to try it, so I put my collar on Spartan and we just ignored him for about 20 minutes. I told Nate to put the eyeglass case back on the table and we went into the dining room which afforded us a good view of the kitchen.

About 20 minutes later, sure enough, Spartan walked into the kitchen with Nate's eyeglass case. I told Nate to just watch and got out of my chair.

"Jesus, Ray, be careful. I don't want to drive you to the ER."

"I'll be fine, Nate."

When I got about six feet from Spartan, I heard the growling begin. With the transmitter behind my back I said with quiet firmness, "Drop it" and pressed level 2. No response. Raising the level to 4, I repeated, "Drop it." I noticed a slight eye change and a quick ear flick. Raising the level to 5 I repeated, "Drop it." Spartan dropped the case but remained lying over it. He then lowered his head and when he put his mouth on the case I repeated "Drop it" again and Spartan jerked his huge head back, got up and left the kitchen. I went over, picked up the case, and brought it back to Nate. Nate got a remote collar and I came back and showed him how to use it. Within a week the problem was resolved and both Spartan and Nate were happy again.

Equipment needed:

1 Remote collar, Garmin Sport Pro or a different high-quality brand.

Food Stealing

Another potentially extremely dangerous problem. Once again, owners end up in the emergency room. I'll refer you, once again, to the chapter on the remote collar. Some dogs counter jump for the food while others just hang around the kitchen, waiting for the owner to accidentally drop a piece of food. If the problem is the latter, you need to set up the dog to begin to end this behavior. I purposefully "accidentally" drop the food and, when the dog reaches for it, I tell him "Leave it" and immediately tap him with the remote. I will do that until he begins to react much more slowly toward the food on the floor. And while cooking after, you need to have the transmitter in a spot that you can reach it quickly, before he eats the food, because then the correction is too late.

Inappropriate Barking

Dogs bark either at something or about something. With the exception of the basenji, dogs bark. It is both natural and instinctive behavior. If you want a non-barker, invest in a basenji. By the way, even they vocalize.

The vast majority of dog owners understand that barking is normal. Owners merely wish to curb nuisance barking. The dog that barks for long periods outside should be brought inside. Common sense. Isolating a dog in your backyard all day is not good for a majority of dogs. They simply do not deal well with the isolation and turn to barking about their condition. This dog should spend short times only outside. If, for some serious reason, you cannot bring him inside, get a bark collar.

Do not get just any bark system, get a good-quality device. There are, unfortunately, a lot of extremely poor-quality bark collars on the market. Garmin makes a couple of good-quality bark limiters. Good bark limiters are activated by the dog's vocal cords, not by sound. Some systems gradually automatically increase the intensity if the dog continues to bark. Be very careful when using this option. Do not use it until your dog clearly understands how receiving stimulation for barking works. If, when introducing your dog to a bark limiter you use the "auto rise" feature, what can happen is the following: Your dog barks, he feels nothing so he continues barking, and the auto rise is raising the intensity level. The dog continues to bark and suddenly feels the stimulation. He reacts to the stimulation by barking again and now he gets a higher level, which may be too high for that particular dog so he begins to panic and may even bark again, so he gets an even higher level of intensity. So, be very careful about using auto rise. Incidentally, if the dog is quiet for 60 seconds or so, the auto rise goes back down, so the smart dogs can learn they can bark until the level eventually rises to the level that is effective. I much prefer the manual set collars. You set the level, beginning at the lowest level, and SLOWLY increase the level until you get the response you want. Your dog stops barking. Then simply leave the collar on that setting.

There are different varieties of bark limiters. Some use sound rather than stimulation. Another system uses citronella as a noxious odor emitted when the dog barks. Some owners swear by this latter system, others swear at it. The choice is yours. I don't like that system. You can use your remote (e-collar) system to control unwanted barking simply by pressing the button at the same time the dog barks. Personally, I like this system. If you reside in a condo or apartment, however, and your dog barks only when he or she is alone, then the remote would be useless.

A wonderful feature of the bark collar is that your dog teaches himself to control his barking. There are two results your dog receives from a good bark collar: first, he learns to control his barking, which becomes music to your ears and second, he becomes more relaxed because he is not wound up and barking at everything. The more relaxed he is, the less stress and anxiety he feels. It's all good.

When the barking is inside the house and is directed at something outside, there is another technique I have employed. When the dog barks, call the dog to you. If he does not come to you, then go to the dog. Quietly take him by the collar, repeat either Come or Here and bring him to where you were when you first called him. When you get there have your dog lie down for a minimum of one minute. At the end of the minute, very quietly give him a "Good dog." Then release him very quietly. If he runs back to the spot and begins to bark again, simply repeat the procedure. This technique can take both time and patience; however, when it works it can be very rewarding for you.

The Dog with a Mind of Its Own

What dog doesn't? A dog without a mind of his own isn't much of a dog. Your relationship with your dog needs to be built upon mutual trust and respect. A dog with a mind of its own is a good, wonderful animal, capable of teaching us a lot about ourselves. When dealing with such a dog, watch your ego! Don't allow your ego to take over when interacting with this dog. Many years ago, before I knew better, I fell subject to my ego in those situations. And I learned the hard way, sometimes painfully so, that your ego is no friend when you're dealing with this canine personality. Indeed, the ego is your enemy. When you decide to go toe to toe with such a dog, your ego can result in your being roughed up, both emotionally and, yes, physically.

I've had many years of working with this canine personality. Be careful with this dog, for this is the dog that knows you inside out, four ways to Sunday. This is the dog with spokes in his wheels, the dog that knows how and when to tick you off. This is the dog some trainers (inexperienced or ego-based) call "stubborn, willful, untrainable, or too smart for its own good." You can learn so many of the great qualities of life from such a dog: patience, forgiveness, respect, understanding, skill in communication, and the wisdom of being a good listener.

Sure, he'll "game" (test) ya. I've seen them set their jaws like a 15-year-old kid who's been knocked around in his young years. "Go ahead," those eyes say, "take your best shot." Monty Roberts, in his marvelous book *The Man Who Listens to Horses,* wrote: "For centuries, humans said to horses: you do what I tell you or I'll hurt you. Humans still say that to each other, still threaten, force, intimidate. I am convinced that my discoveries with horses also have value in the workplace, in the educational and penal systems, and in the raising of children."

My friend, it's the same with your dog. The way many people still deal with the dog is to break it. Break its will, prove you're dominant, you're alpha. Bully your way through the conflict and confrontation. It's what I did many years ago. I'm not proud of it; I simply did not know any better. I didn't know there was another way.

So how do I deal with such a dog? I use what I call Quiet Firmness.

Let's suppose you have such a dog. I'm thinking of a client's 14-month-old female Rhodesian ridgeback. The owner had a trainer working with her and this dog for months. The trainer quit when the dog was a year old, saying she was feisty and very strong-minded. She said the dog would never work out and the owner should get an easier dog. When I saw this dog the first time she jumped on me, bit my hands, and put a few holes in my jacket and, in general, behaved like a brat. Try as they might, the previous trainer and owner had never been able to get Moxie to Heel in the presence of distractions, come when called when she decided not to, nor to not jump on everyone. Additionally, she had begun to show some aggression toward her owner when she was corrected.

What to do with Moxie? How, even, to begin? Through my early learning years I've learned some wonderful lessons from dogs like Moxie. I can recall any number of them as I put pen to paper this morning. A few sent me packing to the local emergency clinic to get repaired. That's pretty much how I learned the best way not to work with dogs. Long ago, dogs like Moxie helped me to change my entire philosophy on how best to work with dogs, particularly dogs like Moxie. The answer to how best to work with a troubled dog is not found by breaking the dog's spirit. It should never be a battle of wills. So how did I begin to work with Moxie? I began with the remote collar. You see, I wanted to work with her, not against her. I wanted to help her to learn that when she did the right thing, that was the smart choice of right action. Remember Ray Hunt's sage words: "Make the wrong thing difficult and the right thing easy." Did it work? If you've read the prior chapters you already know the answer. I saw Moxie a few months ago and she is doing brilliantly. Plus, she has a very happy owner.

Pica

Pica: an abnormal desire to eat (ingest) inedible objects. There are those in the medical field who feel that dogs that swallow objects—rocks, for example—may be experiencing some form of chemical imbalance or some vitamin or nutritional deficiency. I cannot, with authority, speak to that. I do not doubt, however, that in some cases, they may be spot on. If you begin to see pica with your dog, it's always a prudent move to speak to your vet about it. He or she may recommend some medical tests to see if everything is okay medically and nutritionally with your dog.

I do believe that in some cases pica is used by the pet as an attention-seeking behavior. Flo grabs one of the children's marbles and runs off with it. The owner chases down the four-legged thief, forces open its mouth, and either probes for the object with his fingers or else shakes the dickens out of the poor animal's head in an effort to dislodge the thing. Over time, the dog learns to grab the object, run off with it, and swallow the object before the now horrified owner even has a chance to retrieve it.

Veterinarians will tell you how serious a problem this can become. In many cases, surgery is necessary to remove the object which has now become a blockage in the stomach or elsewhere in the digestive tract. The operation is not inexpensive. Furthermore, the operation doesn't solve the problem because the dog turns around and repeats the whole procedure.

Many of these dogs are very overindulged pets. The solution to the problem begins with a massive dose of boundary and limit setting. Stop spoiling the dog. Petting such a dog for simply breathing in and out may make an owner feel good but it sure as heck doesn't help the dog. Tasking can go a long way toward solving a pica problem. And attempting to punish the dog for the behavior without first establishing yourself as a leader in the dog's mind is absolutely pointless. Giving the pet structure begins to help the dog learn that it is no longer his place to seek attention by engaging in acts of willful disobedience. However, in some situations the above by itself does not solve the problem. I recommend going to the remote collar. Use it similar to using it for object guarding.

Coprophagia

The above is a fancy word for poop eating. Once again many feel this problem may be related to diet. It can, on the other hand, be the result of a hungry animal with nothing else to eat. After all, to a dog it's merely recycled dog food. At any rate, it is a socially unacceptable behavior, and is more prevalent than most dog owners are aware.

If you discover your dog is eating poop, I suggest first to truck pup off to your vet. He or she may offer meaningful insight regarding the behavior. There are dogs that only eat their own poop. Others eat practically anything lying on the ground within reach. The latter can present a serious health issue for the dog. I had a client whose wonderful Labrador contracted pancreatitis as a result of ingesting some animal's feces. That poor dog survived, but her owner came very close to losing her. Do not take this problem lightly. I have had a high success rate using the remote collar to solve such a problem.

Digging Up the Yard

The digger is a bored dog. The exception is the northern breed types that will dig a "cool hollow" to escape the heat. Ingredients in the soil such as bone meal are an invitation to dig.

Let's say you put your dog Digger out in the yard because he's a big dog and you want to give him exercise. Ninety percent of dogs will not self-exercise in your yard. After 20 minutes of being outside by himself, what in hell is there for him to do? Chase the intruding squirrels? Bark at the neighbors going off to work? Sniff all the new scents from the night before? Pretty soon he's bored. What if you put your three-year-old son or daughter out there in the identical situation, with no swing set or anything? He or she is going to get into trouble, pulling logs off the woodpile or whatever. Why? Nothin' to do.

So, bring your dog inside before he gets bored. If he must be outside for long periods, see if you can join up with a neighbor or friend with a friendly dog in the morning, so they both can run around together and blow off steam. Also, do some playing with him in the yard. Retrieving is excellent for this. Toss a frisbee or retrieving dummy. Make the yard a positive place for him to be.

When at all possible, bring him inside. Your dog is a social, not solitary, animal.

Destructive Behavior

Historically, February is Boston's coldest month, and January ain't August. It was a cold, but sunny, Saturday morning as I pulled my VW Golf into Bob Miller's drive, killed the engine, pulled on the parking brake, turned around, and told my 10-month-old black Labrador, Jake, to "Be good," then walked up the snowy path to my clients' door and rang the bell. Bob met me at the door and I followed him into the kitchen where I slipped out of my down jacket and thanked his lovely wife as she slipped a mug of hot coffee into my hand.

I had been doing some work with their three Golden retrievers and they were progressing well. After about an hour of work with them, the conversation drifted over to which retriever was the better, the Lab or Golden. The Millers were Golden lovers and you now know which way I lean. I was extolling the Lab's virtues, particularly Jake's, as I had been extremely pleased with his work as a "Derby dog" in the retriever field trial game. Jake spent most of his days with me, unless it was simply too cold, or hot, for him. His crate fit nicely in the rear of the VW Golf, and I would give him breaks and exercise between visits with clients. I had recently ordered him a new crate, custom sized for a Mitsubishi Montero I had just purchased and, in the meantime, had given away my old one to a client, so Jake had been without a crate for about 10 days.

After listening to just how wonderful the Golden is (they are great dogs), I said I had to get going. I made a follow-up appointment for the next week and left. I got back into the VW, gave a quiet "Hi, Jake" to my incredibly perfect Lab, turned the key and fired her up. The engine ran for perhaps four seconds and then died. I turned the key and kicked in the starter and—nothing. One more attempt proved futile, so I popped the hood and got out to have a look. Everything looked fine underneath the hood. I'm no mechanic but back then I did all the minor mechanical work on my vehicles. I thought I'd take Jake out for a short walk and pee, then I'd ask the Millers if I could use their phone (I didn't have a cell phone then) to call home. I walked around to the back, lifted the hatchback, and jumped back in horror and disbelief. Jake was sitting, looking at me, his tail wagging. A green wire hung from his nose and a light grey wire stuck in the fur behind his left ear. Other variously colored pieces of wire were everywhere.

Looking down, I now understood the mechanical problem, or rather the electrical problem. Jake got bored and in my absence had decided it might be a jim-dandy idea to completely demolish the Golf's main wiring harness. Every electrical component from the front seat on back was exposed and useless. Furthermore, because the wiring for the electric fuel pump was, most probably, somewhere under a paw, that was the reason the damn engine ran only until the fuel already in the engine had burned. No tail or brake lights, no directional signals, no rear wiper/washer. In short, no nothing. Well, I removed the wires from my perfect dog, took him for a pee, put him back in the Golf (what further damage could he do?), trudged back up the walk and reluctantly rang the bell. Bob opened the door and, with a somewhat puzzled look inquired, "Yes, Ray, can I help you?"

"May I please use your phone, Bob?"

"Of course. Anything wrong?"

"My car won't start."

"Gee, I hope it's nothing serious."

"Well, it is, sort of," I muttered.

"What is it?" nosey Bob inquired, probing further.

"The damn dog devoured my entire main wiring harness." I finally managed to get the words out. Bob simply stared at me for several seconds. Then a hint of a smile began to pull at the corners of his mouth. Finally, he could contain himself no longer. He completely convulsed in laughter at my plight. Turning his head he hollered toward the kitchen, "Hey, honey, you've got to hear this. Ray's great Lab, Jake, just destroyed his car."

His wife appeared shortly with three cups of coffee and we sat at their kitchen table and talked and laughed (mostly laughed) at the sheer fun of the whole disaster. Bob let me use his beautiful Jaguar to get home and return with some electrical wire, electrician's pliers, and my Golf service manual which, thankfully, I had previously purchased. It took half the day but I was able to splice new wire to what remained and get my car running. I surely made the Millers' weekend. And Jake? Jake was an incredible companion to the McSoley family, passing over the bar after 14 years. Do I still think of him? You bet.

Destructive behavior doesn't seem to be the problem it was years ago. Crate training is one reason. It does, nevertheless, still occur and when it does it's not pleasant. I have worked with dogs that have, literally, done thousands of dollars' worth of damage to the interior furnishings of both their cars and homes.

There are really two causes for destructive behavior. The first is boredom or frustration. The second is what now is called separation anxiety. Both cases can result in the identical outcome—damage, and a very angry dog owner!

Puppies can do their share of damage. Crating pup when he/she is alone solves that problem. But being crated too long can result in a hyperactive pup, which can result in damage. Older dogs sometimes destroy things, usually from boredom. Proper, consistent exercise alone can solve the problem. A tired dog is a good dog, the saying goes.

Separation anxiety is a totally different animal. It is usually easy to identify dogs prone to this behavior because they begin the destruction shortly after the owner leaves.

Boredom and Separation Anxiety

If it's a relatively young dog, introduce him to the crate and crate him when he's alone. Don't make a big deal out of it; simply crate him, tell him "See ya later," and push off. It's a crate, not San Quentin. As I said before, exercise is critical. Exercise before you leave for work is better than after you return home. If there's no alternative, evening exercise beats none.

Proper chew objects can play a major role, good or not so good. I have limited chew objects for my Labs, pretty much sticking with chicken-flavored (hard) Nylabones. Don't simply take it out of the wrapper and give it to pup. Get down on the floor and tease him with it. Make him want to get it into his mouth. Hold it on the floor, moving it back and forth while being excited. When he goes for it, move it quickly from your left side to your right, when he goes to the right, switch back to the left. Get him really excited, then give it to him, showering him with praise when he gets it. You want him to think that putting that silly thing in his mouth really makes you happy. And if you're happy, he's happy. Don't play tug games with the Nylabone. In fact, it's really never a good thing to play tug, even though they might like it. Playing tug teaches your dog three things, none of which are good.

1. It teaches pup the power of his mouth (never good).

2. It teaches him not to give up an object to you.

3. It teaches him to challenge you for possession of it. It can expand to other things and can lead to aggression for possession of objects.

Give pup the Nylabone shortly before you leave. Don't just leave it around the house for him all the time. You want this to be special. Every once in a while, perhaps for a time during the evening, give it to him. Don't horseplay with him. Never allow him to get mouthy with you (biting).

It's interesting that when a dog owner begins to see destructive behavior beginning, he/she will buy more and more toys for their pup to chew. The danger is that the more objects he is given, the more he wants to chew. You might well wind up with an orally fixated pet. Not good.

I once visited a client whose Golden retriever welcomed me with half a Levi's pant leg clamped firmly in his jaws. "Did the victim survive?" I inquired. "Or did you bury him quietly in the back yard?" The owner laughed and then told me that Ranger had to have something in his mouth all the time. You guessed it, the reason I was called was because he was very destructive.

I learned long ago with my own dogs not to make comings and goings a big deal. Why would you want to do that? Perhaps because you feel bad about leaving? That's natural, but not helpful for the dog. I suppose I can understand why you would want to make a really big deal out of returning. After all, Tiger hasn't seen you in how long? Two hours? Oh my. When you make a big deal (emotionally) out of coming and going, then that's precisely what your dog learns, that there's something special in those two acts. He then begins to get perked up between his ears prior to your leaving. And now because he's all worked up and you suddenly aren't there, how might he react? You guessed well, by dealing with his stress which YOU induced the best way he can, through destruction.

Boy, I wish I had $10 for every client who throughout the years has said to me, "Ray, Charlene knows it's wrong, but she does it anyway." Or, "Cleo's getting back at me for leaving." Give me a break. That is pure bull.

"If he's trying to get back at you, what is he getting back at you for?"

"He's angry we left him."

"So when you return, you give him attention?"

"Yes, until we see the destruction, then we yell NO at him."

"So you still are giving him attention."

"Well, we're certainly not going to allow him to get away with it, if that's what you mean."

"And how long has this been going on?" I then ask.

"For well over a year," comes the answer.

I hope you now understand my point, dear reader.

The classic line goes something like this. "Ray, Fifi knows it's bad, but does it anyway."

"So," I ask innocently, "how do you know Fifi knows it's bad?"

"Because if she hasn't chewed on the priceless Steinway in the study, she runs to greet us. However, if I see she's been gnawing on that gorgeous African mahogany leg, she'll be hiding somewhere."

"So let me pose a question here. When she's devouring the precious Steinway family heirloom, do you think she's saying to herself, 'Boy, are they gonna be furious when they see the damage I've done today'?"

After thinking on that for a bit, most owners will answer, "Well, no, I guess not."

Then I ask, "At what point does Fifi look guilty?"

"Well," the retort comes, "after we return."

If therefore, the dog is not conscious of the behavior at the time, what earthly good does it to punish the dog upon your return? You see, punishing the dog may make you feel better, but it does nothing to make the behavior change, and it just might make things worse.

Let's take the case of the accountant who arrives home each evening at 6:00 p.m. Each time he arrives home, he finds that his dog has destroyed more of the plants in his Florida room. So he drags the poor dog into the room, and yells at it, while he points at the offended plants. He does this every time; he's perfectly consistent. But the behavior becomes worse. Why? Because around 5:00 p.m. the dog's biological clock rings, telling him that The Punisher is arriving shortly. He now begins to become stressed and anxious, and his only outlet for the stress is to chew the plants. Hence the vicious cycle.

Incidentally, a dog doesn't understand guilt; that is something the human (mind) projects onto the dog. Your dog knows when you are upset with him and he is responding by showing submission.

When a dog displays separation anxiety when his owners leave, it's common for owners to personalize it. He's spiteful, they say. Not so. The dog, in his anxiety, is that way simply because he's alone. However, if someone comes to dog sit him, no such behavior takes place. The dog simply needs a warm body present, anybody's warm presence. The following story doesn't involve a destructive pet; however, the reason(s) for the inappropriate behavior is the same.

Amy Kaufman was a very attractive, single, elementary school teacher in her mid-twenties. She lived in the city of Newton, a large, pretty Boston suburb that I mentioned earlier in my book. At any rate, Amy had a three-year-old female American Cocker spaniel named Florence, but Amy always called her Flo. Flo was energetic, nonaggressive, cuddly—and extremely insecure. When it was time for school in the morning, Flo would begin to look depressed, as Amy had described her to me. Amy would prepare to leave. She'd get her coat, her briefcase, car keys, and then turn out the lights. All the while Flo would hang her head, drag herself into the living room and curl up in a corner. The last thing that Amy would do before leaving would be to go over to Flo, get down on the floor with her, hold and stroke her for five minutes. Then she would get up and leave. And after Amy left, Flo would pee on the scatter rug in front of the door through which Amy had just left. The interesting thing was that if Amy had forgotten something and returned before even backing out of the garage, by the time she had re-entered the house, Amy would have already peed on the rug! What in the world was causing this, Amy wanted to know. More importantly, she wanted to know if there was a cure.

I asked Amy why she spent five minutes the way she did before she left.

Why not just say, "So long," and leave? "She looks so sad, so depressed," Amy explained. "I want to reassure her that everything is all right, that I will be coming back."

I reassured Amy that she was, most assuredly, not reassuring Flo at all, but rather doing just the opposite. Here's Flo, all worked up, and here's Amy, petting her, and unknowingly, reinforcing her anxiety rather than calming her. And then, to top it off, she suddenly leaves! How would Flo, now in an acute state of anxiety, attempt to deal with it? You sly fox you. You figured it out right away. She pees on the floor. It could have been by destroying the rug, not peeing on it. Or trying to scratch through the door which Amy uses to leave. Or trying to tear through the window screen.

It took time, but eventually I was able to help Amy to understand how her interaction with Flo was counterproductive to what she truly wanted from Flo. I asked her if she understood what co-dependency is about, and that finally clicked for Amy. By helping Amy to rethink the type of relationship that she had with Flo, I was able, eventually, to change the pattern of behavior of both Flo and Amy. I told her the following points and we worked on them.

1. Cease overindulging your dog.

2. Begin a daily program of positive structure (tasking) for your dog, setting limits and boundaries, thereby increasing self-confidence and decreasing insecurity in your dog.

3. Stop all emotional comings and goings. Simply leave. When returning, ignore your dog completely for five minutes, or until your dog is calm. Then acknowledge your pet, but do it quietly and for a short time, maximum time, two minutes.

4. Provide proper chew objects for your dog. Nylabones and Kongs are good.

5. Provide sufficient exercise for your dog. If you can't, hire someone you trust to do it for you.

A discussion on destructive behavior and separation anxiety would not be complete without bringing up the subject of pharmacological intervention. I am neither a veterinarian nor a pharmacologist. Therefore, it is not my place to even attempt to make a recommendation. That is, as we would say in the Marines, above my pay grade. Before considering medicating a behavior problem, I will say that I strongly believe you should first try solving such a problem through any of the approaches I have laid out in this book. I do believe that in a small minority of situations, the proper medication, properly monitored and as part of an ongoing modification program, can assist. I also know that certain medications are prescribed as a first resort and on a much-too-frequent basis, at times with little foundation or validity to substantiate its use.

In summary, you're not going to solve a destructive behavior or separation anxiety issue overnight or, for that matter, next week. You're going to have to take your "patience pills." And please understand that your dog's not engaging in the behavior because he's spiteful. That's a human failing, so let's not drag your dog down to our level. Keep a written chart. Charts can be very helpful. They make up for an imperfect memory. A consistent chart lets you know if the problem is getting better, staying the same, or getting worse.

Remember to crate as a last resort with an adult dog that has never been crate trained, never as a first resort. Solving one behavior issue while gaining another is no solution. Destructive behaviors are, in a majority of cases, resolvable. Enlisting the support and help from an experienced behavior therapist or long-time trainer can be well worth the investment. And make certain if you choose the former, that he or she knows how to actually work with your dog, and doesn't simply tell you what to do.

Chapter 12

Puppies: Total Openness
To The Path

How's the horse going to learn if you don't know what to do?
~Ray Hunt, Horseman

$\mathcal{F}$our thirty-seven a.m. probably seems to be an ungodly time to be out on the road, but that is what the clock reads on the instrument panel, next to the tach which is hovering at 2300 rpm. Whenever I have a long distance to drive to a client, I prefer leaving as soon as possible. That way, my nonproductive hours are kept to a minimum. So it is on this particular morning. I am westbound on the Massachusetts Turnpike heading for a town in New York's beautiful Catskill Mountains. My clients there have acquired an 11-week-old female Rhodesian Ridgeback from a wonderful breeder. I am on my way to assist them in starting out the right way.

The pike at this time of morning has very little automobile traffic. The majority of vehicles consist of the big 18 wheelers, plus an occasional "double bottom," those enormous double full-size trailers, stretching well past 100 feet in total length.

When the highway is clear, as it is this morning, I find my mind becomes quite active. This trip will take approximately four hours, giving me plenty of time to think. I'm thinking, if more people who were going to get a dog would give at least eight hours' time (my round trip to and from my client) to consider what type of dog to get, there would be far fewer dog problems.

You see, problem behavior begins even before that puppy is purchased. We devote hours toward making a decision on what our next vehicle will be. The same goes for our vacation, the landscaping around our house, the new paint scheme or wallpaper for our dining room. But the dog? Oh, the new dog? Oh, what's the difference? Let's just go out and get one. After all, the twins have been asking and I think a puppy would be fun for them. After all, they're four years old, so I think that's a good time.

The thing is, you really don't get a puppy, what you get is a young dog.

The average lifespan for a dog is anywhere from 10 to 16 years, largely depending upon breed. We have a car for four. See where I'm going here? A dog is not a short-term commitment. If we get a pup at 10 weeks of age, the same day we bring our newborn baby home, that dog may well be with us until our child is going into his or her senior year of high school. If we choose badly because we failed to do our basic homework, our dog must suffer along with us, simply because of our lack of responsibility and our thoughtlessness. I deal with clients every week who, at some point down the road, realize sadly the mistakes they made early on.

Several years ago, I was invited to go out to a place where angels live and work. It's called Best Friends Animal Sanctuary and it's located in Kanab, Utah, in Angel Canyon. I was asked to come out for five days to assist the good trainers there with a few extra difficult dogs they had. They would typically be providing haven for around 500-

550 dogs at a time, and have a very high placement record, which is a great testament to the fine work they do. Many of the dogs were there not because they were troubled, per se, but rather because they were troubling their previous owners. I worked with several hounds there because their howling upset their owners. I worked with a big yellow Labrador named Whitney (with whom I fell in love), there because she was a runner who had been placed a couple of times and had run away from the new owner both times. And there was the cow dog mix, Marianne (on the book cover), a screamer and biter no one could get near. Many arrive as unwanted puppies and because Best Friends is a true, No Kill sanctuary, a few of the residents will spend the remainder of their lives residing at Best Friends. Think about that for a bit. Best Friends also has cats, birds, horses, and rabbits, all there for the same reasons. Incidentally, if you happen to be traveling out west, and your itinerary includes the big canyons like Zion, you should add Best Friends to your places to go. Call ahead and plan to stay for a couple of days. The wonderful staff will be happy to put you to work. I worked my butt off while I was there. I was asked to return about six months later for a second five-day training experience with the trainers there. It was an incredible experience for me, both teaching the trainers and, at the same time, learning valuable lessons from them.

Many of the dogs with which I worked were later adopted. Rehabilitation, however, is not of and by itself the answer. Nor is simply neutering and spaying programs. Helpful, yes. And because they assist, they're important. But more is needed. More what? you ask. Simple—education.

It's a little past 6:00 a.m. and I'm almost in Hartford, Connecticut. I'm ahead of the morning commuter surge and hungry, so I'm going to pass through the city, then exit I-84 and enjoy a great breakfast at this little diner outside of Farmington. I'll continue this discussion about pups and you on a full stomach.

Okay, back on the road, draining the last of my coffee. Let's get back to dogs and a list of questions I have for ya.

1. First dog? Some breeds are probably not good first-dog choices. A Rhodesian Ridgeback would be one. My New York clients are dog savvy, so the Ridgy is, for them, going to be perfect. Dobermans, Standard Poodles and Rottweilers are all great breeds but are, once again, left to those with prior dog know-how. Airedales, Briards and Bouvier des Flanders all fall into this category. A good breeder of any of these breeds, and others, may well decline to sell one of his or her pups from their breed, not because you're not a nice person, but rather because you first need a dog or two to gain the experience necessary to handle a pup of their breeding. You should thank them. Getting a dog is not like trying on a pair of shoes. You don't just put one on, see if it fits and, if it fits, purchase. A dog is not a "try on." Do your "trying on" before you buy.

2. Purebred or mixed breed? I have clients who prefer purebreds, and I have others who have had many dogs, none of them purebred. They have always selected their pups from respected shelters, where the chances of acquiring a good purebred are not impossible, but are very limited. If you've decided to get a rescue dog from a shelter, please do as much "homework" as possible before committing.

Remember, it is a long-term commitment. Try to find out any and all background on your dog choice from the rescue service. If he was fostered, what was he like there? There's more to it than purchasing a used car. A car does not have a mind that is open to all sorts of conditioning, both good and bad. And my hat is off to you for deciding to save a rescue.

Some owners look for traits particular to certain breeds. Some enjoy the "always up" demeanor of the West Highland White Terrier (Westie), or the feistiness and independent persona of most of the terrier grouping. There are those who fall in love with the "Hi ya, buddy, hi ya, pal" of the Labrador, as well as his enormous heart and desire when it comes to retrieving. Lots of outdoors folks want the endurance and "Can't tire me out" energy of the German shorthair (not all in the

Sporting group have that energy level). You may gravitate toward the giant but family-oriented and generally docile Newfoundland. I could go on and on; however, I don't pretend to be an expert on all dog breeds. Truth be told, I'm probably not an "expert" on any of them, even though I work with hundreds of them each year.

PLEASE, don't pick a puppy because he/she is cute. All puppies are cute - for a while. Just last week a woman friend of mine told me she had been looking at a minnie Aussie for her six-year-old daughter. I asked why? She answered, "She desperately wants a dog and those are so cute." Now I'm not a big fan for turning pure bred medium or large breeds into small ones. Why? Because I've worked with so many with all kinds of issues. So, I mentioned a Cavalier King Charles Spaniel, an adorable-looking breed with a lovely temperament. She's looking into the breed. While I'm at it, I implore you to think long and hard before running out and purchasing one of the many "Doodles." For example, a Golden Doodle is a whole lot more than a hypo-allergenic, nicely tempered Golden retriever. There's Poodle there as well. I love Standard Poodles; however, they're smart as hell and can be very bossy. I've worked with several hundred various Doodles, the majority had major issues. I suppose now I'm going to need to hire a food taster and car starter. I'm sorry if I've offended anyone. It's simply my experience.

3. Who's going to be responsible for the dog? Having a dog is a large undertaking, requiring considerable responsibility. In my own case Mary, my wife for 46 years, assumed a greater degree of responsibility for my Labs than was her preference. She did it nonetheless, beautifully, with justifiable yet minimal grousing, and a never-ending pure love for all of the dogs.

Getting a puppy for the kids is never a sound basis for a purchase unless the parents understand fully just who is really going to end up with the major responsibility for the pet—one or both parents. More on this in the chapter on children and dogs. Truth be told, Mom, in probably 90% of the situations I'm involved in, the pup's gonna end up your responsibility. And please, don't have hubby Al take the pup to training class while you stay home with the kids. You both should attend. However, if only one can go, then mom should be the one because in so many cases she's the one home with the dog. Having Al train pup means that pup will respond to Al, when he's home; however, when he's at work, why should the quickly growing dog respond to mom? Because you're Al's spouse? Sorry, it doesn't work that way with dogs. Leadership is earned, not passed down by Divine Right.

4. Where are you getting the dog? Most certainly not from a pet shop. Would you buy a diamond from a guy on the corner? Not hardly. You would know nothing about the stone, its quality, where it came from, the number of imperfections, etc. It's the same with a puppy. Is it possible to get a good puppy from a pet shop? Of course it's possible. Is it wise? No. Don't do it.

So, get yourself a book that lists the breeds and both their negative as well as their positive genetic traits. As you know by now, I love the Labrador, but they're not for everyone. There really is no dog that is perfect for every home. That's why they make Fords and Chevies and Dodges.

After you've read a bit about the different breeds and you've whittled it down to, say, a couple, then what? Take in a couple of local American Kennel Club (AKC) dog shows. Look over the full-grown version of both breeds. Talk to the exhibitors; most are wonderful people more than willing to talk up their breed. Just don't bother them when they're busy, and never pet their dog without first asking to do so. Never assume it's okay. Contacting the AKC can also prove helpful. They list breeders in your area.

5. What breed? I've covered this already. Several years ago, while my wife Mary and I were vacationing at a resort on Mexico's Yucatan Peninsula, I struck up a conversation with a gentleman from Wisconsin. After discussing his Green Bay Packers (those cheeseheads really love their team), he told me about his Rottweiler. Great family dog, wonderful with the neighborhood children, a perfect dog is what he called him. On the other hand, I've worked with Rottweilers that ruled the house, whose owners had zero control. Do your homework before you pick a pup. A Rottweiler is not a wise first dog. *The Right Dog For You*, a book authored by Daniel F. Tortora (Simon & Schuster 1980) gives valuable information to the reader interested in choosing a pure bred canine. There were, in the year 1980, 123 separate breeds registered with the American Kennel Club (AKC). I do not know the present number that are registered.

6. Who is the breeder? As I pass over the city of Waterbury it begins to rain. Not hard, just a mild yet steady drizzle, sufficient enough for me to drop my speed by 5 mph. If you look off to your left, you see the most beautiful church, highly visible from I-84. Several times, while passing, I have thought about pulling off and stepping in for a visit, but never have. File under opportunities lost.

Joanne, both a friend and client from many years ago and, I might add, the world's greatest lover of soft-coated Wheaten terriers, rang me up. "Ray," she gushed excitedly into the phone, "you know that Wheaten breeder in Ireland I've been writing to and speaking with? Well, the litter has arrived and she says they're gorgeous. We're thinking seriously of getting one from her. They'll be ready to go in about eight weeks and I'm thinking of flying over to get one of the females. Do you think I'm crazy?"

I simply answered her, "Go for it, Joanne." Well, they went for it, and Tara is, without doubt, the finest example of a Wheaten temperament and look I've ever had the pleasure of working with.

A good puppy begins with good breeding, and good breeding begins with a good breeder! Knowledgeable, responsible breeders get high-quality pups. It's not that they just look good, they've got solid temperaments and good brains to go along with not being hard on the eyes. The breeder of the Rhodesian I'm on my way to see has a marvelous motto on her business card: "Sound Temperament in Sound Bodies." I can always spot one of Ulla's dogs. There is a certain personality about them as well as a great look. So always begin with a good breeder. How do you find one? Ask around, vets, people you know who have one, folks at dog shows, your animal control and rescue officer, and breeders. Lots of breeders. After you've been looking around and asking questions and comparing pedigrees for a month, you will be amazed at how much you've learned about the breed. Make it a fun experience for you. In the end, go with that breeder who "feels right." Intuition, when listened to, is never wrong.

7. Inside or outside dog? Read the chapter on aggression and you will understand better the reasons why. I know there are certain situations that dictate an outside dog. There are, for example, many gun dogs that are kennel dogs. They are true working dogs first, pets second. And they are dearly loved by their owners. Most of those owners are very good "dog people." They're experienced trainers who understand the value and implications of early, proper socialization, and therefore are more than able to keep problems at a minimum.

I saw a husband and wife a while back with a six-month-old Golden retriever. She's a sweet, sensitive dog with a great love for people. When I first saw her she was outside all day long, coming in the house for the evening and then sleeping in the finished basement. When outside she was on an underground electrical fence system with room to run the entire yard. Whenever people came onto the property she would jump all over them. That was the problem they wished for me to resolve. I got them to bring the dog inside, explaining that a dog is a social animal. I also had them keep the dog on the first-floor rooms, whereby she would get used to being around mom, dad, and the children. After that I was able to get their pup to stop jumping on people when they entered the home.

8. Can you afford it? The purchase price is merely a down payment. Vet charges, food, boarding fees, grooming fees, possible day care or professional dog walking service, a quality crate, a good dog bed or two, adequate fencing for the yard (I know breeders who will not place a dog with owners who do not have a satisfactory fence already installed), perhaps a quality dog barrier for the SUV. And good insurance. Oh, how could I forget? Training costs. Not merely puppy school, but a continued program with an experienced trainer as your dog matures.

9. Is it for someone other than yourself? Please, never give a puppy as a gift. It is patently unfair to the dog, to the breeder (who may get it back), as well as to the recipient, who just might not want a dog. I see a lot of this situation—more than you'd think. Are there any exceptions? Perhaps, but very, very few.

10. Are you still certain you want a dog? Okay, you're certain. You've selected the right breeder, or animal shelter with a sterling reputation. Now, how in the world do you pick the RIGHT pup from that bunch of little beasts running around, chewing on and what looks like beating up on one another so it looks to you like they're trying their hardest to kill each other, and the breeder laughing her head off as you stare, wild-eyed, mouth agape, concern plastered all over your face? In many cases, it's best to allow the breeder to pick the pup that's best for you. The breeder knows his or her litter better than anyone. They know each pup and what their temperament will be. And, that good breeder has learned a good deal about you, your lifestyle, as well as your personality. Then again, if the breeder wants you to select, or you're at the shelter, where do you begin?

Temperament Testing

In my last book, *Dog Tales,* I described the test as designed by William Campbell. That initial test has been modified and upgraded. Your breeder may already have had the litter tested. The tests are designed to determine who's a leader, who's a follower, and who's independent, among other traits. Shyness, timidity, and boldness are all traits that are categorized. Remember, however, they are temperament TENDENCY tests, so nothing is cast in stone. In other words, don't bet the farm on one test. And don't you administer the test. Your emotional state, your chi, will affect the outcome. Far better to have someone experienced with testing administer the test.

Picking Your Pup

How to go about it? Do you simply reach in, pick one up, and leave? Well, that's been done in thousands of cases and it may work perfectly. There is, however, a better way to do it. I have done it many times and it has worked well for me.

See how each pup approaches you. I suggest you look for one that approaches in a friendly manner but not the one that immediately jumps all over you and begins to mouth (bite). Also, don't allow your heart to fall out of your shirt and pick out the sad-looking creature huddling in the corner, clearly frightened of you. What you're looking for is a "middle of the road" pup, neither overly excited nor overly timid.

The Right Age to Take Your Pup

I was, for many years, a strong advocate of taking a pup between seven and eight weeks of age, as that is a peak socialization period for a puppy. More recently, the last 10 years or so, I have had reservations about taking a puppy at that age, depending upon the environment to which it is going. Allow me to explain. Providing the environment is not overly hectic or "wound up," then between seven and eight weeks is fine. If, on the other hand, the puppy will be moving into an environment that is high energy, having the puppy remain with the breeder until 10 weeks of age might well make for an easier transfer for the puppy. The breeder, however, must have an environment that provides healthy socialization during this critical time frame (up to 11 weeks). Ulla, my Rhodesian breeder and friend, was telling me about a particular young pup she had in a litter that was just a little too bossy with the others. Kind of like a young bully. He was going on 10 weeks of age. I asked her whom she'd place him with. She told me she had decided to keep him around for another couple of weeks and put him, from time to time, in with a couple of her adult Ridgies. They would set him straight on boundaries and limits, and do it much better than a new owner could do. So when he went to his new home at 12 weeks rather than 10, he would be a bit more mature while also understanding clearly that being a bully was just not a smart thing to be. You can learn a lot about dogs from a wise breeder.

PUPPY DEVELOPMENT: FIRST 12 WEEKS

Neonatal: 1-14 days

Basically, your puppy eats, sleeps, and eliminates. Pup needs his momma most during this period for survival. He can't be taught anything during this time. Around 14 days, the eyes open and the first incidence of avoidance responses can be observed.

Transitional: 14-21 days

Pup still needs mom during this time. He begins to look like a puppy. A lot of internal growth is taking place as well. Permanent separation from mom and litter mates would be disastrous during this period.

Socialization: 22-70 days

From the time you get your pup until he reaches (approximately) 14-15 weeks of age is a critical period of socialization for you and pup. By 12 weeks the bonding should have taken place! That gives you from two to four weeks to establish that. By the time the pup is between 16-17 weeks old, if you follow the guidelines in this book, you will have an adolescent dog well adapted to you, to other dogs, and to other people.

"Okay, Ray," you say. "I'm with you up till now, but I've read that the end of seven weeks (49 days) was the ideal time to take pup home. Now you're telling me that's not necessarily correct. How come you've changed your mind?"

I now believe it simply makes more sense to let the pups live with each other as well as the breeder for a bit longer. However, this belief is based on personal experience and, by the way, I'm not the only voice in the wilderness on this. There are a lot of voices speaking out on this, so I'm not the first by a long shot. But you also need a good breeder, one who's thinking is in line with the 9 or 10-week period rather than the end of seven weeks.

Over the last 15-20 years I have witnessed a virtual explosion in the degree of interspecific dog aggression, dogs fighting dogs. I'm not speaking of the illegal dog fights that, most unfortunately, still exist. I'm speaking about the dog owner walking his dog and when another dog shows up, one or both dogs are ready to have at each other. I believe there are several reasons for this drastic increase, and I do suspect that some of it has to do with puppies leaving their littermates and their mom too early. I've spoken with Ulla-Brett Ekengren, my Rhodesian breeder friend, and she is aware of it as well, but not with her line of dogs. She does, however, feel as I do, that some puppies should not leave the "nest" at seven or eight weeks. Ten weeks is better.

But that's just our opinion.

Picking Up Pup at the Breeder's

A couple of things to ponder before you get to the breeder.

Here's a truism. You're not simply picking up your puppy and taking him to his new home. You're actually dognapping him/her away from the only world it has ever known. You're transporting him to a world he has never before experienced, ripping him away from the safety and comfort of his momma and his littermates. Try to imagine how traumatic that sudden change is. Imagine that happening to you as a child. So, now that you know you're a dognapper, we want to do what we can to make his new home have some connection with his existing one. Contact the breeder ahead of time and purchase a crate similar to what she uses, even though the pup might not ever have been in a crate before. Ask her for a towel that the litter has used for sleeping, so you can take that with you and pup can snuggle on it. You want to let him pee at the breeder's before you start your trip home. Please, allow him to get settled in the car—on the seat next to you is ideal. Or, if you have a passenger, snuggling on that person's lap is great. Pup will be fully weaned so find out from the breeder what she's been feeding him, and find out a week or so before you pick him up in case you need to order it. Of course you will find out how much to feed and what times she presently feeds the pups. Make certain you remember to take your breeder's written instructions with you. If you have young children and bring them with you, be firm with them, making certain that they allow the pup to settle and, hopefully, sleep. Ask the breeder what size collar to get so you have it with you, along with a puppy lead, when you arrive. That way, if the ride home is long, you can safely stop for a pee call on the way.

Upon your arrival home, take pup to the area (previously selected) where you want him to eliminate. Make certain you bring him there before you bring him inside! Put him down, say nothing until he begins to pee, poop, whatever. While he's going, repeat quietly, "Do it, do it, do it." As soon as he finishes, praise him quietly and then bring him inside.

As difficult as it is, resist the temptation to have extended family, friends, neighbors, the bowling and bridge clubs, golfing, fishing, and hunting buddies, the mayor, governor, and the entire state legislature present for the homecoming. Simply let pup settle. There will be plenty of time for everybody to come over and "ooh" and "ah" over the newest family member. Oh, when they do come over, why not do as I do. Place a sign on both the front and side door which says, "Please ignore the puppy, including eye contact, for 5 minutes." I'm a bear about this and will threaten anyone who disobeys with immediate expulsion from the house. I do this for one simple reason: I never want my dogs to make a big deal out of people coming and going. And, as a result, I have never owned a Labrador that jumped on people. When they do pay attention, make certain that they remain calm, speaking in a normal, pleasant voice tone. Baby talk should not be tolerated, nor should a high-pitch voice. Those things simply wind pup up, then he gets all excited and pees on the floor, whereupon everyone present laughs. Pup thinks, "Gee, I guess peeing on the floor was a winner." So use common sense. When he tires let him pick a spot (usually under a table or chair), or simply pick him up and place him in his crate. One more thing. Please no "treats" at this time. When he does get a treat, make it a piece of his dog food; that way you're minimizing the chances of the treat disagreeing with his digestive system. Once again, use common sense.

The Value of Touch

This is something women intrinsically understand. God love them. Guys, you need to learn that as well. A bit of confessing here. I had a very hard time understanding the importance of touch, as it was pretty foreign and therefore, uncomfortable for me. I'm pretty good now. Study after study has demonstrated how proper touch both strengthens the bonding process and helps to lay the foundation for a mutually trusting relationship. Periodically, pick pup up and hold him against your chest so he can hear and feel your heartbeat. That beat should be both calm and slow. With your head right next to his, stroke him and tell him in a quiet, low voice how glad you are that he has come to live with you.

The First Night

My pup's crate is in my bedroom. For the first four weeks that is where my puppies have always slept. Usually the first few nights, pup will wake you up around 1:00 a.m., 3:00 a.m., and yep, 5:00 a.m. When he cries, take him out immediately. After he goes, put him back in his crate. If he cries after going back in, I strongly suggest you ignore it. Respond ONLY when he cries to go out because he really needs to. It's a good thing to discuss this with your breeder as she can give you a good picture of his bathroom needs. Pretty soon he'll sleep from 10:00 or 11:00 until 5:00 or so. Usually the three o'clock wakeup is the first one that he begins sleeping through. Then the one o'clock. After four weeks, I remove his towel from his crate and put it at the foot of my bed, on the floor. I attach a 30" groomer tub choker (mentioned previously) to the leg of the bed. Snap it onto pup's collar and let him begin to sleep right there. Within another three to four weeks, you will be able to get ready for bed, and pup will, on his own, snuggle on his towel without being hooked up. He can sleep there for the remainder of his life with you. Pretty neat, huh?

Getting a Head Start: Learning to Learn

Well, we've got pup through the first couple of days and nights.

He got you up a couple of times, but he peed after you carried him outside, and he was good in the crate when you brought him back inside. You're following my chapter on house-training, and he did okay the second day. It's now Sunday morning (remember you brought him home on Friday), so let's begin to help him learn to Sit when you ask him to. He already knows how to sit; he's been sitting since he was a few weeks old. He just hasn't learned to associate the cue, "Sit," with the action.

There are a few simple, yet critical, standards for helping pup to learn.

First, teach with love for him. Please, never forget that. Second, teach with patience, understanding, and quiet confidence. After all, you know he's gonna get it. Third, you cannot teach what you don't know. My role is to impart to you some of what I've learned in the past

50 years of working with dogs and their owners. Knowledge inspires confidence, and training with confidence is pivotal. Lastly, never allow frustration or agitation to become involved in the learning process. Both are simply low-level anger, and anger is always counterproductive to the learning process as well as to the heart of the very relationship itself. So be very careful here; you don't want to end up with an insecure dog. Over the next seven weeks you and pup are going to learn a lot together.

You will need a notebook listing short-term (tactical) goals as well as long-term (strategic) goals.

Examples of tactical goals:

Learning to Sit when asked, as well as Stay, Down, lying quietly next to you, and being brushed.

Examples of strategic goals:

House-training, learning to Heel (walking next to you with a slack lead), Here (coming when called), responding to tasks when distracted.

Got the idea? With a puppy your tactical goals will outnumber strategic ones. It doesn't mean we won't be working on some of those early on, it simply means that strategic goals require a longer time to achieve.

Your puppy is a what I call a self-directed animal, a free spirit. Given his choice he would prefer to do what he wishes when he wishes, rather than considering your wants or needs. He needs to learn how to learn from you. This is what the head start program is all about. During the next seven weeks you will help pup learn the fundamentals: Coming when you call him; Heeling (walking properly beside you). He will learn also the fun of proper socializing with both people and dogs. He will learn to not be "mouthy," that is to not puppy-bite your hands, trousers, the sash on a robe. He (and you) will learn my relaxation technique.

Allow me to pass on a few additional suggestions. When working with your pup, don't raise your voice, not unless you want him to learn to ignore you when you speak to him in a normal tone. The tone of your voice is merely a vocal expression of your emotional state. Yelling, for example, is nothing more than your frustration, and means that you haven't helped your pup to learn with you using a normal, but firm, voice. So, keep the lessons fun for that puppy of yours. And keep lessons short, a couple of minutes at the most for starters, closer to a single minute is even better. Short, multiple sessions with a pup are always better than one long session. And, if you've had a bad day at the office, forget the training altogether. The entire day may well wind up coming down on pup's head. There is an ugly saying that goes like this: The boss yells at you. You yell at your wife. Your wife yells at the kid. The kid kicks the dog.

Week One: Helping Pup Learn Sit

Okay, time to wake up pup; we've got a game to play. It's called Sit.

Make certain that you are standing on a carpet rather than a slippery bare floor. Get down on one knee, holding three or four pieces of pup's dog food in either hand, not both. Extend your hand so pup can smell the food. Now bring your hand back toward you and hold the food between your thumb and forefinger. When he's close and your food bit is just in front of his nose, slooooowly raise your hand slightly above his head, keeping the food right at his nose. Now move the food a little above his head and backwards, so his head now is looking at the ceiling. Because his neck is stretched and it is a tad uncomfortable, it is natural for pup to sit. As soon as he does, reward with the food and praise him. Then repeat it two or three times and quit. It is not necessary to use the Sit word at this time. Later in the day, before feeding time, repeat the exercise. By the tenth repetition, begin to say "Sit" immediately prior to raising your hand. Take your time with this method. Three or four reps are enough per session. You can do three per day. By the end of the second day, providing all is going well, change your body position.

Stand but bend over so that your food fingers are at pup's nose level. Now say "Sit" and slowly bring your hand up to your belt level. Pup should understand the game well enough to sit for you. By the fifth day you should be able to give the cue "Sit" and bring your hand up to your chest and pup should sit. Move your hand up as though you were zipping up your jacket. Keep your hand moving up your clothes, don't wave it out in front of you.

Congratulations. It's the end of the week and when pup is standing in front of you and you say "Sit" and bring your hand to your chest, pup does two things: A) he sits and B) he sits with his head up looking at you. You have his focus along with his sitting, and proper focus is the initial element in learning.

Week Two: Walking on the Lead Next to You and Whistle Work

So you and pup have survived the first week together. You're getting to know one another. He's still getting you up at all hours of the night, or maybe he's going through half the night on his own. You've read my chapter on house-training so you're able to understand and stay ahead of things. And pup's sitting has come along really well. So expand his sitting so that you're bringing it into your daily lifestyle. Periodically throughout the day, ask him to sit. Remember, it's not a command, but rather a task. Each time he completes the task, he feels a bit more self-confident, but also begins looking up to you a little bit more as his leader.

So now it's time to add to the games. This week we're going to add heeling and have some fun with a whistle. Of all the basic tasks that pup will need to learn, the two most important ones are, in my philosophy, heeling first, and coming when called second. We'll begin with helping pup learn first the concept of heeling, walking next to you.

For this exercise you will need a 6-ft puppy lead (leash) and a simple buckle puppy collar, plus 50 pounds of dog food (just kidding). The only other requirement is a container of patience pills for you.

To begin, you must decide which side you will want him to walk, by your left side or your right. Most right-handed dog people prefer to heel their dog by their left side, leaving their right hand free to carry a package, unlock a door, etc. If you hunt and shoot right-handed, then you most assuredly will want your dog to heel by your left, your off-gun, side.

Which side did you select, the left side? Good choice; let's begin. First, pup's already used to a collar since either you or your breeder got him used to wearing one. If he hasn't had a collar on him yet, let him wear it for a couple of days prior to beginning the heeling game. Good, your pup's been wearing his collar for several days already. So, hook up the lead to it and bring pup outside to your driveway, unless you have a long hallway, say 20 feet. Starting heeling on grass is more difficult for pup because the grass holds scent much better than concrete or asphalt.

A long hallway is, usually, ideal. You want an area with little to no distractions. Hold the lead in your right hand with some slack. Bring your left hand down to pup's nose so he knows you've got some dog food. You did remember to bring several pieces of his dog food, right? I thought so. See? You already have his focus. With some slack in the lead, and your left hand down by pup's nose (I know it's uncomfortable for you but it's short term), tell him "Heel" and step off with your left foot, wiggling your fingers in front of pup's nose to hold his attention. Talk in an upbeat manner as you walk along with your left hand right next to the seam in your jeans. Don't let that hand get ahead of the seam. After 30-40 feet, stop and give him a piece of food. He does not have to sit at this time. After a bit of praise, start off again with "Heel," repeating this exercise. Gradually, increase the distance between stops, giving him a bit of food every 25 feet or so. Remember, you need to keep his attention on you. I'd do this exercise for five minutes (before your back gives out) and end it. Do two or possibly three sessions daily, before he eats. Little by little, extend the distance, periodically rewarding the correct position with the food. After several short sessions you should be able to walk in a more comfortable position while pup maintains his focus on you. When you take him out to pee/poop or for a walk around the block, do not expect him to heel. Instead, tell him "Break" as you start walking. Eventually he will understand that hearing the break word means he does not need to walk next to you. Remember, when heeling, no tension on the lead! Pretty soon you will be walking him on the sidewalk with him heeling next to you. Now begin making 180-degree right turns, turning away from the dog. When he turns with you, praise and give pup a piece of food. In a few days, when the right turn is working well, begin making left turns, moving into him rather than away from him.

This is phase 1 of heeling. Phase 2 begins three weeks from now. Incidentally, when you're heeling pup, tell him "Heel" only when you start from a stop. Do not keep saying "Heel, heel" as you and pup walk along.

Whistle Work - Coming When Called the Easy Way

I use the word "Here" rather than the commonly used word, "Come." Come, to me, is a dead-sounding word. Delmar Smith, one of the truly great dogmen and upland field trainer, believed that the word "Here" simply carried better phonetically. I believe Delmar was correct. So, before you begin, you're gonna need a good dog whistle. I'm not speaking of the kind humans can't hear. I'm speaking about a good, solid-sounding whistle, one that carries in high winds, at long distances through leafy trees, and is easy to blow. The small British-made Acme Thunderer is still a solid choice. So is the Roy Gonia Special, which I prefer. You can go online to Lion Country Supply (lc-supply.com) and purchase either whistle. You will also need a package or two of good old American cheese, which I want you to cut up into pieces about the size of a dime.

Okay, you have your whistle and three pieces of the cut-up cheese. And pup is with you as well.

Whistle Work Phase 1

For three consecutive days, twice daily, I want you to execute the following. With pup in front of you, do the following exactly as I say. Trill (3 quick toots) the whistle quietly, not so loud you scare pup, and immediately give one piece of cheese to pup and much praise. Wait 20 seconds and repeat. Then wait another 20 seconds and repeat. I don't want pup coming to you as he's already there. I simply want him to begin associating the sound of the whistle with cheese. Perform this simple exercise for three consecutive days. So you're giving pup a total of 18 pieces of cheese over the three-day period.

Whistle Work Phase 2

Beginning on the fourth day, and from then on, do the following. Begin at some distance, 8 or 10 feet from pup is fine. Say nothing to pup, just squat down, making certain you are in pup's line of sight, trill the whistle and, when pup comes to you, give him the cheese and a ton of praise. Do this ONCE in the morning and ONCE in the evening. Do not call pup with the whistle more than twice daily. That works out to two pieces of cheese a day. Do all the training inside the house. As this game begins to become exciting to pup, perhaps after a week or ten days, begin making this a hide-and-seek game with him. You hide, he seeks. Make it simple in the beginning, perhaps hiding behind a sofa a mere 10-15 feet from pup. Eventually expand it to hiding in your office downstairs, hiding in another room. Puppies love this game and what you're really teaching pup is to drop everything whenever he hears the trilling whistle, and come a-runnin' to ya. He should never know when he's going to be called. That's why I want the cheese pre-cut and in the fridge. Also, never have pup associate whistle work with the refrigerator door opening. Do the game that way and in three days you'll have a pup come running every time that door opens. So here's how I avoid that. If I plan on calling him at 7:00 p.m., I go to the fridge at 6:15, remove a piece of cheese and place it on the stove or on the back of a counter away from the fridge, and then leave. At 7:00 I quietly return and remove the piece of cheese and quietly go to where I'm planning on calling him. With pup settled, I trill the whistle. Pup jumps up and begins searching for me. When he finds me I reward him and give tons of praise. If he has trouble locating me, I'll trill again. This is a tons-of-fun game for both pup and you. Most dog owners also want their dogs to come to a word, a verbal cue. So, after three weeks do it this way: Trill the whistle and follow immediately with the word "Here." Do that for one week. The following week, reverse the order. Call "Here" and follow immediately with the whistle. After that, some of both, with much more emphasis on the verbal rather than the whistle. Never overuse the whistle.

Week Four: Down, Stay, Dealing with Puppy Mouthiness

Begin helping pup learn Down with the following steps:

1. Get down on your right knee.

2. Holding a food reinforcement in your right hand, direct pup around until he is in front of you, but not facing you. You want him so that when you look at him you're looking at his right side, so he's 90 degrees to you, facing straight ahead.

3. Tell pup "Sit" and give slight praise when he responds.

4. Hold the food at pup's nose, say "Down" and bring your right hand down sloooowly in a vertical line to the floor. Hold it there.

5. If pup begins to follow your hand to lie down and he goes down toward the floor, quietly slide your right hand forward about six inches. This helps pup to stretch out comfortably as he completes the Down. Praise him and give him the food.

6. Repeat this exercise three or four times, then end the session.

7. Remember, always release using the word "Break."

Teaching "Stay"

Helping pup learn stay is quite easy; after all, he doesn't need to do anything—just stay where he is. I find that teaching stay is easier if you begin following the down task. So stand in front of pup and tell him "Down" and from a standing position bring your right hand (with food in it) straight down to the floor. As soon as pup completes the down, raise both hands, palms extending toward pup. Your hands should be at (your) face level.

As your palms go out slightly toward pup, tell him "Stay," and take one step back. As you step back, move your palms in a circular motion to help pup right there. Now return to your pup's right side, turn so you're facing forward just like pup, then reach down and give the food and praise him. What? You forgot the food. Come on people, let's get with the program.

Once pup begins to grasp this concept, it's a good idea to wait three seconds before giving him the praise and food reward. This helps to "Steady" pup to the position. Hey, he just got up and walked away. You forgot to use the "Break" word as his release. Repeat this simple exercise two or three more times, then end it.

If he breaks prematurely, say nothing. Simply bring him back to the same spot and repeat the exercise. Remember, never get frustrated if pup is having a bit of trouble here. It will come very shortly. Your pup will learn faster not by being corrected, but rather by being praised and rewarded for doing it correctly. Remember, your pup has a short attention span, just like a young child.

Puppy Mouthiness

Almost all puppies get mouthy with their owners; it's what pups do. Remember though, puppies don't do that with their moms. She will let them know quickly and firmly that you don't bite mom. This is what I do. When pup gets mouthy with me, I simply press down on pup's tongue, not hard, with the finger that's in pup's mouth. I do this matter-of-factly without saying a word. I simply press down, firmly, not hard. Pup will pull his head back to spit out your finger. Then I begin to pat pup again and, if he gets mouthy, I simply press down on the tongue. Just use enough pressure so it's uncomfortable for pup. It should take but a short time for pup to decide that's not what I want to do. Because you're not saying anything, it becomes pup's decision to stop the biting. Never praise after pup releases!!! You don't want to reward the mouthiness do you? Didn't think so. If you have a difficult time with this technique, then forget it. As an alternative, have a hard Nylabone always with you. When he grabs your finger, give him the Nylabone instead. It's called trade-off.

Week Five: Getting Things Right

This week is all about simply reinforcing all the previously acquired tasks. Let's say you're at the stove reducing the risotto. You look and pup is about five feet from you. Turn to him, raise your hand saying, "Sit." When he sits, give him a little praise, but no food. Then give him the break word. Later, after dinner, you're sitting in front of the television watching your favorite team or you're reading a book, and pup's nearby. Give him a down. Then give a stay and walk to the TV and then come back and sit down. Give pup quiet praise and the break word. I also want you to begin getting a bit more leader-like with heeling. Check back to Chapter 5 and the section on heeling to sharpen pup's heeling work.

Week Six

Pup should be getting lots and lots of good socializing. You should be taking him into town on heeling walks, and giving him a chance to be praised and petted and told "what a beautiful puppy" he is. Trust me, you cannot over-socialize pup at this time. He should love everybody. Incidentally, a simple yet effective way to prevent pup's jumping on people in these situations is the following. When someone approaches, asking if they can pet your pup, tell him or her, "By all means." While they are approaching, stop and put your foot on the lead, loose unless he starts to jump. The lead should be short enough so that if he begins to jump, it will prevent him from jumping, yet long enough so that when he's sitting, there is slack in the lead. As pup gets calmer with these meetings, begin having him Sit prior to being petted, but keep the lead under the shoe, just in case. I always brought my Labs, when they were pups, to Cambridge, a large city across the Charles River from Boston, and home to such distinguished universities as Harvard, MIT, Vassar, and a number of others. I would take my pup into the local small bookstores and place my foot on the lead, then tell him "Down." Pretty soon he would become very used to browsers stepping over him, petting him, as well as those who chose to ignore him. I must say we have always been treated very nicely in these stores, even though they most probably had regulations regarding dogs.

Of course you're not even thinking of roughhousing or, heaven forbid, playing tug games with that pup of yours. I once caught my daughter Kristen's fiancé just beginning to play tug with Kitt, one of my wonderful, field trial Labs.

I gave him the "Dutch Uncle" talk and that never happened again. Those games can encourage as well as condition aggressive behavior. Some years later they divorced, though I doubt very much it had anything to do with the tug-game incident.

For many years, to help teach my Lab pups retrieving, I used a short nap, white paint roller as a retrieving dummy.

It resembles the white larger plastic or canvas dummies for older dogs but the paint roller weighs practically nothing, so it's very easy for the dog to pick up and retrieve. The paint roller is not a toy, something to leave around for pup to chew on. My pups all learned to chew

either the original ham-flavored Nylabone or the newer chicken fla-
vored one. Both are very hard and will last for several months. They
also have a Kong toy. I do not give them rawhide, pigs ears, feet, any
of that stuff. I would go along with the new deer sheds if you wish, but
they're expensive.

Another thing I do is that I make certain pup is used to my placing
my hand in his dog food bowl while he's eating. I do this by holding
out some of his dry dog food, and when he is almost finished, I reach
into his bowl and deposit the last bit of food. My hand then becomes
the dispenser of good things into his bowl.

My puppies play with other dogs at this age, provided the other
dogs are not aggressive toward puppies in an angry way. If they are
overly rough, that is not a good thing.

Something else I should pass along that I have done with my own
pups for many years and that is to introduce them to the house early
on. The best way to do this is to put a lead and buckle collar on pup
and bring him into a room. Sit in a chair with the lead under your foot,
short enough so that pup is comfortable lying down. A good time to
do this is when he is tired, probably like you are, later in the evening.
Have him lie there while you watch television, read a book, play the
guitar. The next evening pick another room. You might have him like
this from 30 to 60 minutes. Later on, when he is accustomed to those
rooms as being yours, he is far less likely to pee or poop in them. Then
you can begin letting him in there with you without the lead.

The importance of crating should be clearly understood. If your
pup is introduced to it properly and at an early age, he'll adapt to it
nicely. I have encountered a very few clients' pups who simply could
not adapt to a crate. This is a rarity. Not only should the crate be used
at night, preferably in the master bedroom, but it can be used during
the day for short periods for sleeping, or those times when he gets
totally out of control with excitability bursts. Do not, in the latter case,
put pup in the crate to punish him. If you simply pick him up, saying
nothing, and put him in the crate, he will never associate it with pun-

ishment. If, however, when you pick him up you say, "Bad dog," and then crate him, you've just punished him. Don't do it; you will regret it later on. The value of crate training also comes into play when your dog is an adult and must be kept quiet at home after having had some surgery. Crating for long periods is, however, not ideal when they're young, since it can contribute to hyperactivity, simply because the puppy has no way to release his energy.

Many complaints I get from clients relate to puppies interfering with breakfast or dinnertime for the owners. Here's what you can do when eating your breakfast bowl of steel cut oatmeal or your baked salmon for dinner and pup is a pest. Many groomers, above their bathing tubs, rig what is called a Tub Choker. It is simply a short (30-36 in.) steel cable encased in a plastic sleeve. He can chew on it but cannot chew through it. The line has a conventional snap at one end and a ring at the other. The ring is large enough to slip through the snap, creating a loop. This loop can be looped around a chair leg, table leg, etc. Simply bring pup to wherever you want him when you eat, although he should, ideally, be in the same room. Then simply hook him to the line and enjoy your dinner. You can leave a blanket or pup's bed for him to lie on. End of problem.

One last thing, once he's hooked up, ignore him completely. If he whines like a three-year-old child pulling a tantrum, please don't reward it by talking to pup, telling him everything is all right. That becomes his "Place" for every meal. Pretty soon he'll adapt to it nicely. Later, when he's an adult and your friends come over for dinner, place pup's bed or towel in the room, tell him "Place," and he'll go over and lie down and sleep. Your friends will ooh and ah, thinking you're the best trainer of dogs. One last point that I almost forgot to tell you. I introduce pup to the groomer's tub choker while sitting in my TV room. I snap in to my pup's collar and place my foot on the line. I make it short enough so pup's head is pulled toward the floor by 2-3 inches. After a while pup will lie down, which releases the slight pressure on his neck. After he lies down I quietly give him a couple of pats. I have him lie there for, perhaps, 30 minutes. After a few evenings of this my pup chooses to lie on the floor next to me, comfortably, wearing the line. Then I simply begin hooking him up where we eat. The line is portable so you can move it to wherever you wish your pup to be. They are a wonderfully helpful tool.

Week Seven

As the weeks go by, your pup will have increasing control of his bladder and, therefore, you should adjust his going-out schedule based on this. You should change your schedule as well. Leave him at times without feeling pangs of guilt. Never make a big deal out of coming and going. That's a great way to wind up with a separation-anxious animal. In fact, I completely ignore my Labs when I return. I never want them to think it's a big deal.

When you enter the house, greet everyone first. Only then acknowledge the dog. As soon as he learns sit, after he calms down on your return, have him sit before you pet him. In that way, it reinforces the no jump in the dog. None of my Labs has ever jumped on people—that is a simple fact. So, by the seventh week you and pup should have accomplished the following:

House-training: Pup should be well on his way, if not perfect, to minding his manners by eliminating outside only.

Tasking: Pup should be doing well on sit, stay, here, heel, whistle work. Not perfect, but darn good.

Limits: Pup should be past his being mouthy.

Play: Pup should be chewing his Nylabone, playing with his Kong and, if a retrieving dog, retrieving the paint roller.

Integration: Pup should now be a solid part of his family; familiar with the entire house; and a gentleman during mealtimes, lying quietly while the family eats.

Exercise: Pup should be going on longer walks and should be getting off-lead runs in a big field.

After 7 weeks

Remember I mentioned that when your dog becomes six months of age, he's no longer a puppy, but rather an adolescent. Around about four months, a few pups will go through a short-term shyness. Pups who were outgoing may now exhibit shyness. Don't panic if you see this. In a couple of weeks, if you pay it no mind, it will disappear. Just ride it through. Next thing you'll see is a four-legged teen.

Your major concern during this time should be that you continue to earn your leadership with pup. You need to be incorporating structuring (setting boundaries and limits) into your daily activities with your pup in a variety of ways. Here's how, for example, I recall working with Jake, one of my black Labs, when he was five months of age. I was building structure in small doses through such simple activities as my going out the door first, helping him learn to "Load up" into my truck, retrieving drills, and good exercise both with and without other dogs.

I began this way. Standing in the kitchen I'd call, "Jake, here." When he arrived, I'd tell him sit and I'd put on his slip lead. We'd walk to the door and I'd tell him "Sit" and then "Wait" (most prefer to use "Stay"). I'd open the door and step outside. I'd tell him "Break" and then he'd come through the door. Sometimes I'd say "Heel" just to keep him thinking. When we'd "Heel" to my truck I'd have him "Sit" and open the door. I'd tell him "Load up" and he'd jump into the truck and into his crate. I'd drive to a nearby field and when I arrived I'd open the door of his crate, and put his lead on. Jake would wait until I said "Break," at which time he'd jump out of the truck. Then we'd heel into the field together. I'd remove his lead and we'd heel another 40-50 feet into the field. Then, and only then would I tell him "Break" and off he'd run. The reason I didn't release Jake when I removed his lead at the edge of the field was simply because I never wanted him to get the idea that when the lead came off he was free. Many ignorant dog owners do this and, once learned, it then needs to be unlearned. Never allow your dog to do something at five months that is not going to be acceptable later on.

Does this simple schedule sound overly rigid? I assure you it's not. Your pup is fully capable of doing all this at five months of age. I'm merely doing what pretty much every owner does when he takes his or her dog for a walk. The difference is I'm adding some structure into the routine—very important structure. And it doesn't take any longer for me to give my pup his run than that other fellow whose young dog runs the show. It's not difficult to do it my way, it just requires both you and pup getting into that routine. The more you do it, the easier it becomes. Continue to exercise your pup every day. Consult with your vet and breeder as to the correct amount. They both will, probably, tend to be more cautious with you as to the proper amount. Jake got a minimum of 30 minutes every morning—rain, sleet, snow, or sun— and I took him before breakfast. Remember, never feed your dog and take him for exercise soon after he eats. It may make him sick—dangerously sick! Far more seriously, he could get "stomach torsion," a life-threatening condition caused by the stomach twisting inside the stomach wall. Ask your vet to explain this condition to you. Probably thousands of dogs die from this condition annually.

During the four to five-month period, you have a wonderful opportunity to introduce your young dog to the real world, the world in which you live. This is vital to your dog's development because he needs to learn that the world can be a friendly and interesting place. This reduces the possibility of aggression problems that occur when dogs think the world is a hostile place, and it is the owner's responsibility to ensure that that does not happen. At the same time, it helps you develop control with your dog in an increasing variety of situations. So let him meet everyone and go everywhere.

Well, I've just exited off I-84 and I have about 10 minutes before I get to my client's home. I hope that my thoughts have been helpful to you and your pup, or your future pup. My program's been working for both me and thousands of my clients. Please remember, establish mutual trust and respect early, and never lose it. And keep the training upbeat, quietly firm, and fun for the both of you. Pup's little brain is like a sponge, so help it to soak up a whole bunch of "the right stuff."

Chapter 13

Kids, Throwaways, And The End Of The Path

Notice the smallest change and the slightest try and reward him.
~RAY HUNT, HORSEMAN

"*R*ay, the temperature has been hovering around 108 degrees for the past week. It's so hot the dogs aren't even venturing out of the shade because the sand will literally burn their paw pads. I don't know how we'll be able to get any training in."

"We'll get it in, Sherry," I answered, "if we have to work dogs late in the evening and early morning. Don't worry, we'll get the work done." I hung up the phone, my mind unsettled. Sherry was right, I reasoned. There's absolutely no way we could work with the dogs under those conditions. It would be inhumane to do so.

So there I was, sitting at my kitchen table in Westwood, Massachusetts, some 14 years ago, staring at an airline ticket for Las Vegas, more than 2,000 miles away. From there I would make the roughly three-and-a-half-hour drive to Kanab, Utah, to the Best

Friends Animal Sanctuary in triple-digit temperatures! Well, it was out of my hands. It was in His hands now. If He wanted me working with the dogs nobody wanted, He'd sorta have to reroute a few highs and lows on the national weather map.

Two days later, my compact rental car was humming along northeast out of Vegas on Interstate 15. It was a little after eleven in the morning and the voice on the radio proclaimed the temperature to be 105. Between Vegas and St. George, signs were posted on the interstate that read, "Turn off Air Conditioners." Though the message made perfect sense, the AC would make my car's engine run hotter; it would have taken a gun to my head to make me shut it off. I passed several disabled and abandoned automobiles before I picked up Route 59 in Hurricane, Utah. It was mid-afternoon by the time I pulled onto the side road marking the entrance to Best Friends, my car creating a massive dust cloud behind me.

Best Friends is located just outside Kanab, a small town in southern Utah in beautiful, big-canyon country. In fact, the sanctuary is located in Angel Canyon. My late wife Mary accompanied me on my first trip out there, describing the area as "absolutely breathtaking." Of course it was wonderful to see the great staff again, friends this time around. The heat, though, was overwhelming. Even a short walk left me drenched in sweat. Needless to say, we did no hands-on dog work that afternoon. Later that evening in my motel room, I prayed for a break in the weather. If the weather held, the trip would a complete disaster for me.

The following morning the weather had indeed broken. In fact, during the rest of my five-day stay, the weather remained in the low to mid-nineties, allowing us to have two dog sessions per day. It was such fun to once again greet some of my dog friends. Pancho was still shy, but had made significant progress since my first trip in March. Forest, the big hound, continued to be a handful but he had improved as well. There was Max, the Great Dane, a lifer at Best Friends and a fellow Buckeye from Cleveland. Whitney, the runaway, the big yellow Lab I loved working with, had been adopted, as had Maryanne, a reformed screaming biter who had settled down with an architect somewhere in Alaska—dogs adopted by wonderful people who want to do their part to relieve suffering by giving a dog a second chance. Even as I write this, images of Angel Canyon, the staff, and the four-legged residents fill my mind.

Five hundred and fifty. That's how many dogs on average call Best Friends home. One writer called Best Friends, "A Last Resort for the Unwanted and the Unforgiven." Between dogs, cats, birds, and horses, the big canyon is home to somewhere around 1,500 animals, the vast majority of them simply "throwaways." The great news is that Best Friends places well over 85% of the animals they take in. There are saints working there. Faith Maloney, the former director, was a saint.

So were the trainers with whom I worked. Sherry and Jana, both gifted trainers, have moved on, but I remember them so well. Others, whose names I cannot recall, were equally gifted dog people. Vacation there next year and volunteer your services for a few days or longer. You will then know firsthand of what I speak. Or visit a local shelter; they employ saints as well. There's something seriously wrong with a society which feels free to dispose of pets like empty bottles tossed along the roadside. We kill well over a million dogs annually, the majority for behavioral issues! Yet puppy mills continue to crank out thousands upon thousands of puppies, many of them purchased and brought home on impulse only. Six months later, after the novelty has worn off and the reality of the responsibility of a maturing dog sets in, the dog is tossed away.

Easy come, easy go. Even purebreds now have rescue clubs in all the states. Those clubs are run by volunteers. They love their particular breed and do their utmost to find suitable homes for dogs taken in from owners who either no longer want the animal or, for some more legitimate reason, divorce for example, can no longer keep the dog. These are truly wonderful dogs that simply ask for a second chance at life.

So you say a purebred isn't for you, but you still want a dog. You want to save a shelter dog. Or perhaps you'd like an older, mature purebred, so you're going to one of the purebred rescue clubs. What a wonderful gift you will be giving that dog, taking him or her home to live with you, giving it a second chance! Before you do, however, might I offer a few suggestions?

First, be completely honest in your conversation with the shelter people. They're there to help you select the right dog for both you as well as your environment. They want to know a few things about you, you see, because they don't want that dog coming back. Why? Because it's brutally unfair to the dog. They hate recidivism with their dogs. So they'll be brutally honest with you.

Second, NEVER FEEL SORRY FOR A DOG. What's in the past is in the past. If Ace has had a tough past, there is nothing you can do to change that, so don't try. By giving him a good home you're already giving him more than he's ever had. Feeling sorry for the dog is dangerous. It flies in the face of a proper relationship. So don't just cuddle and talk baby talk to him. Love him! There are many dogs I work with that are badly troubled. I have a lot of empathy for those dogs; however, I cannot allow myself to have sympathy for them. Why? Simply because if I do then I cannot do my job. I cannot help the dog. The dog doesn't need or want sympathy. What he needs and wants is a compassionate leader. Loving him involves helping him to learn boundaries and limits. Within 48 hours begin helping him to learn how to heel. Heeling is the most critical task he needs to learn. Later on follow with the other basic structures. Establish the leader/follower role early. Remember this, it is impossible to feel sympathetic and to be quietly firm at the same time.

Third, help him to understand that he need not take on a lot of responsibility—that's your job. And it's a critical job. And it may be difficult for you. But you will find that it's well worth all the work. Learn the virtue of Quiet Firmness together.

Fourth, be fair to your dog. Don't begin the relationship by yelling or scolding him. In fact, never yell at him. If he pees in the kitchen, say nothing, simply clean it up quietly. Establish a secure relationship based upon mutual trust and respect, remember? We talked about that earlier in the book.

Fifth, don't spoil the dog. If you spoil him and you end up with a monster, look in the mirror. Blame the person looking back at you. I've worked with literally thousands of shelter dogs, rescue dogs, former racing dogs, abused dogs. The vast majority of them have, in time, worked out well. Notice I said in time. It may take quite a bit of time; however, it will, down the road, be well worth it. Adopted dogs make some of the finest companion dogs. They are so grateful for having been given that second chance—provided you establish a proper relationship as early as possible. I believe it's best to think of your new dog as an adolescent foster child. When that child is placed with foster parents, he or she needs two things from the outset—affection and positive discipline. Notice I didn't say love. Love is both affection and positive discipline. Let the dog know precisely where he is in the pecking order. He'll then become a much better companion for you. I know whereof I speak. This has been my life's work for five decades. Be restrained in your corrections during the first month or your dog will wish he was back at the shelter. That initial month is for you to begin setting small positive boundaries and limits, like working on heeling.

Sixth, the three watchwords are patience, patience and, oh yeah, patience.

Seventh, remember that the first month with your new dog is crucial for your relationship. Zak may be quite calm or subdued during this time frame, since he's adapting to a strangely new environment and making an assessment of his new owner(s). He's learning whether you're a leader, a pushover, or merely an overindulgent attendant. Within a month's time, the dog's real personality will emerge, so don't be shocked when you see this change; it's simply nature taking its course. Just keep tasking and setting limits, lovingly. Be certain to involve the family in this endeavor so he won't end up thinking he's second-in-command. I see that a lot.

Eighth, within one week after you bring Ace home you should schedule an appointment with a veterinarian. His or her examination may provide you with medical explanations for any problems you've observed. Your vet can also set up a proper exercise regimen as well as a proper diet.

Ninth, please give him a chance. If you find he's not perfect within the first 24 hours, please don't return him. Contact a Damn Good trainer or a behavioral therapist (who should also be a very good trainer) and get your new pet evaluated. If the evaluation is positive, then make a commitment to your dog that you will work toward building mutual trust and respect. You owe that to the both of you. Many of the finest dogs I have worked with were former shelter dogs. It's a special person who gives a second chance to one of these dogs, and I have the greatest respect for such people.

Best Friends is easy to find—just look for the angels.

Dogs and Children

Webster already had a few years behind him when baby Patrick arrived. Webster was an Irish Setter/Golden retriever mix, and he had always been a wonderful people dog, though I doubt I'd feel comfortable breaking into his home to walk off with the family jewelry. Patrick's mom, Robin, had endured a difficult delivery and afterwards her doctor told her she needed lots of rest and to get some help with the newborn. Patrick's new grandmother lived down in Augusta, Georgia, and as soon as she heard the news about her daughter requiring help with the newborn, that was all she needed to catch the next plane bound for Boston's Logan International Airport.

Not being much of a dog person, Grandma had heard all the stories about vicious canines murdering and even cannibalizing infants, virtually snatching them out of their bassinets while they slept. No mongrel mutt dog was going to do harm to her little Patrick, by god, not if she had any say in the matter. So, Grandma put a plan into action. Whenever Patrick was up being fed, Webster was sent out to the backyard. Later, after Patrick was fed and changed, read to and eventually put back to sleep, only then was Webster permitted to reenter his homestead.

Two weeks later I was called to be part of a family consult concerning Webster. It seems Webster the wonder dog had begun growling whenever he even laid eyes on little Patrick. When Robin told me what was going on, I said to her, "It's pretty clear to me why he's growling around your son—he hates the little kid."

Why in the world would Webster not like Patrick? Robin, her husband Don, and Grandma all wanted to know. I explained to them that if they looked at the situation from the dog's perspective, everything would be perfectly clear. Webster had quickly learned that whenever Patrick was around, he (Webster) was put outside, essentially isolated from both the child and his beloved pack. On the other hand, whenever Patrick was not around, things were like they used to be, with Webster included as part of the family.

I proposed just the opposite, with the plan to be put into action as soon as we could get Grandma on a Midnight Train to Georgia, that great song by Gladys Knight and the Pips. Then, whenever Patrick was brought into the room, Webster got attention along with Patrick, by the person HOLDING THE CHILD. Within two weeks the growling had ceased, and years later, I have a photograph in my first book, (*Dog Tales*), of Patrick, about five or six, standing next to Webster, patting him in their backyard.

When someone asks me what age their child should be when they get a puppy I tell them five years minimum and, preferably, seven. I base that recommendation on my many years working with frustrated parents, their upset three- and four-year-olds, as well as one totally frustrated dog. Several years ago I had a consult with a client regarding her 16-month-old male Newfoundland, a breed I truly love.

It seems that this immature 120-pound behemoth, when in the back-yard with the woman's twin three-year-olds, would run around, pull their pants down, push them down, and then chew on their sleeves. I inquired as to how much training she had given the animal and she responded that he had had "no formal stuff." We chatted for a while and then I said to her, "It sounds to me like you got the dog as a nanny for your children."

"Well," she answered, "I researched the breed extensively and they are supposed to be simply marvelous with children."

"That is true and they are," I answered. "If you don't train them, however, they might well behave as you're seeing yours behave. You have a responsibility to help him learn how to act appropriately around your twins."

If you're getting a purebred you should, most definitely, research the breed you're thinking about getting. Read books. One book I recommend is *The Right Dog For You* by Daniel F. Totora, (Simon & Schuster, 1980). It is well written which is why I mentioned it earlier in this book. I would agree with him on his assessment of the breeds with the exception of just a couple. It is over 40 years since its publication date but still has very good information. Speak with responsible breeders. Talk with a few veterinarians. They may be biased for or against certain breeds, and that's okay. The more people you talk to, the more educated you become. Some breeds tend toward being superb with children, some are so-so, and a few, in my humble opinion, should not be in a home with children, pure and simple. The other side of this coin is this: are the children good with dogs? I've been around children whom I, were I a dog, would not take kindly to. Children who have never had limits and boundaries regarding how to interact with dogs. It works both ways. I know children who should never be in a home with a dog. It's most definitely a two-way street.

Remember, a young child should never be expected to accept responsibility for a dog. That responsibility belongs to the parents. A child can be shown how to ask a dog to sit and to lie down, and, under the supervision of a father or mother, could heel a dog for a short distance, absent distractions. Any corrections with the dog, however, should be the sole responsibility of the parents. Never allow a young child to attempt to discipline your dog or anyone else's!

A child will naturally mime his or her parents, so be extremely careful of interactions with your dog when your child is present.

Watching a child with a good dog is a heart-tugging sight. There is that sense of innocence, of all that is good, of a time perhaps when we ourselves were that very child. We want for our child what we ourselves experienced, or perhaps we want for the child what we never had. Just make certain you do all you can to get the right dog for you.

When the Path Ends

Murph's is a great breakfast/lunch restaurant located in the heart of Norwood, Massachusetts. Early Sunday morning you could usually find me on the second chair from the end, talking baseball or football or simply sitting quietly reading a book. It's a place where good food is served up to the "locals." The waitresses are always pleasant, and that is simply reflective of Carolyn, the boss. Blonde, with a bright smile and personality to match, she has that special gift of making you feel better after you've left than you were feeling before you arrived. You know the kind.

That's precisely the reason I knew something was wrong. I seated myself, pushed my hat back, put on my glasses, and opened the Sunday paper. Carolyn came over with my usual cup of tea and I looked at her, prepared to kid her about something or other. Something in her demeanor held my tongue in check. The smile was there, but the brightness surrounding it was missing.

"What's new?" I queried, sensing something was definitely amiss. Her eyes began to fill as she stood there, saying nothing. Finally, she said quietly, "Pebbles was hit last week. She was running across the quiet street back to me, and a truck was coming, and she just got hit."

I'm certain the guy driving the truck never knew he hit her, she was so small. It was late in the evening and Carolyn had gone outside with her as she always did. Pebbles would do her sniffing around, pee, and they would go back inside for the night. Yet, for some completely unexplainable reason, this night was different. Pebbles did something she had never, ever done. She ran across the road. The little Lhasa sniffed around, ignoring Carolyn's calls for her to come. That was when Carolyn first saw the truck rolling towards them, its headlights stabbing through the blackness. Carolyn pleaded once more for her to come back to her. Pebbles ignored her call. Panic began to overcome Carolyn. She now was afraid to call her again, in fear she would respond, and turn into the road as the truck arrived. Wisely, she remained silent. Then, inexplicably, Pebbles looked up, turned, staring at Carolyn for a second, and bolted into the street, heading for Carolyn and home. She never made it. The heavy truck rumbled on, its driver totally unaware of the tragedy unfolding behind him.

Over the years I've heard similar stories. Some have been clients agonizing over the loss of their companion, their most trusted friend. I never really know what to say to them, although I understand the emotional turmoil inside each of them. My late wife, Mary, was much better at helping them deal with their grief. She did it with complete openness, sympathy, and honesty, all of it straight from her heart. I think they always felt a bit better after talking with her, simply because they knew she understood their profound pain and they were doing their best to cope.

So I listened to Carolyn while she told me what a great little dog Pebbles was. I listened as she told me stories about her, how at times she made Carolyn angry, how much joy she gave her, the unconditional love. I listened and I watched. I watched her wipe away her tears. I watched as she smiled despite her sadness, her loss. I watched, and I listened.

Each of us says good-bye to our dog(s) in our own way. When the dog is gone, buried, or his ashes scattered across a cherished spot, most of us will get another when we feel and we know the time is right. And what remains of the passed dog? Years ago, *The Oregonian's* Ben Hur Lampman knew the place where a cherished dog is really buried:

> For if the dog be well remembered, if sometimes he leaps through your dreams actual as in life, eyes kindling, questing, asking, laughing, begging, it matters not at all where that dog sleeps at long and at last.

> On a hill where the wind is unrebuked, and the trees are roaring, or beside a stream he knew in puppyhood, or somewhere in the flatness of a pasture land, where most exhilarating cattle graze. It is all one to the dog, and all one to you, and nothing is gained, and nothing lost—if memory lives. But there is one best place to bury a dog. One place that is best of all.

> If you bury him in this spot, the secret of which you must already have, he will come to you when you call—come to you over the grim, dim frontiers of death, and down the well-remembered path, and to your side again. And though you call a dozen living dogs to heel they shall not growl at him, nor resent his coming, for he is yours and he belongs there. People may scoff at you, who see no lightest blade of grass bent by his footfall, who hear no whimper pitched too fine for mere audition, people who may never really have had a dog. Smile at them then, for you shall know something that is hidden from them, and which is well worth the knowing. The one best place to bury a good dog is in the heart of its master.

Carolyn has recently got herself a new dog, a Shih Tzu, no less. He is indeed keeping her busy. In fact, just last week my lunch was "on the house," Carolyn insisted, because I gave her a few suggestions. You know what, friend? I might just end up finding 20 pounds before this dog is trained!

Chapter 14

Different Paths: Getting Involved With Your Dog

The greatest strength is gentleness.
~Iroquois Proverb

*T*he last of the morning mist drifted off the lake a few minutes ago, exposing a surface as still as glass. I see two distinct swirls from rising fish. The distant wooded hills, shimmering in peak fall foliage, gently slope to the water's edge, mirroring themselves perfectly against the water's surface. It's early morning, quiet and peaceful. Eight ducks, so distant they appear as miniatures, paddle out from the shadows to my right, and as they make their way across, a single turkey buzzard soars, flaps it mighty wings, then soars again across the lake from the other side.

I witness all this from my bedroom window, two stories above the lake, sipping Earl Grey tea while I put my thoughts to paper on an oak antique desk in a guest bedroom of my host's estate. The birds remind me of yesterday morning and some of the most magnificent gundog work I have ever seen. I had been pheasant hunting as a guest of the gentleman whose black Labrador retriever I had trained and started on birds earlier that year. Connaht is young, a mere 17 months of age, and lacking experience. He loves people and is foremost a homebody. He'll approach me, his face screwed into a submissive "grin," sit and wait to be petted. But he also is learning to love working birds and although this is his first season, he's growing into it with enthusiasm and intelligence.

Dickens, a six-year-old English setter, was the other dog belonging to my host, and he is indeed a pleasure to watch—or should I say marvel at—in the field. Dickens was professionally trained by one of the country's top Midwest pros and he lives to hunt. He is also a wonderful family dog. Yet, you can see in those eyes a longing for autumn, when the chill of an upstate New York morning signals the beginning of yet another bird season.

To watch a good dog quarter a field in search of game birds is a treat many people never have an opportunity to witness. In my opinion, a good dog, or a brace of dogs, is what makes the day. It's what the sporting breeds were originally bred for. Regrettably, areas that once held coveys of quail or the majestic ring neck pheasant now hold cars for the mall shoppers. But back to yesterday morn. Jack, my host, and I walked the still damp fields for a couple of hours, watching his dogs working a short distance out front. I was nervous, though I made no mention of it. What if Connaht failed to do what he and I had trained for? My reputation was on the line, and although my host said nothing, I knew he was thinking the same.

Connaht, a bit tentative at first, hesitated in flushing his quarry and, when he did, he found it difficult marking the fall in the high sorghum cover. As the sun rose higher and the magnificent colors of the trees splashed reds, yellows, greens, and golds upon the landscape, and Jack and I talked and laughed as the morning aged, the dog gained confidence. We watched him slowly settle, allowing his nose to tell him where the birds held, camouflaged, his eyes learning to watch for a running bird.

By noon we had unloaded and racked our guns, watered the dogs, and I had used up my roll of film. Jack was pleased with both dogs. I was awed by Dickens' ability, but I was thrilled with Connaht's work. He located, flushed, marked, and retrieved birds. Of course I was relieved and happy my training had paid off, but I was thrilled for Jack and Connaht. They were becoming a team on this morning, a team that would, through the years, become stronger.

Later, as we were driving back to Jack's home where I was staying, Connaht lay between the driver and the passenger seats, his head pressed into my side. I know that in his own way he was saying "thank you" to me for opening the gate to many more autumns yet to come and birds to work.

I have a neighbor who once remarked, "Ray, you are a man of the '90s. Not the 1990s, mind you, but the 1890s." Well, if that's true, so be it. I'd have it no other way. I'll remember Dickens the master and Connaht the student, both working birds on an autumn morn when, for a fleeting moment, time stood still and good friends formed lasting memories. Thanks, Jack.

Most people will never have the experience of watching a good gun dog at work. If they did they would learn a lot about the true nature of the dog. I sometimes regret that, due to time constraints, I'm no longer able to participate in retriever field trials. Some of my happiest days were spent both training and trialing.

Many of you do, on the other hand, have time for a hobby for you and your dog. Today, there is so much out there in which to participate: obedience trials, conformation classes, retriever hunt tests, agility, Schuzthund, flyball, frisbee, yep, even freestyle dancing.

So, challenge your dog and yourself. You'll meet some great dogs as well as some truly wonderful people. For more information contact the AKC (American Kennel Club), and they can provide you with a listing for local clubs. You'll be amazed at what's in your own area.

A few years ago I was watching a flyball match in Houston, and there was a team of older women. They were having the time of their lives competing, laughing, and slapping each other on the back. They did not win, but winning was completely secondary for them. They were having great fun with their dogs. If you don't have a purebred, don't let that stop you. There's lots to do with that dog of yours. You'll have more fun than you ever thought possible! And guess what else— so will your dog.

Epilogue

We need another and a wiser and perhaps a more mystical concept of animals. Remote from universal nature, and living by complicated artifice, man in civilization surveys the creature through the glass of his knowledge and sees thereby a feather magnified and the whole image in distortion. We patronize them for their incompleteness, for their tragic fate of having taken fate so far below ourselves. And therein do we err. For the animal shall not be measured by man. In a world older and more complete than ours they move finished and complete, gifted with extensions of the senses we have lost or never attained, living by voices we shall never hear. They are not brethren, they are not underlings; they are other nations, caught with ourselves in the net of life and time, fellow-prisoners of the splendor and travail of the earth.

That quote from Henry Beston's *The Outermost House* has hung on a wall in my office for some 46 years. It was a gift from one of my very early clients. They were a lovely couple and he, like me, was experiencing a change in life. They had a German shepherd dog and I'd like to think that I helped them out a bit.

A lot of water has flowed under the bridge since then, as they say, and here I am, putting some last thoughts to paper. I believe I have a better understanding of what Mr. Beston was thinking about when he wrote the above words, and yet I know I still have a ways to go before I can fully appreciate it.

I hope you have found this book helpful, and that as a result, your relationship with your dog becomes stronger and more complete. The quest of the Samurai as a martial artist was perfection. To reach that state he never stopped learning, he never ceased practicing his art. He knew there was always more to learn, that achieving perfection was always just beyond his grasp, and yet he never quit.

From the dogs I have learned the virtue of patience. Furthermore, I am a better listener, both to the dogs as well as my clients. I'm a better listener today because the dogs have taught me the importance of being a good listener. Along the way should anyone tell you that either he or she is an expert in this field, do not pay them mind for they do not know what they do not know. Always remember that you and your dog, together, are on The Path and, in a few places there are bumps and holes. It's not always paved, but by learning to work together, you can learn how to get around them.

Oh, one last thing. Remember what Ray Hunt said: "By the time you get to square ten, all of square one will be in it." May God bless you! Thank you for inviting me into your home to spend a bit of time with you, drinking coffee and talkin' dogs.